MARI AND THE EARLY ISRAELITE EXPERIENCE

MARI AND THE EARLY ISRAELITE EXPERIENCE

ABRAHAM MALAMAT
The Hebrew University of Jerusalem

THE SCHWEICH LECTURES
OF THE BRITISH ACADEMY
1984

Published for THE BRITISH ACADEMY
by THE OXFORD UNIVERSITY PRESS

Oxford University Press, Walton Street, Oxford OX2 6DP

Oxford New York Toronto
Delhi Bombay Calcutta Madras Karachi
Petaling Jaya Singapore Hong Kong Tokyo
Nairobi Dar es Salaam Cape Town
Melbourne Auckland

and associated companies in
Beirut Berlin Ibadan Nicosia

British Library Cataloguing in Publication Data
Malamat, Abraham,
Mari and the early Israelite experience. – (The Schweich lectures of the British Academy; 1984)
1. Mesopotamia. Mari, ancient period
I. Title II. British Academy III. Series 935

ISBN 0-19-726072-1

Printed in Great Britain
at The Bath Press, Avon

To Naama

דְּרָכֶיהָ דַרְכֵי־נֹעַם וְכָל־נְתִיבֹתֶיהָ שָׁלוֹם

CONTENTS

LIST OF PLATES ix
LIST OF FIGURES xi
PREFACE xii

I. OF PALACES AND ARCHIVES: A WINDOW ON MARI 1
A. Old Babylonian Mari—The Setting 1
B. The Mari Palace 5
Archives reveal 11
Sealed doors and sealed chambers 14
The king's table 20
The royal ceremonial complex 22

II. THE EARLY ISRAELITE EXPERIENCE: A VIEW FROM MARI 27
A. The Comparative Method 27
B. The Chronological Aspect 29
C. Ethno-Linguistic Facets 30
D. Societal Components—Nomadic and Sedentary Modes of Life 34
Gāyum/gā'um/gōy 38
Ḫibrum/ḥeber 39
Ummatum/'ummāh 41
Nawûm/nāweh 43
Ḫaṣārum/ḥāṣēr 47
Patrimony as a tribal institution 48
E. The Geographical Scene 52
Hazor 55
Entanglement of the quadrilateral: Mari, Aleppo, Emar and Hazor 62
Conceptions of space and time 66

III. PROPHETS, ANCESTORS AND KINGS: ASPECTS OF WEST SEMITIC RITUAL 70
A. The Ban 70
Spoils of war 75
B. Intuitive Prophecy 79
Two types of diviners at Mari 80
Prophecy at Mari and in the Bible—similarities and differences 82
Affinities in terminology and contents—Mari and Israel 87
Lay prophets and message dreams 90
Prophetic credibility 94
C. The Royal Ancestor Cult 96
D. Kingly Deeds and Divine Exploits 107
The Sacred Sea 107
The Sacred Forest 112
The Lebanon, Gilgameš and a Hebrew Psalm 116

ABBREVIATIONS 122

BIBLIOGRAPHY 125

INDEXES
I. General 145
II. Akkadian words and Sumerograms 153
III. Hebrew and Other West Semitic Languages 156
IV. Biblical References 159

LIST OF PLATES

at end

I. Air-photograph of the Mari palace during excavations, looking north-west. *From A. Parrot*, Mari *(Collection des Ides Photographiques 7), 1953, Photo 4 ('Photograph taken by the French Air Force, April 1937)*.

II. *a*. The letter concerning the proposed visit of the son (?) of the King of Ugarit to the Mari palace. *From Claude F.-A., Schaeffer*, Ugaritica *(Publications de la Mission Archéologique Français III), 1939, p. 15*.

b. Tablets as found, *in situ*, in room 115—part of the 'diplomatic archive'. *From A. Parrot*, Le Palais I: Architecture *(Mission Archéologique de Mari II), 1958, pl. XXII, 2. Reproduced by permission of Librairie Orientaliste Paul Geuthner, Paris*.

III. *a–c*. Clay sealings of King Zimri-Lim, Queen Shibtu and Mukkanisum. *From A. Parrot*, Le Palais III: Documents et Monuments *(Mission Archéologique de Mari II), 1959, pls XLVII, 3 & 69; XLVIII, 43. Reproduced by permission of Librairie Orientaliste Paul Geuthner, Paris.*

d. The initial discovery of tablets in the Mari palace: André Bianquis removing tablets a mere metre below the surface, in Room 5, early in 1936. *From A. Parrot*, Le Palais I: Architecture *(Mission Archéologique de Mari II), 1958, p. 218, Fig. 25. Reproduced by permission of Librairie Orientaliste Paul Geuthner, Paris.*

IV. *a*. Looking through Room 6 to Room 5, from Room 1. *Ibid., pl. XLVII, 1.*

b. Room 7, with two bathtubs and a privy, *Ibid., pl. XLVI, 3.*

V. Room 116, possibly 'the sealed store-room for fine oil in the Court of the Palm', with Room 115 (the 'diplomatic archive') beyond; Courtyard 131 to the right. *Ibid., pl. XXVI, 1.*

VI. Wall-painting of a West Semitic (leading a sacrificial bull), from Courtyard 106. *From A. Parrot*, Le Pelais II: Peintures murales *(Mission Archéologique de Mari II), 1958, p. 20, Fig. 18. Repro-*

duced by permission of Librairie Orientaliste Paul Geuthner, Paris.

VII. *a.* A cake mould depicting the goddess Ishtar (Astarte). *From A. Parrot*, Le Palais III: Documents et Monuments *(Mission Archéologique de Mari II), 1959, pl. XIX, 1044.*

b. Cake moulds as found among the debris of the upper storey, in Room 77. *From A. Parrot*, Le Palais I: Architecture *(Mission Archéologique de Mari II), 1958, p. 222, Fig. 259. Reproduced by permission of Librairie Orientaliste Paul Geuthner, Paris.*

VIII. *a.* The pottery 'doorbell' of Room 108, *in situ. Ibid., p. 103, Fig. 105.*

b. Two clay liver-model fragments from Hazor in Northern Israel. *From Y. Yadin*, Hazor *(The Schweich Lectures 1970), 1972, pl. X, a, Oxford University Press for the British Academy.*

LIST OF FIGURES

1. Map of the ancient Near East in the Mari period. 3
2. Plan of the Mari palace (after Parrot). 7
3. Mari in the Old Babylonian period—schematic chronological chart. 9
4. The north-western part of the Mari palace, showing the locations of 'doorbell' installations. 17
5. Schematic reconstructions of (a) doorway 109–108; and (b) a doorway sealed from the 'inside'. 18
6. The route between Mari and Hazor. 65

PREFACE

The fascinating discoveries at Mari, the Old Babylonian royal city on the banks of the Middle Euphrates river, have been a major facet of the author's scholarly endeavours, and have represented a continual challenge within his pursuit of early Israelite and biblical history. At times, the broad scope of the material from the Mari archives, astonishing in itself, became the author's main preoccupation, especially when seeking to apply it to biblical research, and particularly to the initial, formative stages of the history of the Jewish people.

Though only a part of the some 25,000 tablets from Mari have been published so far, we have recently been witness to a renewed impetus in their decipherment and publication, over twenty volumes of texts having already appeared (see *ARMT* XXV for the most recent volume). This development is indeed portentous for Bible studies, and an intriguing picture of Mesopotamia and northern Syria is ever growing clearer as the milieu which had hosted the earliest rootlets of Israelite existence.

No one would dispute that Mari represents one of the most important discoveries for Bible research; indeed, the author would regard it as most significant, for among all the extra-biblical sources it is unique in illuminating the protohistoric phase of the Jewish people in its ethnic, social and cultural aspects. The Mari documents generally reflect a West Semitic ascendency—dominating politics and demography alike—throughout the greater Mesopotamian sphere. It is to this milieu that the Israelite forefathers were tangent in their ethnic crystallization, rather than to the Canaanite sphere.

The broad pallet of the Mari material—from diplomatic and political intrigue to pastoral life and exotic prophecy—inherently beckons comparative study with Israel, and with the Bible in general, and even with Biblical Hebrew. The present volume utilizes numerous possibilities provided by the Mari texts for comparing the two cultures, emphasizing not only the similarities and parallels, but also the differences and contrasts. This, in turn, introduces a new perspective into earliest Israelite history, and enhances our understanding of the Bible and its world. Moreover, the author seeks to apply a concept of the 'West'—Syria and Eretz Israel—as a sphere unto itself, though closely tied to Mesopotamia by ethnic, cultural and commercial factors; an entity which has left a distinct impression on the history of the ancient Near East in general.

The mode of research characterizing this volume is readily revealed by perusal of the subtitles to its three main parts: 'A Window on Mari'; 'A View from Mari'; and 'Aspects of West Semitic Ritual'. The author has adopted an historical approach which regards a culture from without (despite the 'dangers' underlying such a method): a proper understanding of one culture can be obtained only from the vantagepoint of another culture. And thus the volume's topic—Mari and the early Israelite experience.

* * *

Many are those to whom I am in debt, in one way or another, for their support and assistance in the preparation of the Schweich Lectures for 1984, and of the present publication. Foremost, I wish to thank the Schweich Committee of the British Academy (particularly Professor E. Ullendorff), for the honour they paid me by inviting me to deliver the lecture series. My primary debt to two of my teachers—Benjamin Mazar, of the Hebrew University in Jerusalem, and the late Benno Landsberger, of the Oriental Institute of Chicago—reflects my principal realms of interests.

Two of my colleagues—Professors P. Artzi, of Bar Ilan University, Ramat Gan, and Baruch Levine of New York University—have most kindly read the manuscript and offered significant comments; and Dr Alan Millard, of the University of Liverpool, critically read the manuscript of the lectures per se. Some advice on Akkudien matters, received from Professor A. Shaffer of the Hebrew University, Jerusalem. Finally, I must thank Mr Rafi Grafman, of Jersualem, whose skills in translation and editing have so felicitously culminated in bringing the present volume to fruition.

The Perry Foundation for Biblical Research at the Hebrew University has long supported my Mari studies and is facilitating the publication of a Hebrew version of this book; the Basic Research Foundation administered by the Israel Academy of Sciences and Humanities has sponsored several years of my research; and the Dorot Foundation was most generous in providing for the final preparation of this English edition.

Jerusalem, December 1988 A.M.

I

OF PALACES AND ARCHIVES: A WINDOW ON MARI

A. OLD BABYLONIAN MARI—THE SETTING

Some fifty years ago, in writing of the texts newly discovered at Mari in Syria, William Foxwell Albright, the late doyen of Palestinology, noted that nearly half a century had then passed since the discovery of the El-Amarna archive—texts which had revolutionized the study of the Late Bronze Age in Hither Asia.[1] Today it is just over half a century since French archaeologists began excavating at Mari, under the late André Parrot. After only three years, the now famous Mari archives from the Old Babylonian period began coming to light—a discovery which has, in its turn, also revolutionized the history of that region, but this time concerning the Middle Bronze Age. And even more recently, the discovery of an archive at Ebla, still in the early stages of study, may well be revolutionizing the history of a somewhat earlier period, the end of the Early Bronze Age. This first lecture concentrates on the Mari palace and its archives, here and there touching on our central theme, Mari and its relationship with the lands to the west, including the Land of the Bible. The second lecture proceeds to examine the people and places in the sphere of Mari, and the social and ethno-linguistic affinities with the earliest Israelites. And the final lecture delves into several religious phenomena exhibiting West Semitic affinities, especially intuitive prophecy.

What have we gained from these Mari discoveries, after fifty years? And how have they affected and benefitted the study of ancient Palestine, the Bible and early Israelite history? The time span represented by the Old Babylonian archives, and by the splendid palace in which they were found, is also only about half a century—that is, roughly, the first half of the eighteenth century BC down to about 1760 BC.[2] The palace came to a violent end at that time, when the famous Ḫammurabi of Babylon sacked the city, reducing it to a state from which it never recovered.

[1] See Albright 1937, p. 26, basing on Dossin 1937.

[2] The dating used throughout this volume is based on the 'Middle Chronology', which ascribes the reign of Ḫammurabi of Babylon to 1792–1750 BC. See the basic study, Smith 1940. For other chronological schemes, in particular the higher ones, see e.g., Landsberger 1954, and the chart there on p. 115. Recently, an ultra-high chronology was put forth by Huber 1982, 1987. For the 'Low Chronology' (Ḫammurabi, 1728–1686 BC), preferred by many archaeologists and Egyptologists, see Albright 1965. For general surveys, see Rowton 1970; Tadmor 1970.

What sort of world surrounded Mari in its Old Babylonian prime? This period can be regarded as the first truly international age—with open diplomatic channels and bustling, far-reaching commerce, and even commercial banking of a sort. In comparison with the Amarna Age, some four centuries later, the Mari world was still limited toward the west: though it included Anatolia and even far-off Crete, Egypt and even southern Palestine seem entirely to have been outside the picture.[3] Geographically, Mari's location was more or less central, and it was therefore able to serve as a middleman between Babylon, the southern Mesopotamian city-states and even Iran, on the one hand, and Syria including northern Palestine and the coastal Levant (that is, the 'West') on the other hand.[4]

Now Mari fostered a special relationship with northern Syria at this time, especially in its political, commercial and cultural ties with Aleppo, capital of the major kingdom there, Yamḫad, and with Ugarit, the important emporium on the Mediterranean coast. Some 500–700 years earlier, the city of Ebla, about sixty kilometres south of Aleppo, had occupied a similar superior position in the west. Ebla has gained much publicity in the recent decade, but the picture to be gleaned from the discoveries there is still somewhat unclear. In that earlier day, there was much trade between Mari and Ebla, and Mari might even have been dominated by Ebla for a time, and vice versa.[5] In short, Mari already then held a prominent position as an emporium on the Middle Euphrates river, through which Mesopotamian commerce was funnelled to and from the west.[6]

Several centuries later, in the Old Babylonian period, we see at Mari (as well as at Ebla) a largely West Semitic or Amorite population with a thick veneer of early Babylonian–Akkadian civilization, with all its refinements. It is in this light that we can understand the words of a Mari official, addressed to his lord, the Amorite king Zimri-Lim: 'You are the king of the Ḫaneans (a major Amorite tribe), but moreover you are the king

[3] The southernmost place in the West, mentioned at Mari, seems to be the city of Hazor in Upper Galilee. The damaged toponym in *ARMT* VI 23: 23—in the sequence Yamḫad, Qatna, Hazor, [. . .]—might refer to some place in central or southern Palestine, but certainly not Egypt. See Malamat 1960, p. 15. Alt 1954 suggested the possibility of Gaza, or even Egypt, in this context. Albright 1968, p. 73 and n. 77, also opined that Egypt was mentioned at Mari, in the name *Maḫ(ḫ)an* (which in reality refers to Maḫanum, a well-known Mariote toponym), but this is baseless; Albright noted: 'I have been promising a paper on this subject for years and hope to find time to publish before long.' But he never did so. And see below, p. 62, n. 125.

[4] See, e.g., Kupper 1982.

[5] Relations between Mari and Ebla in this early, pre-Sargonic period were quite intense; besides their strong cultural ties, both centres belonged to one and the same linguistic sphere. See the recent articles of Archi 1985; see also Michalowski 1985.

[6] See Finet 1969. This riverine trade is well attested in the Old Babylonian period, as are the tolls imposed by the Mari authorities; see in particular Burke 1964. The Akkadian term for toll is *miksu* (*AHw*, p. 652), cognate of Hebrew *mek̲es*, the latter appearing only in religious contexts (Numbers 31: 28, 37, 41); in Talmudic times the Hebrew word has a strictly secular meaning, similar to the one at Mari and in Akkadian generally.

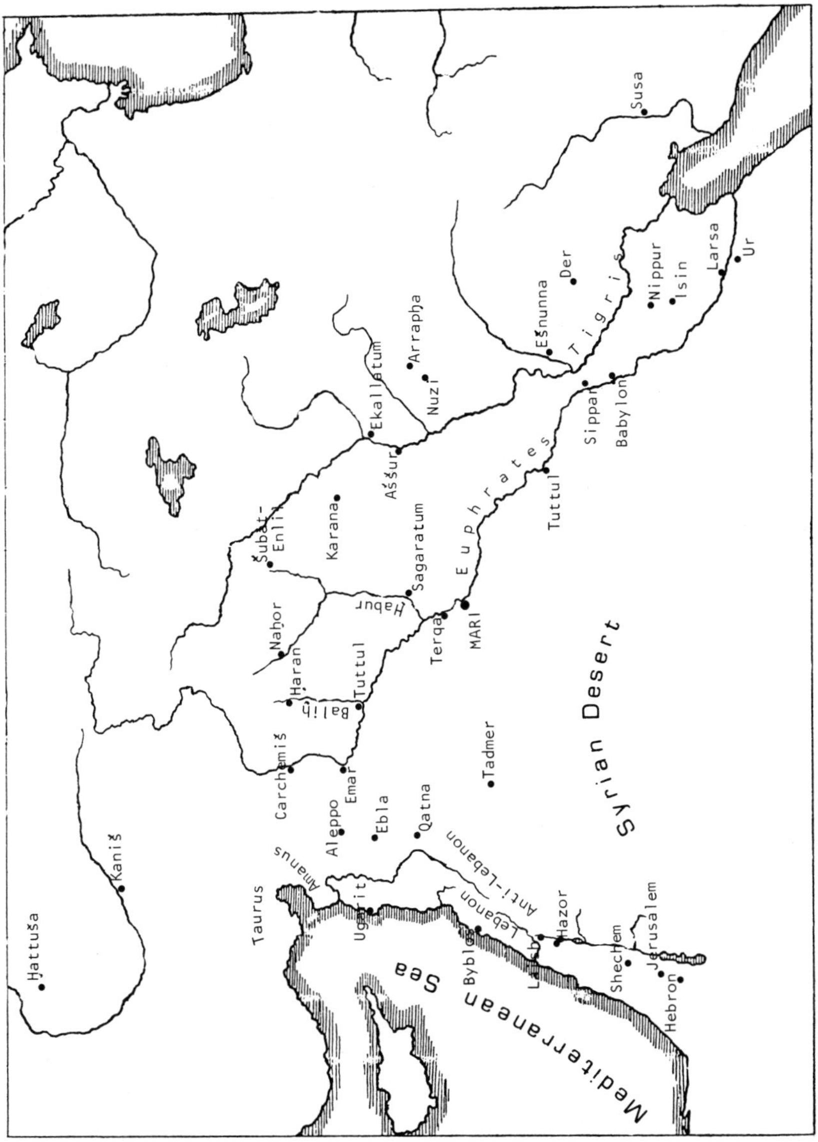

1. Map of the ancient Near East in the Mari period.

of the Akkadians; my lord ought not ride a horse; may my lord ride in a chariot, with mules, and thus honour the dignity of his royal office' (*ARMT* VI 76: 20–24) (see below, p. 80 and n. 42).

The status and position of Mari in Mesopotamia–Syria in the Old Babylonian period is silhouetted in a tantalizing Mari document which, though often quoted, has not yet been published definitively (A 482).[7] Mari, of course, was not the only kingdom or hegemony there, and this text sums up the political constellation of the region as it appeared to one high official. In a letter sent to Zimri-Lim by one Itur-Asdu, then an agent of the king at the city of Nahor, we read a sort of high-level diplomatic report, incidentally containing an overview of the political configuration of the day, revealing five major states besides Mari in the Mesopotamian–Syrian sphere.[8] Itur-Asdu, on the king's instructions, had called a meeting of various local sheikhs or kinglets (*šarrāni*) in the city of Šarmaneḫ[9] to the north of Mari, on the occasion of a festival of the goddess Ištar. The convocation was apparently held with the intention of concluding covenants with these sheikhs, a practice often associated with sacrificial ceremonies. Itur-Asdu reported: 'With regard to what my lord wrote here to the sheikhs, saying, "Come to the sacrifice in honour of Ištar"—I gathered the sheikhs to Šarmaneḫ and conveyed this message to them: "There is no kinglet (*šarrum*) who is strong (*dannum*)[10] in his isolation. Ten [to] fifteen kinglets are vassals of [literally 'go after'] Ḫammurabi the ruler (*awīlum*) of Babylon; so, too, Rim-Sin the ruler of Larsa; so, too, Ibal-pi-el the ruler of Ešnunna; so, too, Amut-pi-el the ruler of Qatna; [and] twenty kinglets are vassals of Yarim-Lim the ruler of Yamḫad. . . ."'[11]

Itur-Asdu's report thus reveals a multi-polar system of six leading powers, including Mari, in the region. The last two kingdoms mentioned by him, Qatna and Yamḫad, were in Syria; and Yamḫad seems to have been the strongest of them all at that time—a situation generally reflected in Zimri-Lim's correspondence. Politics and commerce, of course, go hand in hand, and in an inventory of a shipment of tin, four of the same kingdoms again appear, while Ešnunna and Larsa, at the eastern end of the arc, are replaced by Ugarit and Hazor (and a third, damaged name) at the western end

[7] Published only in transliteration and translation, in Dossin 1938, p. 117. The initial English translation is noted in n. 1, above; a fuller one can be found in *ANET*, p. 628.

[8] It is noteworthy that Assyria does not figure among the current powers in the region; this may have reflected the specific political situation at that moment, after Zimri-Lim had recovered his throne at Mari, a time when Assyria was in eclipse.

[9] The city, to be sought in the land of Idamaraṣ, is a *hapax legomenon*; the reading has been amended in Durand 1987a, p. 230, to read Tarmanni, a well known toponym.

[10] For the royal epithet *šarrum dannum*, common in Akkadian, see the parallel biblical usages *melek̲ 'az* (Isaiah 19: 4) and *'oz melek̲* (Psalms 99: 4).

[11] I am grateful to Professor J.-M. Durand for examining the tablet, to clarify my proposal that the name of an additional kingdom might have appeared after Yamḫad (Assyria? Hazor?). In a letter dated 25 May 1985, Professor Durand notes that the tablet (A.482) is indeed broken at that spot and suggests certain possibilities; unfortunately, they leave the matter unresolved.

of the arc.[12] Apparently Hazor in northern Palestine, though within the commercial sphere of Mari, was beyond its ordinary political horizon—that is, it was south of Qatna, the southernmost kingdom within the Mariote sphere of influence. That Hazor too was in the nature of a kingdom much like the other powers noted by Itur-Asdu is reflected in the Bible, in such glosses as 'Hazor formerly was the head of all those kingdoms' (Joshua 11: 10),[13] and in the much later coalition of several kings in northern Palestine, assembled by Hazor against the invading Israelites (Joshua 11: 1–5).

What was Itur-Asdu seeking to convey to the tribal chiefs at Šarmaneḫ? He was trying, of course, to persuade them to ally with Mari, for it was hopeless, so he implied, for small peoples to remain unaligned, that is, in political limbo, vulnerable and insecure, liable to be set upon and gobbled up by one or the other of the powers of the day.

This picture seems to shed new light on an interesting passage in the Bible which, till now, has been rather obscure in meaning. In the Book of Numbers, the seer Balaam was brought by the king of Moab to curse the Israelites but, instead, God placed a blessing in his mouth. In Numbers 23: 9, he says: הן־עם לבדד ישכון ובגוים לא יתחשב, 'Lo, [Israel] is a people encamped in isolation (*lᵉḇādād*), not considering itself among the [other] nations.' This passage has generally been taken to mean that Israel would be isolated and weakened—which makes little sense in its context. But the Hebrew term here, *bādād*, literally means 'isolated, alone'.[14] According to the commentators, it carries two possible nuances, one of strength—Israel dwelling securely and peacefully (cf. Deuteronomy 33: 28);[15] and the other of exclusiveness—Israel having nothing in common with the other nations, being of a somewhat aloof status.[16] The nuance of strength is actually intimated in Midrashic literature, which understands *bādād* in Deuteronomy 33:28 and in Numbers 23:9 as connoting self-reliance, and not weakness,[17] which is incompatible with the context of Numbers 23.

Thus, what Balaam was actually beholding was a self-confident, 'isolationist' nation, independent of other nations. Itur-Asdu's argument now puts this biblical passage into bold relief—despite the fact that, or rather because, it is its very antithesis.

B. THE MARI PALACE

Having taken a mere glimpse of Mari in its geopolitical setting (and cf. below, pp. 56ff.), let us now take a closer look at the Mari palace itself,

[12] On the tin inventory, see Malamat 1971; and cf. the recent collation of the text, in *ARMT* XXIII, No. 556, pp. 528–529, introducing several improved readings; and see also below, p. 57 and nn. 108–110.

[13] See Malamat 1960.

[14] For the biblical occurrences, and the meaning of 'isolation, separation', see *BDB*, pp. 94–95; and *HAL*, p. 105.

[15] Cf., e.g., Gray 1912, pp. 346–347; and there for further opinions.

[16] See von Gall 1900, p. 25.

[17] See Sifre, *Wᵉzo't Habberaḵah*, para. 256.

where almost all of the Old Babylonian documents have come to light. Now this palace, the nerve centre of the kingdom of Mari, is one of the most formidable finds ever made in Mesopotamian archaeology or, for that matter, in Near Eastern archaeology in general. Unique for its period in size and splendour, its most noteworthy feature is surely the very bulk and the mundane character of the aggregate archives and their close relationship to the palace itself. The 25,000 or so tablets are a clear indication of the early bureaucratization of life at the palace, and of the penetration of scribes *per se* into the administrative apparatus—and to the advent of literacy to the apparatus itself. The interplay between palace and documents unveils a broad panorama of history, commerce, administration, bureaucracy, crafts and even family life in Old Babylonian times, as well as religion and a glimpse of literature. It has also yielded many 'spin-offs' for the study of the lands to the west of Mesopotamia—the greater Canaanite sphere—as we shall see in the following lectures.

To obtain the 'feel' of the palace and a general impression of the impact of the Mari finds, let us take a sort of tour of the palace, with occasional digressions on a variety of its features and on some of the documents found there. What we have before us represents, of course, the final phase of the complex—the palace of King Zimri-Lim at the time of its destruction by Ḫammurabi. Several stages can be seen in the development of the palace, but this subject has still largely to be clarified in a satisfactory manner.[18]

Passing through the main gateway complex, on the north, we enter a huge courtyard (131), the old reception area with a small, attached throne room (132) containing early-style frescos. To the left of the throne room is a group of rooms (133–135) in which hundreds of administrative documents have come to light, many of which have been published only recently. Most of these texts are tedious lists of persons or commodities, lists of workers or receipts for goods brought to or taken from the palace. Routine as they may be, much can be gleaned from them, to reveal the daily life and procedures of administration and commerce at Mari. Let us linger over a few examples.

Concerning realia, we read of a vast variety of goods and objects, ranging from musical instruments to precious metals, from arms and chariots to types of pots. Among the occupations at the palace we find such craftsmen as smiths, carpenters, weavers, gardeners, porters, harness makers and armourers, to mention but a few.[19] Many of these persons were of tribes in the Mari region, including *Amurru* or 'Amorites', a rather rare appellation at Mari but often found in the Bible (although not in identical

[18] For the earlier seasons of excavations in the palace, from 1933 to 1974, see Parrot 1958a, 1958b, 1959. For the renewed excavations, commencing in 1979 and continuing still, see Margueron 1982b, 1983, 1984a, 1987b. For Ḫammurabi's destruction of the palace, see Margueron 1984b.

[19] See, e.g., Dalley 1984, pp. 50ff. (and the documentary evidence there), also for their products.

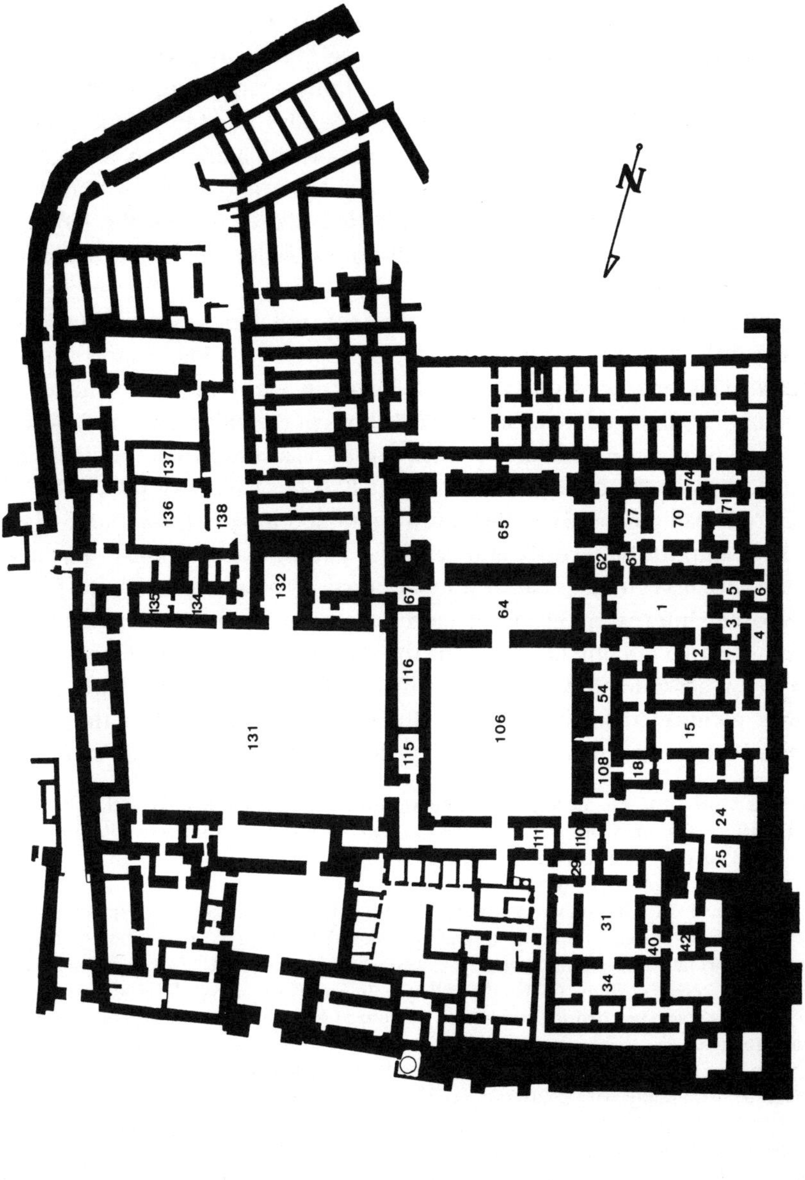

2. Plan of the Mari palace (after Parrot).

usage).[20] Other geographical names also appear in these texts—usually as the place of origin or despatch of persons or goods. Thus, we read of Western locations such as Tadmer (biblical Tadmor, classical Palmyra in the Syrian Desert), Gubla (biblical Gebal, classical Byblos on the Mediterranean coast), Kaptara (biblical Caphtor, better known to us as Crete, but the term is also applied to the Aegean realm, as a whole), as well as numerous other places not mentioned in the Bible.

We also have here more than a passing glance at several of the top officials of the Mari hierarchy, the elite of quite a large bureaucratic corps. To name but a few of them, there was Baḫdi-Lim, the palace prefect; Išar-Lim, a general; Asqudum, a diviner–priest, married to a daughter (or sister) of Yaḫdun-Lim, an earlier king of Mari, and whose own mansion has recently been excavated a few hundred metres east of the palace;[21] and, of course, Zimri-Lim's jack-of-all-trades, Mukannišum, to whom the French have devoted an entire volume (XVIII) of the *ARMT* series, though even that contains but a fraction of the texts touching upon his activities. I have little doubt that rooms 133–135 comprised Mukannišum's suite of offices. This energetic official had a finger in many pies: a confidant of the king, he managed many of the workshops at the palace, was responsible for various treasure and store-rooms, served as a comptroller of goods and often despatched supplies to the king when he was away on one of his numerous campaigns. His office even contained a 'safe' (*pisannum*, where he kept important records and receipts, among other things), which he sealed with his cylinder-seal, several impressions of which have been found.

Another interesting group of facts which can be culled from these dry administrative documents concerns the palace itself. Unfortunately, it has not been possible thus far to identify positively even one of the palace rooms mentioned in the texts.[21a] But we repeatedly read of the 'Court of the Palm in the palace of Mari',[22] the 'divan', the 'bitumen chamber',

[20] De Vaux 1978, pp. 58–64; and see my review of the original French edition, Malamat 1973b, where is pointed out (p. 85) that biblical *Emori* is identical with the cuneiform *Amurru* only in Joshua 13: 4. See also the bibliography below, p. 27, n. 2.

[21] See Margueron 1983, 1984a.

[21a] But see J.-M. Durand's recent seminal study, attempting to identify numerous rooms and parts of the palace with terms appearing in the Mari texts—'L'organisation de l'espace dans le palais de Mari: Le témiognage des textes', in E. Levy, ed., *Le système palatial en Orient, en Grèce et à Rome* (Actes du Colloque de Strasbourg 1985), Strasbourg 1987, pp. 39–110. This study reached me too late to be utilized here, but some of its conclusions are similar to ours.

[22] The intriguing 'Court of the Palm (in the Palace of Mari)' has stirred several attempts to identify it, initially with courtyard 131 (Parrot 1974, p. 114, Fig. 63) and more recently with courtyard 106; see below, n. 62. Since the palm served as a symbol of justice, the following passage from the wisdom literature may be of relevancy; it is from the fable of 'The Tamarisk and the Palm': 'In former days . . . they appointed a king. . . . The king planted the Palm in his courtyard. . . .' See Lambert 1960, pp. 155–156. The palm in the Mari palace, too, may have been symbolic of justice and it may have been in its shade that judgements were delivered. Note in the Bible (Judges 4: 5), Deborah the Judgess 'sat under the palm . . . and the people of Israel came up to her for judgement.'

the 'bureau at the palace gate', the 'fine perfume store-room', the 'fine oil store-room', the 'room of seals' (or 'room of sealed documents'), the 'sealed store-room of the Court of the Palm', and many others (see Pl. V). Incidentally, Mukannišum's office contained more than twice the number of tablets in the El-Amarna archive. This was just one of quite a few archives at the palace, and it was not even the largest of them.

Beyond Mukannišum's office is a sanctuary complex. The excavations here have shown that successive temples had stood on this site for some 700 years prior to the destruction of the palace. At some stage in the Old Babylonian period, however, the sanctuary was reduced in size and integrated into the expanding palace. In order to understand this development, we must look back into the history of Zimri-Lim's line, the Lim dynasty. In very brief outline (see Fig. 3): a local Amorite sheikh named Yaggid-Lim managed to gain control over the Mari region.[23] His main

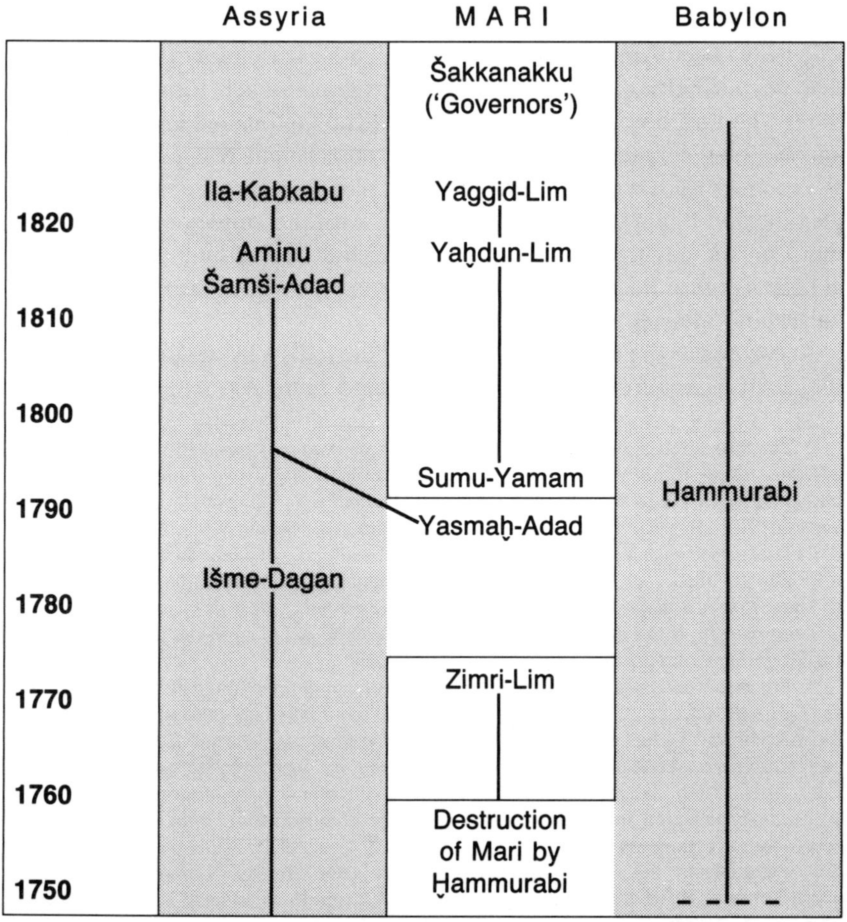

3. Mari in the Old Babylonian period—schematic chronological chart.

rival was a certain Ila-Kabkabu, also an Amorite. Yaggid-Lim's son, Yaḫdun-Lim, was able to bring Mari to prosperity and major status over a reign of many years. He seems to have been succeeded by a brother, Sumu-Yamam, a rather shadowy figure who is never denoted 'king' in the documents, and who soon disappears from history. Yaḫdun-Lim (or possibly Sumu-Yamam) was apparently murdered in a palace *putsch* or rather by rebellious vassals (see below n. 25 and p. 73). In the meantime, a descendant of Ila-Kabkabu, Šamši-Adad, had seized the region and city of Ashur and established himself there as king; at this juncture he then also seized Mari, ousting the Lim dynasty and installing his son, Yasmaḫ-Adad, as viceroy there. After some twenty years of such 'Assyrian' control, Zimri-Lim—probably Yaḫdun-Lim's son—was able to drive the rival dynasty out of Mari and recover the dynastic throne, succumbing to the ambitions of the great Ḫammurabi of Babylon after a reign of fourteen years.[24]

In a problematic 'Letter to a God' (*ARMT* I 3) written by Yasmaḫ-Adad, the 'Assyrian' viceroy, accusations are levelled against the then deposed Lim dynasty. What is significant for us here is the fact that Yaḫdun-Lim—who truly raised Amorite Mari to great heights—is accused of seizing 'things that do not belong to him. [The god's] temple which former kings had [built], he tore down and built a palace. [The god] called him to account, and his own servants killed him . . .' as punishment for his 'sacrilege'.[25] We can now apparently associate this 'sacrilege' against the sanctuary complex located behind Mukannišum's office with the condemnation of Yaḫdun-Lim for having desecrated a temple and having built his palace, or at least a part of it, over the ruins.[26] If this is so, we have here a remarkable epigraphic–archaeological correlation.

According to the recent major study of the palace by the present excavator, Jean Margueron, the sanctuary located there was originally built as

[23] The ultimate origin of the Lim dynasty remains a matter of speculation; one suggestion is Terqa, on the Euphrates some 60 km north of Mari; an alternative is the city of Ṣuprum, located between Terqa and Mari (cf. Charpin & Durand 1985, pp. 294ff.); another is Tuttul, apparently Tell Bi'ya at the Baliḫ-Euphrates confluence (see below, n. 67). Recently, Charpin & Durand 1986 suggested—basing on unpublished evidence—that the Lim dynasty derived from the Sim'alites (see below, p. 35 n. 28), originating in the land of Idamaraṣ, northwest of Mari. *Lim* is a distinct West Semitic theophoric element (Ugaritic *l'im*; Hebrew *lᵉ'om*), and surprisingly, it has appeared in the early Ebla texts, including in the names of the first two kings there, of the 25th century BC; see Archi 1986.

[24] For the several fragmentary royal inscriptions of Šamši-Adad found in the Mari archives, see Grayson 1987, pp. 56ff.; and cf. Charpin 1983. For Zimri-Lim's takeover of Mari, with assistance from Yamḫad to the west and Ešnunna in the east, see Charpin & Durand 1985.

[25] For a revised reading see Charpin & Durand 1985, pp. 293ff., 339ff. It was surely Yahdun-Lim who was slain, rather than Sumu-Yamam; furthermore, these authors suggest that he was actually defeated in battle, fighting against rebellious vassals, rather than in a mere court coup, as commonly assumed.

[26] The difficulty lies in the word for 'palace' in *ARMT* I 3: 10'; Dossin read *bīt ḫilāni*, which can be rejected on several counts. We would accept the reading of Landsberger 1954, p. 35, n. 28: 'Palast' (i.e. é-gal). Charpin & Durand 1985, p. 298, n. 23, however, read é dam-ni, 'harem', the house of his spouse.

a separate entity, which was eventually incorporated into the palace complex. The importance of the sanctuary declined at the beginning of the Old Babylonian period, and gradually it was reduced in size, about a third of its area being taken over for secular use. A shadow of its former self, the temple was reduced to a mere chapel.[27]

Archives reveal

Passing back through the old reception courtyard (131), we enter a corridor (114) leading to the second major wing of the palace—apparently the newer part. Immediately to the left is a small chamber (room 115), the importance of which is entirely out of proportion to its size, for it was here that the bulk of the royal correspondence was found—some 4000 tablets (see Pl. II*b*).[28] For the historian, this is the jackpot—the diplomatic and political archive of the kingdom of Mari, revealing the secrets of the king and his inner circle of senior officials, in the capital and in the provinces. There is also correspondence with other kingdoms and rulers, notably between Zimri-Lim and Yarim-Lim, king of Aleppo, and Ḫammurabi of Babylon, the two eminent rulers of the day. What can be learned from this enormous archive? The possibilities are too numerous to go into here, and include topics entirely unique to Mari (e.g. intuitive prophecy; see lecture III). There is so much material in this one room that we must continue down the corridor without hesitation, lest we spend the remainder of the chapter here (though below we shall occasionally refer to documents discovered in this room).

Passing the entrance to the main courtyard (106), to which we shall return later, we come to rooms 111 and 110, both also archive chambers. Adjacent to them on the north is a rather luxurious palace wing, centred on a small courtyard (31) and a sort of 'divan' (34). Many of the rooms of this apartment have walls painted in rather simple patterns. The excavator long ago suggested that these were the actual royal apartments, but more recent analyses suggest that they comprised a secondary unit—possibly the royal harem (Akkadian *tubqum*, 'corner').[29] Indeed, this is the best defended corner of the entire palace complex. Confirmation of this

[27] See Margueron 1982a, I, p. 375; II, Figs. 248ff., sectors D and E.

[28] Room 115, lying between the two major courtyards of the palace, hardly gives the impression that it originally served as an archive. Indeed, since clay labels bearing year formulae of Ḫammurabi mentioning the destruction of Mari were found there, among the documents, we can assume that the documents had been gathered there for classification and perusal by Ḫammurabi's officials. For the labels, see Thureau-Dangin 1939.

[29] For the word *tubqum*, 'corner' in the Mari documents as referring to the 'harem', see Durand & Margueron 1980. In the Bible, a similar semantic development concerning the term for 'harem' may have taken place; in Psalms 45: 14–15, on the queen of an Israelite king: 'The royal princess, her dress embroidered with golden mountings, is led *inside* (*pᵉnīmā*) to the king' (*NJPS*). Here, 'inside, interior' would appear to refer to the harem, similar to Middle Assyrian *bītānu*, the interior apartments in a mansion; cf. *CAD* B, p. 276a. And see especially, e.g., El-Amarna 29:32, where a harem is most definitely intended.

identification might be found in the fact that the archives in room 110 and scattered documents in nearby rooms included around seventy letters sent to or received by women. Most of this correspondence, which totals close to 200 letters, has been published. No comparable body of material relating to women is known anywhere else in the ancient Near East.

Some years ago I published a study (together with P. Artzi)[30] on the most prominent of the Mari ladies—Šibtu, Zimri-Lim's queen, a true *ēšet ḥayīl*, 'a woman of valour', to use a biblical phrase. Here we can look at only one sample of the intimate letters between Šibtu and her husband. It reads, in part: 'To my lord. . . . I have just given birth to twins, a son and a daughter. May my lord rejoice!' This woman also acted on her husband's behalf during his absences from the capital, handling correspondence, managing the affairs of the palace, and keeping the king's officials in hand. Until quite recently it was thought that Šibtu was the daughter of Yarim-Lim, king of Aleppo, and his chief wife, Gašera. In several documents, however, Šibtu's mother is named as Zizi.[31] Either Šibtu was a princess by a secondary queen at Aleppo, or it might be assumed that Zizi was Gašera's nickname. Such nicknames were not uncommon in antiquity, and even Zimri-Lim was not immune to this phenomenon, for his family often addressed him as 'my Star'. In this context we may also note that, from recently published material, it would seem that Zimri-Lim did not marry Šibtu while he was still in exile at the court of Aleppo, as previously understood, for Zimri-Lim apparently sent the bride-price (*terḫatum*) from Mari only in his fourth year as a sovereign (*ARMT* XXV 616).[32] Also in a family context, there is a document which lists ten of Zimri-Lim's daughters—out of the twenty or so known to us from the archives as a whole; another document mentions over ten of his wives.[33] A further prominent woman at the palace was Addu-duri, perhaps another of Zimri-Lim's wives or, more probably, his mother (for at one time or another she seems to have been queen).

In the documents, we also read of women scribes and of high female officials in the administration and the cult hierarchy. Here at Mari, then, we see a picture seldom seen in the ancient Near East—of upper class women filling major and active roles in the kingdom.

To continue our tour, down a nearby corridor (109) we come to two large chambers of a rather peculiar nature (rooms 24–25). The excavator interpreted them as a school, for they each contained several rows of low stone benches. There were also pottery tubs containing small sea shells,

[30] See Artzi & Malamat 1971.

[31] See *ARMT* XXII, p. 606, index, s.v. *Zizi*; XXIII, p. 631, index, s.v. *Zi-zi*. The name might have been pronounced Ṣiṣi, a sort of *Lallwort* (baby-talk) referring to the suckling breast—something like 'nanny'.

[32] For Šibtu's marriage, see Abdallah 1987.

[33] For Zimri-Lim's daughters, see Lafont 1987. For his harem, much of which may have been 'inherited' from his predecessor, Yasmaḫ-Adad (and cf. 2 Samuel 16: 21–22), see Durand 1985a; and for the royal ladies of Mari in general, cf. Batto 1974.

supposedly for learning arithmetic. However, no analogous schoolroom is known before Hellenistic times and, for purely practical reasons, the 'benches' could never have served for study. Most opinions now see in these rooms the royal counting-house or treasury, in which the benches or banks were used for storing precious commodities, and the sea-shells may have been used as tokens in tallying the inventory.[34] From various documents and inventories found in the palace, we know that considerable treasures had been stored there, from the time of Yaḫdun-Lim. This wealth apparently fell into 'Assyrian' hands, for there are tablets from the days of the 'Assyrian' viceroy, listing such items as three sealed coffers of 'gold, silver and precious stones'—a stock phrase for treasure; there was also jewellery, a large amount of bronze, cloth studded with silver and gold-plated musical instruments. Several of the tablets note that the goods were deposited, for instance, in the 'sealed store-room of the "Court of the Palm" of the Mari palace', or in the 'sealed store-room of fine oil'.[35]

Types of 'treasures' and store-rooms similar to those mentioned in the Mari documents and other Mesopotamian texts are also found in the Bible (2 Kings 20: 12–15), though in a later period. In the days of the Judean king Hezekiah, 'Merodach-baladan . . ., king of Babylon, sent envoys. . . . And Hezekiah welcomed them and showed them all his treasure house, the silver, the gold, the spices, the precious oil, his armoury, all that was in his store-houses. . . .'[36] Such an inspection of the accumulated wealth of a vassal is recorded in cuneiform documents, as well, and often preceded a fate similar to that of Mari at the hands of Ḫammurabi. Indeed, Hezekiah was warned (20: 16): 'Behold the days are coming when all that is in your house and that which your fathers have stored up till this day shall be carried to Babylon.' By a quirk of fate, however, it was not Judah which was so plundered, but Babylon: in an Assyrian inscription we read that Sennacherib, king of Assyria, 'entered Merodach-baladan's palace in order to examine the treasures'—which he subsequently appropriated for himself.

Returning to the Mari palace, and continuing down the same corridor (109), we enter another important archive (108), containing over 1000 tablets. This room, and an adjacent one (18), comprised a store-room for various commodities, including a deposit of various 'antiquarian' texts. These latter include such 'incunabula' as thirty-two clay model livers dating from a century or so prior to the days of Zimri-Lim. Indeed, they are the earliest known direct evidence of hepatoscopy—divination through

[34] See the analysis of the Mari palace, in Heinrich 1984, pp. 68–81. For Rooms 24 and 25 as a treasury rather than a school, see there, p. 78.

[35] For list of inventories of treasure continuing over from Yaḫdun-Lim to Yasmaḫ-Adad, see Charpin 1983.

[36] For the biblical incident, see the histories of Israel, and especially Hutter 1982, pp. 69–71, 81; see also Oded 1985. In the biblical episode, almost the same items of treasure are listed as in Mari, and in both they were passed down from one king to the next. The Hebrew term there for treasure-house, *bēt n^{e}ḵōt*, is the exact equivalent of Akkadian *bīt nakkamti*.

examination of the liver of a sacrificial sheep (Pl. VIII*b*).[37] There was an inscription of Zimri-Lim's father, Yaḫdun-Lim, one of the earliest royal historical inscriptions in the Babylonian language, possibly some fifty years old by the time the palace was destroyed (and see p. 107). And there were copies of historical inscriptions of Šamši-Adad and Zimri-Lim,[38] and various religious texts, some of them incantations in Hurrian, the language of a major element of non-Semitic, non-Indo-European origin, which had infiltrated Syro-Mesopotamia much earlier.[39]

Sealed doors and sealed chambers

The archive also contained numerous legal documents and contracts, some going back a century or more. Here, too, were lumps of clay bearing cylinder-seal impressions, interpreted by the excavator as jar-sealings. These latter introduce us to a most interesting feature in the palace, for many of these so-called jar stoppers are actually the sealings from the doors of store-rooms and archives (see Pl. III*a–c*).[40]

By means of such sealings, the official (or officials) responsible for a store-room—whether it contained jars of wine or some other commodity, or even baskets holding documents—could protect himself, for only as long as his seal remained intact was he held responsible for it. Breaking the seal was tantamount to assumption of the responsibility, and anyone doing so became accountable. This, indeed, is reflected in a passage in the Babylonian Wisdom Literature, where a young man entering royal service is advised: 'Guard his (the prince's) seal . . .; open his treasury, enter therein . . ., but do not turn your eye to anything; do not let your mind consider anything stealthy—for eventually the matter will be investigated. . . . The prince will hear of it. . . .'[41] It is in this spirit that we can better understand certain Akkadian documents—among them Old Babylonian texts from Mari—touching upon the sealing of store-rooms and archives. In one Mari letter (*ARMT* XIII 22), we read how Mukannišum, whom we have previously noted, had been instructed by Zimri-Lim to remove certain precious objects from a particular store-room. The official actually responsible for that store-room, however, told him that the objects were not in his charge, but rather in another store-room. At the door of this second store-room, Mukannišum discovered that it had been sealed with the king's seal, and he was reluctant to open it without royal authority.

[37] The clay liver-models were published by Rutten 1938.

[38] For the Disc Inscription of Yaḫdun-Lim, see Thureau-Dangin 1936; Kupper 1976. The historical inscription of Šamši-Adad is still unpublished. For Zimri-Lim's 'Victory' stele, see Dossin 1971; and Sasson 1972a; Charpin-Durand 1985, pp. 319ff.

[39] For the Hurrian documents (notably including one letter), see Laroche 1957.

[40] For the following, see in greater detail Malamat 1986; certain matters have been updated here slightly. For the current views of sealing practices, see Gibson & Biggs 1977, though much work has since been done in this rapidly progressing field. See now Zettler 1987.

[41] Cf. R. H. Pfeiffer in *ANET*, p. 427a; and Lambert 1960, pp. 102–103, *ll.* 81ff.

Since Zimri-Lim was away from the palace at the time, he turned to the queen, who told him not to open the store-room himself, but to have the person responsible for it (probably one of the women-in-waiting) open it, take out the objects and then reseal it herself.

The procedure for opening archives differed slightly. The fact that one tablet closely resembled any other one—despite the great possible differences in content—require the presence of someone who was literate, but not necessarily the same person as that responsible for the store-room in question. Among the Mari texts are several letters describing this situation.[42] In *ARMT* X 82 and XIII 14, we again read of Mukannišum being instructed by the king to send him items—this time certain lists of personnel, documents kept in sealed baskets in a sealed room. Here, it was the princess Inib-šina who broke her father's seal. Igmilum, an official privy to the identity of the required baskets, pointed them out to Mukannišum, and only then was he able, together with another official, to take the baskets out and send them to the king—without breaking their seals.

Further, in *ARMT* X 12, Šibtu writes to Zimri-Lim, confirming his instructions to retrieve certain documents from an archive and to hold them for him till his return to the city. She sent three trusted officials—including Mukannišum—along with the king's messenger who knew where the relevant 'files' were kept. At a certain workshop (in the palace?), the messenger pointed out the right store-room, and the three officials broke the seal on the door, which bore the imprint of Igmilum, whom we have just noted in a previous instance. Entering, they removed the 'files' in question, taking them to Šibtu's quarters. The queen then resealed the store-room (probably by proxy)—in a most revealing manner (*ll.* 33–35): '. . . and the door of the room I sealed the cord (or thong—[gi]š/[ku]š *eb-li*) with my seal.'[43]

As interesting as these written sources may be, how can we relate them precisely to the clay lumps bearing seal impressions? Is there any other archaeological evidence which might shed light on this matter? Actual examples of sealed doors, chests and the like have come to light in Egypt;[44] but in other parts of the ancient Near East, including Mari, only similar lumps of clay have been noted—variously defined as 'bullae', 'jar, sack or basket sealings', 'bouchons des jarres', 'cretuli' and the like. Scattered

[42] Initially discussed by Sasson 1972b; and more recently by O. Rouault, in *ARMT* XVIII, pp. 213–214, 228, 231–234, 249.

[43] Thus *ARMT* X, pp. 40 and 254. But see now Durand 1984b, p. 260, n. 3, for a collated reading of *l.* 34: [*š*]*a ep-tu* . . ., 'et la porte de la pièce *que j'avait ouverte*, je l'ai scellée à mon sceau.'

[44] The sealing procedure in Egypt was very sophisticated; see Boochs 1982. There is a vivid description of the unsealing and resealing of a door, on the Victory Stele of King Piye (Piankhy; 25th Nubian dynasty): 'Breaking the seals of the bolts, opening the doors. . . . Closing the doors, applying the clay, sealing with the king's own seal, and instructing the priests: "I have inspected the seal. No other king who may arise shall enter here"'; see Lichtheim 1980, p. 77.

in such lands as the Sudan, Greece, Crete and Iran, they have generally been found in strata corresponding to the Old Babylonian period at Mari. On the reverse, these sealed lumps of clay bear the imprint of a peg or knob bound with cords.[45]

About thirty sealings of this type were discovered in the 1980 season of excavations at Mari, in an early phase of Asqudum's palace east of the royal palace, from the end of the Šakkanakku period (see Fig. 3). In studying them, the excavators also re-examined the published clay sealings from the royal palace, discovering—as I had suspected for some time—that many of them were also of this type. Significantly, all but one of the latter were found in rooms 29 and 108 (and apparently in adjacent rooms 107 and 54; see Fig. 4).[46] In room 108 there was an archive of about 1000 tablets, as we have noted: royal and official correspondence, legal texts, numerous clay model livers of an earlier period, and a copy of an historical inscription of Zimri-Lim.[47] And it is here, in the doorway leading into room 108, that we seem to have a fixed feature which must be associated with the sealing of the room.[48] This object (see Pl. VIII*a*)—which André Parrot 'irreverently' (as he put it) called a 'bouton de sonnette', a doorbell button—is a pottery disk 11 cm in diameter, with a concentric hole 2.7 cm in diameter. It was found *in situ*, affixed in the door jamb opposite the side of the socket, about 1.15 m above the floor.[49] This location precludes its use as a catch for a doorbolt,[50] but enables us to reconstruct its use in sealing the door (see Fig. 5). It apparently served as an escutcheon for a wooden peg which jutted out some 7–10 cm. The door would have been pierced at about the same height, and a cord attached to the door bolt within the room would have been threaded through the hole, stretched taut and wound several times around the peg. Peg and cord would then

45 These lumps of clay have ingeniously been interpreted by Fiandra 1981, 1982; cf. also Postgate 1980, p. 92, Pl. XI: h; and most recently, on a hoard of door-sealings from as early as the late 4th millennium BC from Choga Mish in Iran, Kantor 1986. As for Mari, see the independent studies of Beyer 1985 and Margueron 1982a, pp. 489–492.

46 In Parrot's official publication, unfortunately, there are no illustrations of the backs of the sealings, and most were regarded as jar-sealings; cf. Barrelet et al., in Parrot 1959, pp. 156–250, Pls XLVI—LII; and Parrot 1958a, p. 101, concerning room 107.

47 The 'antiquarian' nature of part of the archive of room 108 is further emphasized by Yaḫdun-Lim's Disc Inscription, found in the adjacent room 18—which I am inclined to call a 'museum'. In the final phase of the palace, at least, it could be entered only through room 108; see Parrot 1958a, p. 195.

48 Margueron 1982a, I, p. 492, following a suggestion of P. Amiet.

49 Parrot 1958a, pp. 102–103. A similar feature was discovered recently on the wall (not on the door jamb) adjacent to a door at Isin, in a context of about the same time as the Mari palace. See Spycket & Strommenger 1981, p. 57 and Pl. 20: 2–3. The 'doorbell' there was set into the plaster 70 cm above the floor and 14 cm from the doorway. It is made from the base of a pottery jar, 8 cm in diameter and pierced (after firing) by a hole 2.6 cm in diameter, the hole reaching 6 cm into the wall. The excavators assumed that it was related to the closing of the door, and this can now be extended to include the *sealing* of the door. I must thank Mlle. Spycket for providing data beyond that appearing in the above publication.

50 As initially supposed in Margueron 1982a, I, p. 491.

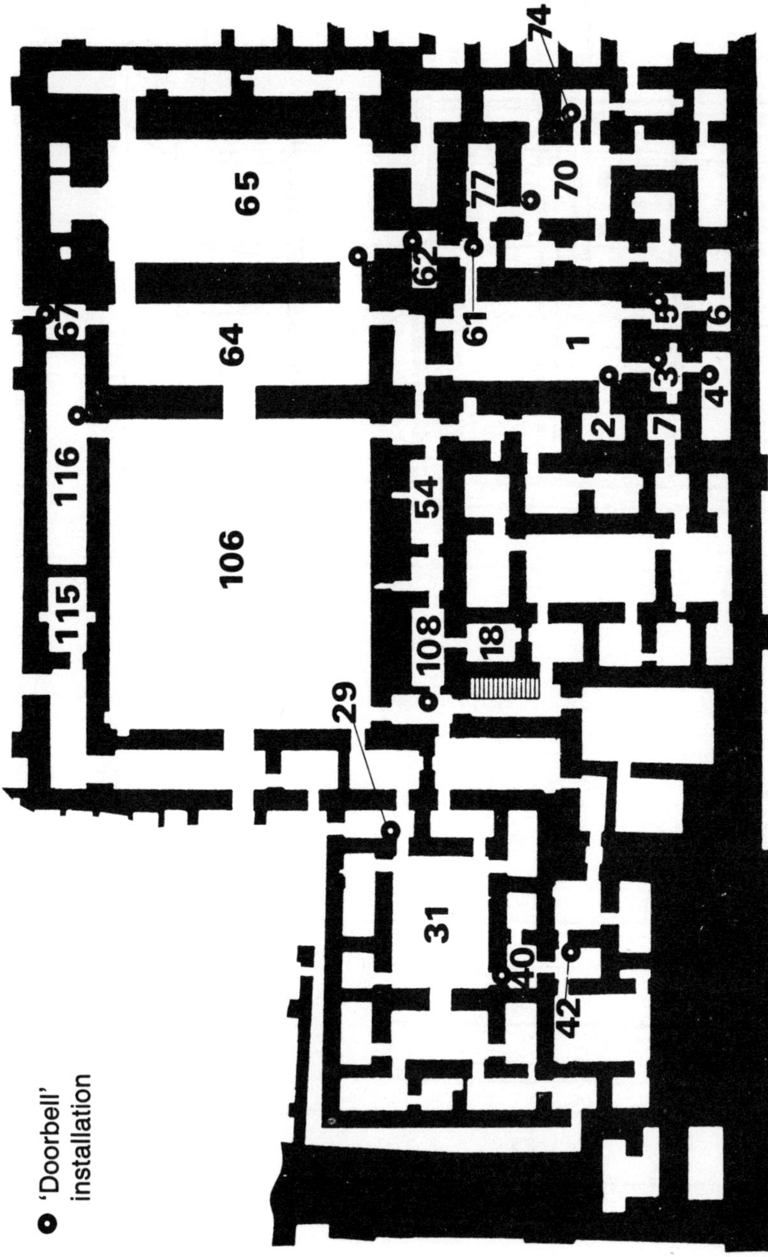

4. The north-western part of the Mari palace, showing the locations of 'doorbell' installations.

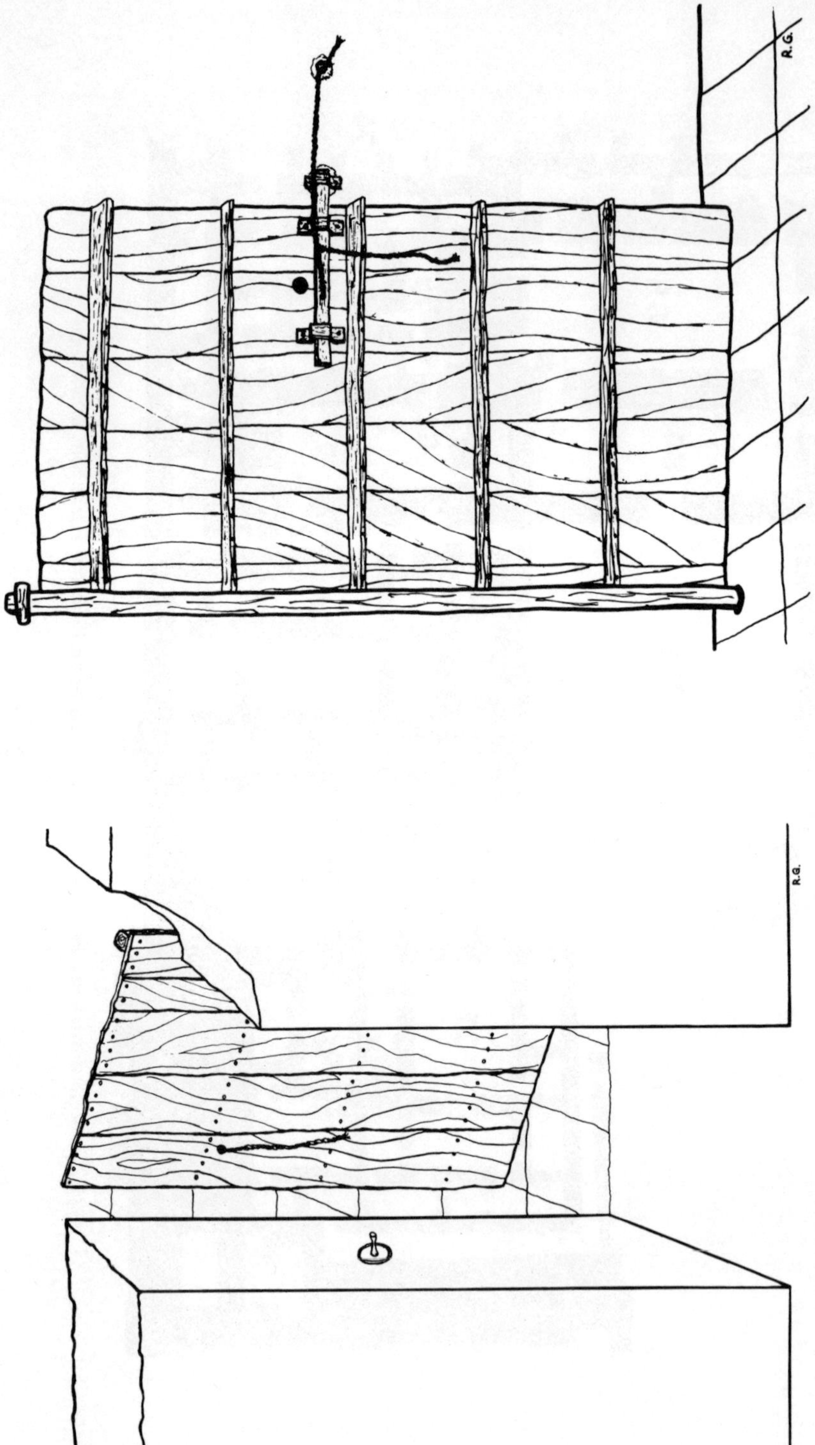

5. Schematic reconstructions of (a) doorway 109–108; and (b) a doorway sealed from the 'inside'.

have been 'wrapped' in an envelope of soft clay which, finally, would have been impressed with a seal. This is precisely what we have seen Šibtu doing in sealing an archive, and anyone wishing to open the door would have to break the clay sealing it, to release the cord.[51]

Adjacent to other doors in the palace[52] there are further features which we can apparently associate with the sealing of rooms as well. Thus, there is occasionally a single or a pair of holes in the wall next to the doorway, opposite the door socket (see Fig. 5b). Here, the bolt was surely mounted on the inner side of the door itself—a common feature throughout architectural history. The single hole or the one of a pair closest to the door would have been for fixing the wooden catch, but the second hole, some 40–50 cm away, would have had a function identical to that of the 'doorbell'—that is, it would have held a peg for the cord used in sealing the door (see Fig. 5b). But here it would be on the same side of the door as the bolt (on the 'inside'). This latter point would, *a priori*, seem problematic. It must be remembered, however, that it was not a room which was being sealed, but a doorway, and the access being denied could be in either direction.[53] This would seem to be the case in ceremonial hall 65, where one of the two main doors bears traces of an external 'doorbell' on one jamb (see p. 24 top).[54] Assuming that the other main door could similarly be sealed, access to the hall could thus be limited to the doorway from room 62, which has a two-hole arrangement. Sealing the doorway within room 62 by its internal 'doorbell', and the two main doors to the hall with their external 'doorbells', would effectively have prevented all access to the entire ceremonial hall complex and its dependent chambers.[55]

Can these revelations concerning sealed chambers shed any light on similar phenomena in the biblical world? Indeed, there are several instances in the Bible where chambers are actually sealed: in the Book of Daniel,

[51] The above description is based, inter alia, on the fact that no traces of a doorbolt were found in room 108, though there may well have been one there. In other doorways in the palace where bolt mechanisms are in evidence (see below), the closing cord of the doorbolt would have been used for sealing the door, in the same manner as described above (and see Fig. 5).

[52] See Margueron 1982, I, chart on p. 490, série a. We can now add to his list our example in room 29 (see Parrot 1958a, p. 163), one in room 61 (p. 221; and see below), and a third in room 127, alongside a blocked doorway (p. 73); but his 'salle S-ext.' and '65–64' there are problematic and doubtful.

[53] Contra Margueron 1982a, I, pp. 489ff.

[54] Parrot 1958a, p. 119 and Pl. XXXII, 2, concerning which Parrot commented: 'Nous ne voyons pas à quel usage précis tout cela pouvait servir.' This example, too, should be added to Margueron's list, under série b, as should one in the doorway to room 4 (cf. Parrot 1958a, p. 217); see Margueron 1982a, I, chart on p. 490. Note also what appears to be the hole for a 'doorbell' in the passageway to room 7, visible on the left in Parrot 1958a, p. 201, Fig. 233; in any event, room 7 certainly did not begin its career as the best preserved '*w.-c.* ... dans les annales de l'archéologie orientale' (Pl. IV*b*).

[55] Similarly with the two doorways leading into room 77; in both courtyard 70 and room 61, the relevant doors have the two-hole arrangement, and these two sealed doors would in conjunction also have effectively prevented all unauthorized entry into room 77.

the stone closing Daniel within the lions' den is sealed by King Darius 'with his own signet and with the signets of his lords, that nothing might be changed concerning Daniel' (6: 18); and in the New Testament, Matthew relates how Pontius Pilate ordered the Jewish priests 'to make the sepulchre [of Jesus] secure by sealing (*σφραγίσαντες*) the stone (door) and setting a guard' (Matthew 27: 66)—a detail often clearly depicted in Renaissance art. Finally, a revealing passage in an Elephantine Papyrus, written in Aramaic in the fifth century BC—the so-called Passover Papyrus—relates: 'Bring into your chambers [any leaven which you have in your houses] and seal it up (*ḥtmh*)'[56] for the duration of the festival since leaven is forbidden to the Jews during the Passover week.

To return now to the Mari palace, one room which could be sealed with an external 'doorbell' was room 5, opening off courtyard 1. This same room 5 was one of the first to be excavated in the entire palace, and it was here, early in 1936, that the first tablets came to light on the site—just a metre below the surface (Pl. III*d*). Several things are extraordinary here. First, over 1500 tablets were found in the debris of this one room, from floor-level up to a height some three and a half or four metres above. And some of them were found stored in pottery jars stacked up against one wall. This situation would indicate that at least part of the tablets had fallen from an upper storey, upon the collapse of the ceiling. Thus, the group of tablets here actually represents two separate archives which, today, unfortunately, can no longer be distinguished.

The king's table

Many of the tablets found here deal with foodstuffs, especially daily provisons for the royal meals (*naptan šarrim*) prepared at the palace. This room 5 gives access to two other rooms (6 and 57), in one of which were large quantities of dishes and jars—surely also for service on the royal table. Thus, we appear to have here a store-room cum archive belonging to the overseer of the king's table—in other words, the royal butler. Interestingly, many of these lists are dated, and occasionally the daily lists of foods are found to be totalled up in monthly accounts. Copies of some of the same accounts have been found in room 111, which we passed earlier. Thus, the butler probably had to submit his monthly accounts to his superior, whose office seems to have been in room 111.[57]

These tallies of 'king's meals' are another genre unique to Mari, and much clever use of them is currently being made by several scholars to

[56] In the 'Passover Papyrus' (Cowley 1923, No. 21), *ll.* 6–8, as restored by Porten 1979, p. 91.

[57] For these royal meals see, inter alia, Glaeseman 1978; Bonneterre 1985. For the texts on the king's meals from room 5, see *ARMT* IX and XII; from room 111, *ARMT* XI. And cf. Materne 1985, where an attempt is made to distinguish between the several scribes writing the tablets.

unravel the annual course of life at the palace.[58] Careful perusal reveals daily, monthly and yearly cycles.

Thus, two meals were eaten each day—a sort of early, heavy lunch and a much lighter evening dinner. In the course of the month, there were special feasts on specific days, such as the *kispum* ritual meal, in commemoration of dynastic forefathers (a topic to which we shall return later; see p. 98). And over the year we see, beginning in the spring, a holiday season involving large quantities of food and numerous celebrations; followed by a slack summer season, when the king was out of town, campaigning at the head of his army; and then an autumn–winter period when the king was again at home.

This material now provides a realistic background for the biblical passages on the royal table at the courts of Judah and Israel, particularly in the days of King Solomon.[59] Here we read that 'Solomon's provision for one day was thirty measures (cors) of fine flour, and sixty measures of meal, ten fat oxen and twenty pasture-fed cattle, a hundred sheep. . . .' And later, 'And those officers supplied provisions for King Solomon, and for all who came to King Solomon's table, each one in his month; they let nothing be lacking' (1 Kings 5: 2–3, 7 [MT]; 4: 22–23, 27 [RSV]). The latter passage clearly reflects monthly totalling, just as at Mari. The daily quantities, however, would fall far short of those needed for some of the larger feasts at Mari, at which as many as 1000 guests might sup.[60] Such enormous banquets at Mari must have been held in the large courtyard 106, but ordinarily the ceremonial hall 65 was probably used, as we shall see later on.

In the immediate vicinity of the 'chief butler's office', there are several other interesting groups of rooms, comprising the royal kitchens. Room 71, containing an archive of several hundred tablets (so far unpublished), and the large adjacent room 72 apparently formed a sort of kitchen or bakery, for in the courtyard (70) just outside there were two large ovens. Furthermore, in a chamber across the courtyard, above room 77, there had been a group of pottery moulds in which fancy cakes had been made (Pl. VII). The moulds had fallen into the room below at the time of the collapse of the upper storey, during the destruction of the palace. These moulds can be compared to modern Continental biscuit moulds for making 'gingerbread men'. The patterns in them include geometric motifs, lions, fish, stags and, most significantly, a nude female figure holding her breasts. This latter figure probably represents Ištar or Astarte, fertility goddess

[58] For several attempts, see Hamlin 1971; Sasson 1979; see also Kerestes 1982.

[59] In addition to King Solomon's table, we may note the following in the Bible, referring to royal tables, on which the parallel Mari material may shed some light: *Saul*, 1 Samuel 20: 5, 18, 24–25; *David*, 2 Samuel 9: 7ff.; *David to Solomon*, 1 Kings 2: 7; *Solomon, Queen of Sheba*, 1 Kings 10: 4–5; *Ahab and Jezebel*, 1 Kings 18: 19; *Jehoiachin* (in exile), 2 Kings 25: 29–30; *Nehemiah*, Nehemiah 5: 17–18.

[60] Parrot 1966, p. 7, mentioning banquets at the Mari palace with up to at least 1000 guests within the vast courtyards.

and lady of the heavens (Pl. VII*a*). It is apparently this very sort of cultic cake which Jeremiah the prophet condemned among the Israelites (Jeremiah 44: 19): '... (women of Judah) burned incense to the queen of heaven and poured out libations to her ... (and) made cakes for her, bearing her image....'[61]

In addition to these chambers, there are also several suites of rooms in this wing which were obviously occupied by various palace officials as dwellings. These are scattered around three courtyards (15, 1 and 70), and they generally include a bed- or sitting-room and a bathroom cum privy. In the bathrooms, there are one or two pottery tubs, and the tiled floors have built-in drains. And in several instances there are corner fire-places for heating the room.

The royal ceremonial complex

Let us now proceed to the focal point of the Mari palace, ceremonial hall 65, by way of courtyard 106 (Figs. 4 and 6). This court—possibly referred to in the texts as 'the Court of the Palm in the Mari palace'[62]—was entirely surrounded by high walls. On the west, two doorways gave access to the administrative and service wings we have just visited. On the east, a single doorway led into a large store-room containing huge jars, probably for wine or oil. Indeed, this might even be the 'sealed store-room for fine oil in the Court of the Palm', mentioned in more than one Mari text. On the north of the courtyard, on the central axis, is the main entrance, which we passed when coming into this newer wing of the palace from the older part. Opposite, also on the central axis, is the broad entrance to the throne-room complex. The walls around the courtyard bore wall-paintings: border designs in simple geometric patterns, as well as much more elaborate scenes, arranged in friezes.[63]

In one fresco fragment here, we see a figure in a sacrificial procession, possibly a high official, leading a bull to the altar (Pl. VI). On the edges of his garment are the fringes mentioned in some texts (as we shall see below, p. 95). This figure seems to reflect the general appearance of the West Semitics at this time, and this is how we might envisage the Patriarchs of the Bible, as well. On another, larger fragment we see more of the procession, with an extraordinarily large figure at the right, probably the

[61] In Jeremiah 44:19, Hebrew *kawwānīm*, most likely cognate with Akkadian *kamānu*, 'sacrificial cake' (*CAD* K, p. 110): 'We made cakes for her *lᵉha'ᵃṣiḇāh*'—probably now to be understood, in the light of the Mari mould, as 'to engrave her image'. And cf. Jeremiah 7: 18. See also Yorkoff 1972.

[62] For this identification, see al-Khalesi 1978, basing on the main frescos on the walls of the court, which show palm trees. Recently, Margueron 1987a arrived at a similar conclusion, but postulated the existence of an actual tree, a single palm. But these opinions do not seem to be sufficiently substantiated.

[63] On the frescos, their dating and their stylistic features, see Parrot 1958b; Moortgat 1964; Moortgat-Correns 1952–53.

king, depicted in the style of an earlier time. On the basis of recent analyses, it is thought that the wall-paintings here, in courtyard 106, are of the period of Šamši-Adad.

Previously, we mentioned in passing the frescos in the old throne room (132), in the older part of the palace. In the main panel there, figures can be seen in two ritual scenes, flanked by mythical animals. The costumes and other features there are typical of an earlier period (Ur III?), even before the West Semitic dynasty took control of Mari and its palace.

Coming back to courtyard 106, just to the right of the entrance to the throne room complex is a panel, the most famous of the Mari frescos. In style it is also the latest of the palace paintings. The central scene was interpreted by the excavator as the 'Investiture of Zimri-Lim',[64] but it is now generally conceded that it reflects some other ceremony or ritual of that king, such as the annual ceremony of bringing the statue of Ištar into the palace. The actual ceremony may have been conducted within the throne room complex, inside the adjacent doorway.[65] Around the painted panel we see a fenced park with idealized, sacred trees beautiful to behold' (Genesis 2:9) and guarded by cherubs (cf. Genesis 3:24)—a veritable Garden of Eden. The upper register of the central panel shows the king with distinctly Old Akkadian features, i.e. as king of Akkad, before a goddess, probably Ištar, holding insignia of royalty and weapons, and flanked by other figures, either gods or priests. In the lower register of the central panel, there are two mirror image figures, each holding a vase from which four streams of water are emerging—reminiscent of the four rivers of Paradise, in the Bible, flowing forth from a single source (Genesis 2:10). Fish swim up the streams toward the vase—as if toward the fertility of their upstream spawning grounds.

Entering room 64, we see opposite the doorway a raised podium flanked by steps. During the excavations, a large stone statue was found alongside the podium, depicting a goddess holding a vase with water flowing down her robes and fish swimming upward—precisely the figure just seen in the painted panel outside, in the courtyard. Here, however, the depiction is in three dimensions. The identity of this goddess, and the original position of the statue, are still matters of scholarly controversy. The problem is further complicated by the fact that the statue's head was found far away, in the courtyard. If the statue had not stood on top of the podium in room 64, then this podium may have supported a throne for the king, used during his more public audiences, for he then would have been in full view of most of the courtyard outside.[66]

[64] For the so-called Investiture Scene of Zimri-Lim, see the initial publication in Barrelet 1950; and Parrot 1950b. See also Haldar 1952, for the wall-painting from courtyard 106.

[65] Hrouda 1971, pp. 157–158, and especially al-Khalesi 1978, associate this painting with the ceremonies conducted within the ceremonial hall (rooms 65 and 66).

[66] See the reconstruction in Margueron 1982a, II, Fig. 244, showing the angle of vision toward the king, enthroned in room 64.

From here we enter the large ceremonial hall 65, through a large doorway. This huge chamber is over 26 metres long and close to 12 metres wide, and the walls are preserved to a height of as much as 5 metres and may have been twice as high, originally. Traces of wooden beams were found at the centre of the floor, showing that the room had been roofed over. At the centre of the western wall there is a low podium, for a throne. Flanking this are two doors, the southern one giving access to the 'wine-cellar', and the northern one opening onto a special suite of rooms (62, 61 and 77)—two chambers and a large bathroom cum privy, probably intended for the king and his immediate entourage as an occasional refuge during the long, drawn-out banquets and festivities in the ceremonial hall.

The ceremonial hall itself is paralleled in layout and location in various smaller halls, such as 'courtyard' 1, as well as outside the main palace, in the *šakkanakkum* palace in Chantier A, for instance, or in the much smaller palace recently excavated at Tell Bi'ya (probably Tuttul) at the confluence of the Baliḫ and the Euphrates rivers.[67]

On the central axis of the ceremonial hall there are two tiled areas which had served as open hearths. The entire eastern end of the hall, for five metres, was paved in bitumen, and the floor there contained a drainage system. In the eastern wall there is a 4 metre wide opening leading by means of a broad stairway to a small, raised cella (66). Flanking this entry are two bases, probably for statues. At the foot of the stairway, the excavators found a stone statue of Ištup-ilum, a *šakkanakkum* or governor of Mari some 200 years prior to Zimri-Lim.

All these features in the huge ceremonial hall bring to mind a text from Mari (12803), published in 1980,[68] concerning one of the central sacrifices made apparently at the palace and associated with a festive meal. This feast, commemorating royal ancestors—the *kispum* ritual already noted in passing—was intended to assure the welfare of the kingdom and of the king. The relevant passages in the document read as follows: 'At the going-out of the first day of Adar (around February), the *kispum* (shall be offered) in the city and in its environs. The "meal" shall be drawn (from) the palace.

[67] See now also Margueron 1985, and on p. 218 the plans of (a) the throne room of the *šakkanakku*, (b) room 1 of the palace, and (c) throne room 65 there. To these we may add the newly uncovered palace at Tell Bi'ya, being excavated by E. Strommenger since 1983; it is practically a copy of the Mari palace, and measures 91.40 × 46.80 m—considerably smaller than the palace at Mari. Its largest hall (throne room? ceremonial hall?) measures 10 × 24 m, with a 'cella' with only two steps. Several tablets were discovered, from the days of Šamši-Adad. For the most recent report, see Strommenger *et al.* 1987, with a plan of the palace on p. 11. The plan of these throne rooms belongs, typologically, to the Syrian 'Mittelsaalhaus' (central hall) type found throughout Syria and even as far south as northern Egypt in the Amorite period; for a representative example, at Tell el-Dab'a, see Eigner 1985.

[68] See Birot 1980; for additional bibliography, see below, pp. 98ff.

A sheep shall be sacrificed in the hall of thrones to the statues (*lamassātum*) of Sargon and of Naram-Sin (two kings of Akkad, who had ruled hundreds of years earlier). ... Before the arrival of the king (the intention here is Šamši-Adad), the sacrifice of the hall of thrones is performed and the meats are cooked, the best meats shall be presented to Šamaš (the sun god). So long as they have not been presented to Šamaš, the *kispum* (to the statues of the two dead kings) shall not be offered. ... After they have been presented to Šamaš, the *kispum* (shall be offered) to Sargon and to Narām-Sin, to the *yaradu* Ḫaneans (*yaradu*, surely meaning "descended", that is, deceased; and see below, pp. 99f.) and those of the Numḫā (another Amorite tribe)....' The text then goes on to mention royal sacrifices in the temples and other matters.[69]

Relating this text to the ceremonial hall in the Mari palace (which certainly could be called a throne room—*bīt kussîmi*, in Akkadian), we can see that the eastern end of the chamber, with its bitumen pavement and drainage installations, would have been perfectly suited for the slaughtering of the sacrificial animals, while the hearths would have been more than adequate for the roasting of the meat for the meal. The statue of Ištup-ilum, found on the floor near the staircase, may have merely been one of numerous statues of 'ancestors' which had stood at the top of the stairs within the 'cella' to the east.[70] This ritual of ancestor worship at the New Moon is an interesting and complex topic having manifold ramifications. It was so essential to the official side of religion at Mari (as in other areas of Mesopotamia and Syria) that we shall devote some time to it in our final lecture (see below, pp. 96–107).

We are now coming to the close of our tour of this fascinating palace. We have not visited all its parts; for instance, we have not even entered the workshops, nor the servants' quarters in the southwest. But even so, we have seen an impressive and extensive, monumental complex. Already in 1937, the French noted that one of the Mari letters, written to Zimri-Lim by Ḫammurabi, King of Aleppo, hinted at the splendour of the Mari palace (Pl. II*a*). The letter relates that the king of Ugarit, on the Syrian coast, was most anxious to see Zimri-Lim's palace, and he sent a person, possibly

[69] From our point of view, the crux here is the term *bīt kussīḫa*, a house or room of thrones, mentioned twice in the text (*ll.* 7 and 10). Birot 1980, p. 146, regards it as a hall in the temple of Šamaš, patron deity of, inter alia, *eṭiemmum*, ghosts of the deceased; others hold that there was a specific sanctuary with thrones for statues of divinities, set on thrones or chairs, to whom the *kispum* was offered. And see below, p. 98 and nn. 100, 101.

[70] For the 'cella' (room 66), see Parrot 1958a, pp. 132ff., Pl. XXXI, 2; and see al-Khalesi 1978, pp. 37–57, and the earlier bibliography there; cf. n. 65 above. It is assumed that the statues of Zimri-Lim, and deities (Ištar?), stood at the top of the 'cella'; it seems to us, however, that statues of the royal ancestors of the Mari dynasties were located there. Cf. similarly Durand 1985b, p. 159, n. 55.

his son, to inspect it for him.[71] We can only regret that we were not able to join *that* guided tour of the palace—for it surely must have been far more fascinating than our 'tour' today—in itself a unique experience in a palace without parallel.[72]

[71] This letter was initially published only in translation, in Dossin 1937, p. 19; with a transliteration, it appears in Schaeffer 1939, p. 16. Durand oddly considers this brief document as an itinerary, rather than reflecting a visit to Mari's marvels; see *ARMT* XXIII, p. 474, n. 50.

[72] It appears to be the fate of splendid palaces to disappear for centuries without a trace, until unearthed by the archaeologists' spade—particularly when they were built in violation of sacred chapels, as at Mari. But then, not more than a dozen miles from the premises of the British Academy in London, King Henry the Eighth also built a palace 'without parallel'—Nonsuch Palace, erected directly over a 500-year-old church which Henry totally demolished to make way for his pleasure. Nonsuch, too, disappeared after a relatively short lifespan, and was revealed once again only some thirty years ago. Cf. Dent 1981.

II

THE EARLY ISRAELITE EXPERIENCE: A VIEW FROM MARI

A. THE COMPARATIVE METHOD

Prior to the discovery of Mari, Northern Mesopotamia and Syria in the Old Babylonian period presented a rather bleak picture.[1] Above we have seen how the Mari discoveries—a virtual treasure-house of historical, cultural and economic data—can serve to shed light not only on Mesopotamia, but also on the lands to the West, and thus also on the Bible and earliest Israel. Here, we shall examine more of this material, and delve much deeper into it.

It seems to me that Old Babylonian Mari—more than any other extra-bibilical material—can place the proto-history of the Israelites in a new perspective. Mari, like the Holy Land, is situated on the fringe of the Syro-Arabian Desert—albeit on an entirely different flank. Now, the city-states of the so-called Fertile Crescent had often been infiltrated, and the West Semitic groups with whom we are concerned here were just one more of these intrusive movements. These West Semites, often simply called Amorites, eventually gained hegemony over the urban areas which they had infiltrated.[2] Old Babylonian Mari, along with early Israel and many other peoples of the West, did apparently share common origins (see pp. 32, 101). Thus, a comparison between early Israel and Mari can, should and must be made—so long as it is a controlled, meaningful comparison. Indeed, the broad spectrum of the Mari archives—the largest extra-biblical body of material within this West Semitic milieu from the first half of the second millennium BC—actually invites such a comparison.

But first a cautionary word on the comparative method in approaching Mari and the Bible. Valid, meaningful comparisons can yield significant results, and can preclude shallow or extreme conclusions. Lack of discretion in this respect has been a pitfall in the past—the outstanding example being the somewhat sensationalist hullabaloo surrounding the early announcements of the epigraphic finds at Ebla, finds which are quite remarkable in themselves.[3] I would reject any romantic or neo-fundamentalist

[1] See, e.g., Maisler 1930. Significantly, Maisler (Mazar) already devotes some space to both Ebla and Mari, prior to their discoveries (pp. 7 ff).

[2] Of the voluminous literature on the Amorite tribes, note the more recent treatments, mainly concerning Mesopotamia: Kupper 1957; Gelb 1961; Buccellati 1966; Liverani 1973; Anbar 1985.

[3] For Ebla, see now the already somewhat dated Matthiae 1980 and Pettinato 1981.

approach to the Mari documents; yet much of the scholarship soon after their discovery, as well as later on, fell into the trap of romanticism. Even André Parrot, the excavator of Mari, never really freed himself of this attitude, and in other scholarly schools too this fever was rampant.[4] Such an approach tends to relate Mari *directly* with the Israelite cradle, almost as if there had been an initial, genetic connection between the tribal populations reflected in the Mari documents and the clans of the Hebrew Patriarchs.

Rather than taking any such 'genetic' view, I conceive Mari and the relevant parts of the Bible as two separate but analogous corpora. The comparative method I advocate would best be called 'typological' or 'phenomenological'. In other words, efforts should be concentrated on examination of typical phenomena, seeking out common sets of concepts and elucidating institutions and practices which more or less overlap at Mari and among the Israelites. When such similarities are revealed in the aggregate, they cannot simply be regarded as representing common patterns of human behaviour, and thus this approach can place our comparisons on a firm and constructive basis.[5]

Proper comparison, however, also involves a contrasting approach. If our aim is validity, then the basic difference underlying Mari and the Bible must not be neglected. This difference—surprisingly ignored in most research—lies in the very nature of the two sources, for they are as different from one another in quality as 'the raw and the cooked', in the words of Claude Lévi-Strauss. The Mari documents are everyday, first-hand material directly reflecting the reality of their matrix. Further, they were intended for limited, internal consumption. In decided contrast, the relevant biblical material—mainly in the genre of folk-narrative—has been 'processed', that is, edited and re-edited, and in part indeed composed, centuries after the events described. This intricate literary, intellectual and, in particular, theological reworking was the 'contribution' of later, often tendentious historiographers.[6] But this would in no way preclude, *a priori*, some erstwhile historical connection with Mari—though there is nothing in the data presently available which would support such an assumption.

We can now embark on a comparative study of Mari and the Bible, based on these assumptions and reservations—with benefit to our understanding of both milieus. An added benefit is the light shed by the Mari documents on the earliest stratum of the Hebrew lexicon, as we shall later see. Mari at first glance appears to be remote from the Bible, in terms

[4] Parrot 1950a; 1962; 1967. There are many other scholars who make genetic connections with the early Hebrews; see, e.g., Albright 1968, pp. 69 and 71 ('these exciting new tablets . . . appear to prove that the ancestral Hebrews founded the First Dynasty of Babylon').

[5] On the comparative approach, which should encompass similarities as well as contrasts, [illegible] al Mandelbaum 1979/80; Hammel 1980. Concerning our region, see Gelb 1980; [illegible] and on the Patriarchal narratives, Millard 1980. On Mari and the Bible cf. also [illegible].

[6] [illegible] mat 1983, esp. pp. 306 ff. and the bibliography there.

of time and space. Indeed, the earliest parts of the biblical text can go back little further than the 12th–11th centuries BC[7]—meaning that we are faced with a gap in time of more than half a millennium between the sacking of the Mari palace by Ḫammurabi and the date when the earliest parts of the Bible as we have it were set down. But the Patriarchal narratives—and it is with that part of the Bible that we are primarily concerned—would seem to present events which hark back much further than the 12th century BC. The problem is, how much further back. And this is a major bone of contention among scholars.[8]

B. THE CHRONOLOGICAL ASPECT

The chronological aspect is probably the least relevant but also the most problematic facet of the Patriarchal narratives. Can the timespan covered by these narratives be synchronized with the Mari period? The so-called Patriarchal Age has often been ascribed to the first quarter, or third, of the second millennium BC—in archaeological terms, the Middle Bronze Age I (as held, foremost, by Nelson Glueck and W. F. Albright), or the Middle Bronze Age II (as held, *inter alia*, by Père R. de Vaux and E. Speiser).[9] As some scholars regard the Mari documents as more or less contemporaneous with Abraham, Isaac and Jacob, one could readily be enticed into adopting a 'genetic' approach, leading to overevaluation of the extra-biblical evidence for the historicity of the Israelite Patriarchs. Another school of thought has gone to the opposite extreme, reviving (in modified forms) the position of classic 19th century biblical scholarship, contending that the 'Patriarchal Age'—and the 'patriarchs' themselves along with it—are no more than pure fable: the creation of the later biblical authors, and consequently possessing no particular time of their own.[10]

My own view is that the Patriarchs should not be assigned to any specific, well-defined set of dates—that is, to a 'Patriarchal Age' as such. Hence, this oft-used term is of doubtful legitimacy. I am in no way suggesting the negation of the very essence of the Patriarchs. But I do regard, along

[7] In chronological order, according to a recent study (Freedman 1987): (1) The Blessing of Jacob (Genesis 49); (2) The Song of the Sea (Exodus 15); (3) The Oracles of Balaam (Numbers 23–24); (4) The Blessing of Moses (Deuteronomy 33); and (5) The Song of Deborah (Judges 5). While all these are certainly of the 12th–11th centuries BC, the sequence proposed above is debatable.

[8] Concerning a 'Patriarchal Age', the scholars accepting such a concept can be grouped into those who date it earlier and those who date it later; among the latter, placing it around the el-Amarna period and the Late Bronze Age II, are Gordon 1963; Eissfeldt 1975; Kaufmann 1942, p. 1, n. 1; Lemaire 1984; the former are noted below, in n. 9, as well as Cazelles 1966 and Yeivin 1963.

[9] See Glueck 1959, pp. 60–110, and in his wake, Albright 1961; de Vaux 1978, pp. 257–266; and Speiser 1964, p. xliii–xliv (18th–16th centuries BC).

[10] See Thompson 1974; van Seters 1975. An intermediate stage is suggested by Mazar 1969, which would place the Patriarchal narratives within the 11th century BC, reflecting the early period of David.

with certain other scholars, the Genesis narratives as an artificial construct, based on a limited, three-generation scheme.[11] This was the product of later biblical historiographers, who used this scheme to formulate what was actually a prolonged historical process. Two devices served to remould the biblical source material, blurring the historical picture. One process is known as 'reflection'—in which the rudimentary source was 'contemplated' anew according to later intellectual and theological patterns, arriving at a reappraisal of past events. Even more distorting, however, is the other process—'telescoping',[12] in which a lengthy series of events is adjusted and simplified into an artificial, spurious account which presents a severely foreshortened timespan. By such tendentious means, the entire fabric of Israel's proto-history could be condensed into a simplistic, narrow chronological framework.

To exemplify the process of 'telescoping'—for of the two processes only it is of relevance to chronology—we can note the obvious case of the Israelite conquest of Canaan. An extended, intricate chain of events was forced into the limited framework of the exploits of a single national hero, Joshua, and attributed to him. Another example of gross condensation, as I see it, is the biblical account of the Exodus from Egypt, which is centred upon the charismatic figure of Moses. Actually, two or more 'exoduses', or even a continuous flow of such movements, seem to have been boiled down into a single account, forming a wondrous story of a prolonged, 40-year wandering of the Hebrew tribes toward Canaan. But the instance of the 'Patriarchal Age' is, to my mind, the outstanding example of reduction to an artificial framework. The cycle of Patriarchal narratives—conveniently arranged under the accounts of 'Abraham', 'Isaac' and 'Jacob'—reflects events which spanned hundreds of years, and probably preserves isolated reminiscences of an even dimmer past, of the early days of the Amorite tribes moving into Syro-Palestine from the end of the third millennium BC on. The literary end-product of all this artifice resembles, by way of metaphor, an accordion which has been closed: in order to recover the full historical span, one must open it out to the proper dimension.

Now, how does all this affect an intelligent, considered comparison with Mari? With all due reservations, the Old Babylonian material at Mari certainly could lie within the 'reconstituted' or 'untelescoped' purview of the proto-history of Israel, and hence its relevance for comparison with the Bible.

C. ETHNO-LINGUISTIC FACETS

From what other aspect can we examine the problem, to strengthen the chronological basis for comparison between Mari and the Bible? One pro-

[11] Malamat 1985, p. 237; and see Gottwald 1979, pp. 308 ff., Westermann 1981, p. 90; Soggin 1985, p. 95.

[12] For this device in a non-biblical context, see, e.g., Munz 1956 (and in a biblical novel, see the preface in Mann 1934, pp. xvii ff.).

minent means would be the onomasticon common to Mari and e
a most potent argument in favour of the antiquity of Israel's proto
core. We shall limit our discussion solely to the names of the Pa
family, some of which find namesakes at Mari. The best docum
these biblical names is Ya‘^{a}qoḇ—Jacob—the common occurrence o ...ich at Mari can serve as hard evidence of its antiquity. It appears in tens of cuneiform documents, in various forms such as Yaḫqub-El, Ḫaqbu-El, (Ḫ)aqba-aḫum and (Ḫ)aqba/u-Ḫammû.[13] The biblical form, as with many other names in the Book of Genesis, is hypocoristic, a sort of nickname lacking its theophoric component, which was apparently -El. This appears to be indicated in the blessing of Jacob by the angel, after their struggle, when Jacob gained his new, historical name: 'Your name shall no more be called Jacob (*Ya‘^{a}qoḇ*), but Israel' (*Yiśrā'ēl*; Genesis 32: 28). His new name, Yiśrā'-El, was surely intended as a substitute, parallel in form to Jacob-El. Indeed, the Bible seems to preserve this latter form in one specific instance, as has recently been demonstrated, in Deuteronomy 33: 28:[14] without any major textual emendation, the words can be read in a non-traditional manner to yield the following translation: 'So Israel dwelt in safety, Jacob-El is settled securely ....' The name of Jacob is also found somewhat later among the Semitic rulers of Egypt—the famous Hyksos kings, but there it appears with a different theophoric component (i.e. Ya‘^{a}qob-Har or, as recently suggested, Ya‘^{a}qob-Haddu).[15]

Other 'biblical' names at Mari are Ishmael, in the form Yasmaḫ-El; and Laban (though some scholars would read the name differently),[16] with theophoric elements, as in El-Laban or Aḫi-Laban. More usual, we find Abi-Ram—Abram (or the longer form, Abraham). A recently published Mari text (*ARMT* XXII 328: 111)[17] contains the personal name *Bi-ni-ya-mi-na*, that is, Benjamin. This is the first time that this name appears in its full form in syllabic spelling, leaving no doubt as to its reading. We shall return to this significant name in our discussion of tribal names, below (see p. 35, n. 29). Admittedly, these names also occur in later periods, a fact which has often been cited as an argument against an early date.[18] However, it must be noted that they are in intensive use particularly in

[13] For the various forms of this name, see *ARMT* XVI/1, s.v. Yaḫqub-El, p. 217; (Ḫ)aqba-aḫum, (Ḫ)aqba/u-Ḫammû, p. 102. For this and other West Semitic names, see Huffmon 1965. The form *Ya‘^{a}qoḇ-'Aḥ* might be hinted at in Jeremiah 9: 3.

[14] Freedman 1963.

[15] On Ya‘^{a}aqob-Har see recently Kempinski 1985, and there the reading Ya‘aqub-Haddu, suggested by O. Rössler, who holds that in the Egyptian of the first half of the 2nd millennium BC the *r* in foreign names was pronounced as *d*.

[16] See *ARMT* XVI/1, p. 142: *La-ba-an*, p. 143, where the reading Lama-El is preferred.

[17] This instance is of considerable importance, for the first element of the name 'Benjaminites' is written at Mari always with the logogram DUMU.MEŠ, merely denoting 'son(s)', whether pronounced as Akkadian (*mārū*) or as West Semitic (*binū*, *banū* or the like). In personal (i.e. not tribal) names, at least, there is a reading which exactly parallels the biblical name Benjamin; see below, n. 29.

[18] Thompson 1974, pp. 17–51.

Old Babylonian (and Hyksos) contexts, and this is especially true of the name Jacob. Such names are much less common in later periods (with the exception of Abi-Ram).

Thus, our comparison is of a two-fold significance: on the one hand, it demonstrates the horizon on which the Patriarchal names should be evaluated. The majority of these names surely belong to the oldest stratum of the biblical onomasticon, representing early models of personal names among the Israelites. On the other hand, these names are clear indicators of the ethnic affinity of Israel's ancestors—the West Semitic or Amorite stock, which gave rise not only to the Mariotes but also to a Ugaritic line, to the Hyksos and, of course, to the Hebrew Patriarchs.[19] Thus, personal names can often serve as ethnic 'calling-cards', so to speak—though serious limitations must be taken into account when using them as a sole criterion.

But we certainly have additional criteria of even greater weight for determining the West Semitic character of many of the population groups reflected in the Mari documents, on the one hand, and of the early Israelites. on the other hand. Foremost at Mari is the linguistic factor. Basically, the Mari texts are written in a chancery style in the Babylonian of the Hammurabi period.[20] But this language is permeated with West Semiticisms in grammar and, more significantly, in vocabulary and idiom. Numerous terms and expressions betray the everyday speech of the scribes, who frequently resorted to typical West Semitic words, or gave specifically West Semitic nuances to Standard Akkadian terms (see below, p. 44, on *nawûm*).

Many of these very same West Semitic idioms are present in the Hebrew Bible as well, particularly in poetic or exalted language.[21] Numerous examples could readily be cited, especially concerning the conceptual world and lifestyle of the West Semites—idioms having no adequate equivalents in Standard Akkadian since their referents were largely foreign to the Assyro-Babylonian social and ideological milieu. Perusal of the short list in Table 1 (which could be enlarged) of West Semitic words appearing in the Mari documents, along with their Hebrew (and other) cognates, is broadly illuminating, as far as the nature of the respective societies is concerned. (Several of these terms are discussed in greater detail below; see pp. 33ff.). The list is arranged by general subjects, to emphasize the societal significance of the corpus as a whole.

The general nature of the words included in the list reflects a clearly patriarchal–tribal system, and hence they found no ready parallels within

[19] See, in particular, Huffmon 1965; Gröndahl 1967; Albright 1954; and still the pioneering work of Bauer 1926.

[20] See Lambert 1967, where the Mari dialect, more widespread than Mari itself, is denoted [illegible] Babylonian'.

[21] [illegible] be assumed that the West Semitic vocables of the Mari idiom, over the course [illegible]ame archaic and as such entered the biblical literature; there, their usages had [illegible]alized and restricted to particular linguistic strata.

Table 1

	Mari	Hebrew	Other[22] West Semitic	Meaning
Geography:	*ḫamqum*	*‘emeq*	U, A	Valley
	gaba’um	*giḇ^{e}‘āh*	U	Summit, height
	k/qaṣûm	*qāṣeh*	U	(Desert) frontier
	ḫēn/ḫīnum	*‘ayin*	(General)	Spring (referring to toponyms in both Mari and the Bible)
	yābiltum	**yaḇal, yūḇāl*	U, A	Watercourse, irrigation canal
Cardinal points:	*aqdamātum*	*qedem*	U, A	East; before
	aḫarātum	*’aḥar, ’āḥōr*	U, A	West; after
	**sim’al*	*ś^{e}mō’l*	U, A	North; left
	**yamīn(a)*	*yāmīn*	U, A	South; right
Fauna (flocks):	*ḫa(ya)rum*	*‘ayir*	U	Donkey foal
	ḫazzum	*‘ēz*	U, A	Goat
	ḫiglum	*‘ēgel*	U, A	Calf[23]
Flora (foods):	*suḫrum*	*ś^{e}‘ōrāh*	U, A	Barley
	ḫimrum	*ḥemer*	U, A	A fermented drink
Military:	*baza(ḫā)tum*	*bṣ‘* (root)		Military outpost
Tribal units:	*gāyum*	*gōy*	P	Tribal unit/territory (?)
	ḫibrum	*ḥeḇer*		Nomadic association
	ummatum	*’ummāh*		‘Mother’ base/unit
Settlement patterns:	*nawûm*	*nāweh*	U, P	Pasturage
	niḫlatum	*naḥ^{a}lāh*	U, P	Patrimony, estate
	ḫaṣārum (pl. *ḫaṣīrātum*)	*ḥāṣēr* (pl. *ḥ^{a}ṣērīm*)	U, A (?)	Hamlet (?)
Leadership:	*šāpiṭum* (cf. *šāpiṭūtum*, *šipṭum*)	*šōp̱ēṭ*	U, P	Ruler, governor
	merḫûm	*mērē^{a}‘*	U (*r‘h*)	Supervisor of the royal pasturage
	malikum	*meleḵ*		(Deceased) king
Verbs:	*naḫālum*	*nāḥōl*	U, P	To inherit, apportion
	šapāṭum	*šāp̱ōṭ*	U, P	To rule, govern
	ḫakûm	*ḥāḵōh*		To wait
	ḫalûm	*ḥālōh*		To be ill
	qatālum	*qāṭōl*	A	To kill
	šalûm	*šālō^{a}ḥ*		To send (on a mission)
	ḫarāšum	*ḥārōš*	A	To be silent
	wašābum	*yāšōḇ*	U (?)	To exercise authority
	**naqāmum/ (niqmum)*	*nāqōm*	U, A (Sefire)	To avenge
	sabākum	*sābōḵ*	A (?)	To intermingle
Varia:	*yagātum*	*yāgōn*		Sorrow
	yaradu	*yārōd*	U, P	Descend (into Sheol)
	ḫakim	*ḥāḵām*	(General)	Skilful, competent
	abi’ānum	*’eḇyōn*	U	Poor
	yalūtum	*’^{e}yāl*	A	Help
	saḫātum	*šaḥat*		Pit

[22] U = Ugaritic; A = Aramaic; P = Phoenician; General = general West Semitic.

[23] Always with the meaning of a zoomorphic vessel. For jars with animal heads—in this case lions—see Deller 1985 (and other animals at Mari, pp. 337 ff.). For *ḫiglum* or *ḫig(g)al(l)um* in recently published texts, see, e.g., *ARMT* XXIV 91: 24 and note; *ARMT* XXV, p. 273, text 47.

the Standard Akkadian lexicon which, as noted, was largely based on an altogether different societal structure. On the other hand, it is significant that Standard Akkadian generally did contain adequate means for expressing matters of cult and religion at Mari.

Terms for tribal leadership in Mari have been the subject of several recent discussions,[24] reducing the need to delve into them below. We can suffice with the term *šāpiṭum/šōp̱ēṭ*; the latter, Hebrew form (conventionally translated 'judge' in the English Bible) is now shown by the Mari term to have a much broader sense, designating a person not merely dispensing justice, but actually governing. Thus, the Book of Judges deals with rulers of a sort (both the major 'deliverer' Judges and the minor Judges).[25] The conventional translation, 'judge', entered West European tradition long before King James, as is attested by the Septuagint. This translation can hardly be abandoned now. The term *šōp̱ēṭ* survived into Classical times—at least among the Carthaginians, as attested in the Latinized form *suffetes*.

D. SOCIETAL COMPONENTS—NOMADIC AND SEDENTARY MODES OF LIFE

Significantly, this West Semitic terminology reflects, in one way or another, a thoroughly tribalistic milieu—mainly of non-urban populations but to some extent also of urban society. This is so at Mari as well as in early Israel, and it is only within these two sources—of all the documentary evidence of the ancient Near East till Islamic times—that tribal society manifests itself in full bloom.[26]

If modern sociology and comparative anthropology are still groping about in their treatment of present-day societies, they are confounded all the more so in seeking to grasp ancient, extinct societies. Despite this serious shortcoming, the variegated patterns and mechanisms of tribal structure and organization are often found to be parallel in our two sources, though they diverge widely in other respects.

In such patrilineal, tribal regimes as at Mari and in early Israel, the basic social and economic unit is the extended family—the *bēt āḇ* of Biblical Hebrew and the Akkadian *bīt abim* at Mari.[27] Such units aggregate to form a 'clan' and, subsequently, broader tribal associations. The best documented of these associations at Mari are the more or less sedentary Ḫaneans, who lent their name to an entire region on the Middle Euphrates,

[24] For *šāpiṭum* and its West Semitic relation, see Stol 1972; Safren 1979; Pack 1981, pp. 109 ff.; and Mafico 1987 (and there also on the derivatives of the root *špṭ*: *šapāṭum*, 'to govern'; *šāpiṭūtum*, 'governship'; and *šipṭum*, 'decision' or 'judgement', like Hebrew *šᵉp̱āṭîm*).

[25] For the most recent comprehensive study on Hebrew *špṭ* in the light of extra-biblical sources, see Niehr 1986a (on Mari, pp. 25–41).

[26] For tribal society at Mari, see inter alia Kupper 1957; Luke 1965; Malamat 1967; Marzal 1969; Rowton 1974 (and other articles by Rowton; see below, n. 34); Matthews 1978; Anbar 1985; and Talon 1986. For the tribal structure of Israel see, in addition to the histories, the recent works of Weippert 1967; Geus 1976; Gottwald 1979; Thiel 1985; Mazar 1986; Lemche 1985.

[27] For the biblical *bēt 'āḇ*, see Scharbert 1982 and Bendor 1986.

and the semi-nomadic Yaminites. The Yaminites, unattested as such outside Mari, are seen as a still somewhat unruly and independent group. Their name—literally 'sons of the right' (DUMU.MEŠ-*yamīna*), that is, southerners—is contrasted by the much rarer tribal designation 'sons of the left' (DUMU.MEŠ-*sim'al*), that is, northerners.[28] The Yaminites or, as some prefer, Benjaminites, are outwardly identical in name with the Israelite tribe of Benjamin—a fact which has occasionally been blown out of proportion. For the present, I can see no connection between the two entities beyond the similarity of name.[29]

The process of tribal settlement as revealed at Mari can be seen to range over a broad spectrum of simultaneous stages of sedentarization—from nomadic to permanently settled. In the Bible we see a *diachronic* view of this same gradual process, the progressive stages being depicted as if in sequence: entrance of the early Israelites into Canaan, roving about it, taking possession of parts of it and, finally, settling it as a permanent, sedentary population. But at Mari we see a *synchronic*, side-by-side picture of this variegated process—at one single, brief point in time (actually about half a century).[30] The stereoscopic picture obtained by viewing these two depictions—the synchronic and the diachronic—yields a depth and perspective otherwise unattainable. Mari shows 'raw facts in the field', so to speak—almost like modern fieldwork—while the Bible, with its historical perception, has broken the process down into typical stages.

[28] See the initial study of the Yaminites, Dossin 1939b; and cf. Klengel 1958/59; Anbar 1985, nn. 74–76. The most recent study on the Simalites is Charpin & Durand 1986, where it is assumed (as noted above, p. 10, n. 23) that the Lim dynasty at Mari originated among the Simalite tribes; it is also assumed there that the Yaminites and the Simalites comprised two branches of the Ḫaneans, that is, southern and northern respectively.

[29] For the different forms of the name of the DUMU.MEŠ-*yamīna*, see *ARMT* XVI/1, p. 39, s.v. *Yamina*. Early on in Mari studies, the term was taken in its entirety as West Semitic; that is, DUMU.MEŠ, 'sons', was read as *binū*/*banū* + *yamīna*, as is still preferred by some scholars (e.g. Cazelles 1967; Albright 1968, p. 69). This might be supported by the personal name *Bi-ni-ya-mi-na* (see above, p. 31 and n. 17). But it has been rejected by Dossin 1958; and Tadmor 1958, p. 130, n. 12, following B. Landsberger's observation that the Mari texts do not employ logograms for West Semitic terms. Thus, the tribal name would have been read *Marū-yamīna* (an 'incredible' reading, according to Albright 1968, p. 69). We are inclined to accept the suggestion in Gelb 1961 regarding DUMU.MEŠ as a semantic indicator, and thus read the tribe's name simply as 'Yaminites'. A semantic indicator—'sons' or 'children'—is quite common within the biblical milieu; see *b^enē Yiśrā'ēl*, 'Israelites', *b^enē 'Ammōn*, 'Ammonites', *b^enē qedem*, 'Easterners', etc. Further, in the Hebrew tribal name Benjamin, the first element, *bēn*, 'son', is not necessarily an integral part of the name, precisely as in Mari, and might be detached or even omitted (cf. the Mari forms without DUMU.MEŠ, in *ARMT* I 60:9; 67:7; XXI 339:7), as in *ben y^emīnī*, *'īš y^emīnī*, *'ereṣ y^emīnī*. Emphasis on the respective eponymic-tribal or territorial nature of the name may have been a factor in the usage of the variant Hebrew forms.

[30] The Mari documents span the reigns of Yahdun-Lim (15–20 years), Sumu-Yamam (3 years), Šamši-Adad + Yasmaḫ-Adad (± 20 years) and Zimri-Lim (14 years), totalling slightly more than half a century. This would correspond, according to the Middle Chronology, to c. 1820–1761 BC, and according to the Low Chronology, to c. 1755–1696 BC. Most of the documents are from the reign of Zimri-Lim.

Throughout the biblical narratives we read of the encounter between tribal society and well-established urban culture—an ambivalent relationship of friction and symbiosis. At Mari, too, such a picture is projected—but from the other side of the lens, and in this latter light we may now better assess the mode by which the Israelites were able to penetrate into urbanized Canaan and succeed in their process of *Landnahme.*[31] In the Israelite–Canaanite encounter it would seem that friction more often than not developed between the two rival social and political systems.[32] A most indicative episode in this context was Jacob's encounter with the townsmen of Shechem, after the rape of his daughter Dinah. Though the inhabitants of the city welcomed him and offered him land and connubial relations, Jacob and his sons preferred to avenge the family honour, despite the fact that their rejection of the offer entailed a considerable loss of potential economic advantage (Genesis 34).[33]

That Israelite tenacity won out is history, but it differs considerably from the experience in Mesopotamia, where there seems to have been much more mutual assimilation amongst the rival societies—the Akkadian–Babylonian culture, on the one hand, and the various tribal, West Semitic elements, on the other hand.

The sociological models applied by scholars, sometimes even today, to this dimorphic situation have generally been based on alleged sharp dichotomy between pastoral semi-nomads and sedentary urbanites—with all the 'inherent', unbridgeable hostility between them. This is often further complicated by the misleading identification of tribalism with nomadism in the scholarly mind. Recently, however, a new type of model has emerged, involving a dual concept of 'dimorphic society' and 'enclosed nomadism'.[34] This model emphasizes the dimorphic structure of the population in a given area, involving a grazing pattern of certain elements on pastoral lands, generally within regions of urban settlement.[35] The result in both Mari

[31] There are currently three major models for understanding Israel's takeover of Canaan: (a) the so-called *Landnahme* process, a virtually peaceful infiltration of the country, set out in the classical study in Alt 1925; 1953 and subsequently elaborated upon in Noth 1956, pp. 67–82; (b) the revolt model of Mendenhall 1962 and Gottwald 1979, postulating a peasant rebellion of Canaanites against the urban Canaanite oligarchy; and (c) the military model, in an extreme garb: a one-time, all embracing conquest of Canaan, or in a moderate garb: a series of skirmishes and battles by various groups and involving sophisticated stratagems but not a single campaign, alongside peaceful penetrations (see Malamat 1979a).

[32] Schmitt 1970; Dietrich 1979.

[33] Hour 1962. For an anthropological approach, see Pitt-Rivers 1977, pp. 126–171; Westermann 1981, pp. 648 ff.

[34] For the application of these terms to Mari society, see the studies of Rowton 1974, 1976a, 1976b, 1977; see also, in reference to Mari and the Hebrews, Malamat 1967, where the dimorphic phenomenon is treated, albeit without explicit use of the term *per se*. The term derives from the noted French sociologist E. Durkheim, while 'enclosed nomads' was coined by O. Lattimore.

[35] In general see the collected papers in Ucko *et al.* 1972; and, e.g., Marx 1977; Salzman 1980. For Mesopotamia and Palestine, see Adams 1975, and Luke 1965; further Matthews 1978; Hermann 1980; 1988; Otto 1984.

and Israel appears as a symbiotic relationship of mutuality and cultural sharing between tribe and city.

This sort of dimorphic society, involving 'enclosed nomadism', seems to be mirrored by recent archaeological discoveries from the Middle Bronze Age II B in Palestine. Most significant in this respect are the many open, satellite villages, often rather small and short-lived, found adjacent to Bronze Age towns.[36] The biblical traditions concerning the 'encampments' of the Patriarchs alongside Canaanite cities such as Shechem and Bethel (Genesis 12: 6, 8), Hebron (13: 18) and Beer-sheba (26: 25) fit in well with such an archaeological picture. In the Mari documents, this mode of life is best illustrated in the concept of the *nawûm*, as we shall see below (pp. 43ff.).

In recent years it has again become fashionable, in some quarters, to discredit the historical reliability of various biblical descriptions of pre-monarchic institutions in Israel.[37] In order to counteract such scepticism we could adduce various biblical references to early social and legal practices which point to the existence of legitimate pre-monarchical institutions. Thus, for example, we see evidence of an ancient family law, including provisions for inheritance and landed property, and marriage customs—in other words, a law not royal in authority. We can also note the recruitment of troops along gentilic lines, from individual settlements rather than the formation of a national army. In short, it is the life of the family or clan that is dominant in these contexts, and not the later royal system.[38] An indication of a different sort can be found in the so-called anti-monarchic pericopes within the Bible, several of which no doubt draw their inspiration from pre-monarchic times.[39] Yet, moreover—and this will be our major argument here—there is extra-biblical evidence, and in this context the Mari documents are of prime importance.[40]

From the list of words in Table 1, we can see that the Mari documents contain a set of West Semitic terms denoting tribal units, forms of tribal settlement and tribal leadership—in short, tribal institutions and customs. A comparative study of these terms with their Hebrew cognates not only sheds light on the meaning of individual words but also serves to illuminate the underlying structures and institutions of the societies involved. We

[36] There are several good examples of such satellite villages, e.g. the Middle Bronze Age II B open settlement at Giv'at Sharett, a suburb of modern Beth-Shemesh, about 1.5 km from the ancient mound (see the preliminary remarks in Bahat 1978); the Middle Bronze Age II B open settlement in the Rephaim valley 5 km west of biblical Jerusalem (preliminary report, Edelstein & Eisenberg 1985); and a recently discovered settlement of the same period, located at Manahat, four km west of biblical Jerusalem, currently being excavated by G. Edelstein. And see the general picture in Finkelstein 1986.

[37] In contrast see Reviv (forthcoming), chapters 3 and 4, and the bibliographical references there to those negating the biblical material; and, e.g., Schäfer-Lichtenberger 1983.

[38] Thiel 1985, chapter 2; Stager 1985.

[39] Cf. in particular Crüsemann 1978.

[40] For a shorter version of the following section, see Malamat 1988a; and the early study of Noth 1960.

employ the concept of institution in a broad sense encompassing *inter alia* various life-styles. Let us first enumerate the Mari–Bible equivalents in the various social realms: tribal units, *gā'um/gāyum/ḫibrum/ummatum—gōy, ḥeḇer, ummāh*; forms of settlement, *nawûm/ḫaṣārum—nāweh, ḥāṣēr*; and finally the institution of patrimony, *niḫlatum—naḥᵃlāh*.

Gāyum/gā'um/gōy[41]

We shall commence our discussion with the term for the tribal unit, *gāyum*, Hebrew *gōy*, which was relatively small in scope. At Mari we witness the occurrence of personal names composed of *gāyum* as well, in particular Baḫlu-gāyim (the leader of a clan notably named Amurru; see below). Besides at Mari, *gāyum* is now also attested in a single occurrence in the contemporaneous texts from Tell al-Rimaḥ (ancient Karana).[42] It should be determined whether this term (as well as *ḫibrum* and *ummatum*; see below) should be treated as an ethnic gentilic concept or simply as designating a group of individuals unrelated by blood ties. Perhaps it may even be understood in a territorial sense. All these interpretations are reflected in the various translations advanced by the editors of the Mari texts, while the *CAD* defines *gāyum* in a non-committal manner, as 'gang or group of workmen'.[43] The difficulty in determining the exact meaning of *gāyum* and similar sociological terms at Mari is due to the fluctuations of tribal structure and the loosening of kinship ties in the process of transition toward a sedentary way of life.

The definition of *gāyum* is further complicated by the fact that the tribes, as a result of continuous raids by the kings of Mari, were exposed to the practices of the royal administration. Hence, this expression is already used in the context of territorial and administrative organization. This additional nuance takes its place alongside the original ethnic connotation, thereby becoming an ethno-geographic, but by no means a purely geographic or administrative, concept. This pattern of settlement was, as a rule, the outgrowth of common wanderings. Thus, the ethnic gentilic connotation as a sort of 'clan' is applicable to all the references of the word *gāyum* in the Mari texts, as well as to the term *gōy* in some early biblical sources.[44] Interestingly enough, the *gāyum* thus far occurs only with reference to the federation of the Ḫaneans. There is a lengthy economic list of 258

[41] See Malamat 1967, pp. 133 ff., and now Talon 1985; Botterweck & Clements 1973; Matthews 1978.

[42] See Dalley *et al.* 1976, pp. 220–221 (No. 305: 18). For a different identification of Tell al-Rimaḥ, see now Charpin & Durand 1987, pp. 294 ff.

[43] Cf. *CAD* G, p. 59a, s.v. *gâ'u*; *AHw*, p. 284a, s.v. *gā'um*, 'Volk'. The editors of the Mari texts translated variously: 'pays, territoire' or 'tribu, clan, peuple'. Cf. the translation in *ARMT* IV 1: 13 (as against *l.* 15).

[44] In Hebrew the transition of the meaning of the word *gōy* as a people, tribe or clan is blurred; thus, in such passages as the following, the sense of clan or tribe is not impossible. Cf. Genesis 20: 4; Deuteronomy 4: 34; and the more obscure Genesis 14: 1, 9 and 17: 4, 5; Judges 4: 13, 16; 2 Chronicles 15: 6.

Ḫanean recipients of quantities of oil; these are divided into thirteen groups, nine of which carry the designation *gāyum* and the clan name.[45] One *gāyum* is of particular interest since it is called Amurrum and indeed almost all of the 35 individual members carry Amorite names, pointing to the ethnic homogeneity of the clan. A further attestation of a *gāyum Amurrum* appears in a recently published document (*ARMT* XXIV 235: 8). The term never occurs in connection with the Yaminites; could the reason lie, as some scholars seem to think, in the different character of the two tribes—the Ḫaneans being more sedentary and already 'clannish', while the still nomadic Yaminites lacked a mature tribal structure reflecting a distinct clan system?[46]

Like *ummatum* at Mari and *'amm* in Hebrew, *gāyum* acquired a distinct military sense (*ARMT* VI 28: 7–9), since in the earliest stages armies were organized along gentilic lines, both in Old Babylonian times and in ancient Israel.[47] Moreover, the Hebrew term *gōy* shares a common semantic development with *'ummāh*, *ḥeb̲er* and *'amm*—whereas the primary meanings seem to be identical with their Mari cognates. In time, the four Hebrew terms came to encompass entire peoples or nations. Contrary to their original, narrow gentilic application, they ultimately expanded their scope—that is, they underwent an 'anaemic' process so to speak, namely, a loosening of blood ties in the kinship system.

Ḫibrum/ḥeb̲er[48]

Another tribal unit or clan of specific character at Mari was denoted *ḫibrum* (in Biblical Hebrew, *ḥeb̲er*, appearing four times in the Bible), and has cognates in other Semitic languages. The term is generally applicable to a group of nomadic or semi-nomadic households whose common wanderings led to a closely bonded life. Thus, this term, deriving from the root *ḥbr*, 'to unite, be joined', denotes a group of closely associated households.[49] In two cases, a *ḫibrum* at Mari received certain quantities of honey and possibly wine. The *ḫibrum* possessed a certain number of sheep, albeit small, in one case a total of 280 sheep for three *ḫibrums* (*ARMT* IX 244). The *ḫibrum* is associated with nomadic tribal confederations

[45] See Birot 1953, 1955. In other sources we find the name of a tenth *gāyum*; see Anbar 1985, pp. 72–73.

[46] Cf. Rowton 1977, p. 189. But Charpin & Durand 1986, pp. 180–182, publish a new text (A 2560: 7–8) which mentions the *gāyums* (*ga-a-šu-nu*) of the Simalites and Yaminites which, however, are included there both within the Haneans.

[47] In a military context in the Bible, *gōy* is in one case even specified by *anšē milḥāmāh*, 'men of war' (Joshua 5: 6; and cf. Joshua 10: 13; 2 Kings 6: 18; Isaiah 29: 7–8 and, figuratively, the army of locusts in Joel 1: 6). As for *'amm* in a military sense, see now Lipiński 1987, col. 192.

[48] For a previous treatment see Malamat 1962, pp. 144 ff. See also Matthews 1978, pp. 65–66; and Arbeli 1981, pp. 101–104, where our hypothesis concerning Heber the Kenite as a symbol of a tribal unit is adopted.

[49] For this root cf. Cazelles 1977, cols. 721–726; *HAL*, pp. 276–277.

(Suteans, Ya'ilites). A most instructive document from Mari (*ARMT* VIII 11) mentions the *ḫibrum* in the context of the transfer of lands belonging to a widespread family named 'bīt Awin', of the Rabbean tribe affiliated with the Yaminites. The transfer was effected in the presence of thirteen heads of the households which comprised the extended family (Arabic *ḥāmūla*) of Awin. This family was not homogeneous, but rather included two groups of households: five households which had already settled in an urban centre (the city of Appan), and the others who were called 'eight sons of Awin *hibrum ša nāwêm*'—a *ḫibrum* of households still nomadic (see below).[50] The *ḫibrum* here is not ascribed to a specific eponym, that is, it is smaller than a lineage, in anthropological terms.

The Bible seems to employ the expression *ḥeber* solely in reference to groups which were not bound by blood ties. Thus, we find reference to 'a *ḥeb̲er* of priests' (Hosea 6: 9), already indicating a gradual expansion of the term. Nevertheless, the erstwhile concept of a gentilic tribal unit, as at Mari, may be inferred from the Bible, as in the personal name Heber, which in several cases appears to carry the symbolic meaning of 'household unit' and 'family' (and see immediately below). Indeed, it was a common phenomenon in the Bible, as well as in Mesopotamian contexts, that the appellation of a tribal unit was conceived as the personal name of its eponym.[51]

Most informative in this respect is the appellation 'Heber the Kenite', mentioned in the Deborah episode (Judges 4: 11, 17). The narrative speaks of a single household, and Heber is the personal name of its head; but in reality the terms probably designated a Kenite sub-tribe, the sons of Hobab.[52] The latter had attached themselves to the Israelites during their journey to Canaan (Numbers 10: 29ff.) and subsequently to the Judahites when that tribe settled in its territorial inheritance (LXX: Judges 1: 16). While still in the south of Palestine, Heber apparently detached itself from the main tribe of Hobab (which had settled in the south) and wandered northward in search of pasturage (or for other reasons), as far as the plain of Jezreel. Accordingly, we may assume that the name Heber here was but a symbolic appellation, a sort of personification of a minor tribal unit which was still nomadic. As such it was comparable to the term *ḫibrum*

[50] An additional occurrence of this phrase is now attested in *Ḫana ḫibrum ša nawêm*, 'the Ḫaneans of the migratory units of the pasture land', in contrast to the Ḫaneans already settled. See Charpin & Durand 1986, pp. 154, 175, where, too, the word *ḫibrum* is ascribed the meaning "groupe en mouvement". Furthermore, *ARMT* XIV 50: 114; 72: 18 attest to a related verbal form, *ḫabārum*, 'to migrate, to set out from one region to another'. In contrast, Birot translates *ḫabārum* in *ARMT* XIV as 'émigrer', 'se réfugier'; and see there, p. 228, No. 50, *l.* 14, referring to the possibility of its being a denominative of the term Ḫabiru.

[51] There are numerous examples of this phenomenon. Concerning the Bible, see, e.g., Nahor (see below), which in Genesis designates an eponymous ancestor, a tribal organization, as well as the city in Aram Naharaim (Genesis 24: 10).

[52] See Mazar 1965. There are other occurrences in the Bible where tribes split up ('fission' in anthropological terms) and moved to separate regions, such as the tribal units of Abraham and Lot (Genesis 13: 11).

in the Mari documents. The parallel with 'bīt Awin', noted above, is illuminating: Awin and Hobab were known eponyms within their respective tribes, the Rabbeans and the Kenites. Each had stood at the head of a group of households, several of which were settled more or less permanently (cf. 'cities' of the Kenites in 1 Samuel 30:29), whereas others persisted in their nomadic ways. The latter were of the *ḫibrum ša nawêm* type (see above), to use the Mari idiom; the biblical appellation 'Ḥeber' suits them well.

Of the nature of the *ḫibrum* as an association of households wandering in common, such as the 'bīt Awin' at Mari, we can also learn from the appearance of the term 'Ḥeber' in the genealogical lists of the Israelite tribes, above all in the genealogy of the tribe of Asher. There, the name 'Heber' could appear to be symbolic of a group of households which, at least in part, had enjoyed a special bond harking back to the days of common wanderings from the central hill-country of Canaan toward the north-western coast.[53]

In conclusion, in view of its literal meaning, the Hebrew personal name Heber in the genealogical lists would connote a specific tribal–sociological concept similar to that of the *ḫibrum* at Mari.

Ummatum/'ummāh[54]

A further tribal unit at Mari was the *ummatum*, neither the etymology nor the precise meaning of which has yet been determined satisfactorily. Despite the prevalent view deriving the lexeme from *ummānum*, 'host, army'—and despite its occurrence in military contexts—one of the many meanings to which *ummatum* is applied suggests a connection with Hebrew *ummāh* and its cognates in other West Semitic languages. Hebrew *'ummāh* derives from Semitic *'mm*, 'mother', and *ummatum* has also been traced to this root. Thus, *ummatum* too may originally have designated some sort of tribal unit or, literally, 'a mother unit'. Granted, there is no way, *a priori*, of knowing the size of this unit, whether a family in the sense of *ḥāmūla* in Arabic, a group of families (Arabic *'ašīra* or *qabīla*), or even an entire tribe. It may represent a matrilineal unit, which had grafted itself on to a matriarch—as with the Leah or Rachel tribes in the Israelite tribal system, which may have been conceived as *'ummāh*—*'ummat* Leah' and *'ummat* Rachel', respectively.[55] In any event, certain personal names

[53] For details on Heber and his significance in the genealogy of the tribe of Asher, see Malamat 1962, pp. 165–166, and n. 13 there, which also treats the specific meaning of the name Hebron (from the root *ḥbr*).

[54] For this section, see Malamat 1979b (and there also the instances of Tell al-Rimaḥ); as well as *AHw*, p. 1414b, s.v. *ummatu(m)*; von Soden also connected this word with the Hebrew for 'tribe' or 'tribal unit', though Anbar 1985, p. 75, n. 14, opposes this.

[55] See Halpern 1983, pp. 148–149, where the biblical matriarchs are regarded as a tradition gaining a fixed form in the Song of Deborah, and hence the title of Deborah as 'mother (*'ēm*) of Israel'.

in which *ummatum* is a component have been explained in this manner, e.g. Ili-Ummati, 'My god is my family'.[56]

The military connotation of *ummatum* surely derives from the fact that early armies were organized on gentilic principles, as seen above. Just as such words as *gā'um/gōy* and *'amm* (see above) acquired a military sense only secondarily (originally having denoted tribal units), this may be true of *ummatum* as well.

Of great interest is the occurrence of *ummatum* in Yaḫdun-Lim's Foundation Inscription. One section of the text records that the 'kings' of three tribes, who were related to the large tribal confederation of the Yaminites, sought to throw off Yaḫdun-Lim's yoke by forming a coalition against him (col. III: 16–18): 'In the town of Samanum, the *ummatum* of the Yaminites (?)[57] gathered against him.' Later Yaḫdun-Lim was to tackle yet another enemy belonging to the large tribal federation on the Middle Euphrates, the Ḫaneans (col. III: 28–30): 'The city of Ḫaman, the *ummatum* of the Ḫaneans (*ummat Ḫana*) which all the fathers (*abbū*) of the Ḫaneans had built, he destroyed . . . .' In both these instances the word following *ummatum* denotes a tribe. Consequently, the term seems to signify a tribal entity, whether of large scale or small. The tribal units gathered in their respective heartlands and either of the two cities could be viewed, in biblical terms, as the hendiadys *'īr wᵉ'ēm*, 'a mother city', of the tribe under consideration, Yaminite, Ḫanean or Israelite (see below).

The Hebrew, Aramaic, Arabic or Ugaritic[58] cognates of *ummatum* would suggest adding it to the lengthy list of West Semitic loanwords in the Mari (and other Old Babylonian) context. Admittedly, *'ummāh* occurs only twice in the Bible, but in each case in a tribal context: once relating to the Midianites (Numbers 25: 14), and once to the closely affiliated Ishmaelites (Genesis 25: 16). In both cases the word signifies a tribal unit, sub-tribe or clan. Since it is applied in the Bible only to foreign tribes, it may be a loanword from the dialects of those nomadic peoples whose tribal organization (as well as the tribes themselves) possibly harks back to an earlier stratum. The leader of the *'ummāh* is denoted *nāśi'* ('chieftain') in the Ishmaelite genealogy, and *rō'š* ('head') in the passage referring to Midian; but the leaders of the Midianite sub-tribes are designated *nāśi'* elsewhere as well (cf. Numbers 25: 18; Joshua 13: 21).[59]

[56] See Stamm 1939, pp. 199–200, where the name is translated as 'Mein Gott ist meine Familie'; and see there additional names of this type.

[57] The tribal name is written here in an unusual manner: *um-ma-at* TUR/DUMU-*mi-im*, which led Dossin 1955, p. 14, to an unacceptable interpretation, 'race perfide'; Oppenheim, in *ANET*, p. 556b, translated simply 'the center (i.e. *ummatum*—A.M.) of *nomads*'. In the Mari texts, however, shortened spellings of DUMU-MEŠ-*ya-mi-na*, like the above form, are sometimes found, and they still have to be explained (see above, n. 29).

[58] Ugaritic *'mt*, 'kinship' (Ginsberg 1946, p. 33) or 'family, clan' (Gibson 1978, p. 143); Aramaic *'umma*; Arabic *'umm* has various meanings: 'mother', '(water) source', 'urban centre' (see below), etc.; and note also Arabic *'ummā*, 'congregation'.

[59] For the role of the *naśi'*, see Speiser 1963; Niehr 1986b. For *rō'š*, see Bartlett 1969; and cf. Schäfer-Lichtenberger 1983, esp. pp. 355–367.

We also find a masculine plural form, *'ummīm*, in Psalms 117: 1, in parallel to *gōyim* (and possibly in Isaiah 54: 4). With time, both *'ummīm* and *'ummōt* were to become general terms meaning simply 'nations'. This broadening of meaning finds parallels (as noted above) in *gōy*, *ḥeḇer* and *'amm*. The corresponding singular form of *'ummīm* was probably not *'ummāh* but **'om*, a form possibly not recognized by the Masoretes, who thus mistakenly gave it the vocalization of the more familiar *'ēm*, 'mother' (and see below).[60]

Finally, the unique but well-known expression *'īr weʼēm beYiśrā'ēl*, 'a city which is mother in Israel' (RSV; 2 Samuel 20: 19) is applied to Abel-Beth-Maacah in north-eastern Galilee. The obvious interpretation of *'īr weʼēm* is 'a mother city', especially since the biblical phrase *'īr u-ḇenotehā* signifies a city together with its 'daughters' (i.e. the surrounding villages). In later Hebrew, *'īr weʼēm* gained currency as a vernacular expression for 'metropolis' or the like. But the true interpretation of this phrase is not so simple; the *'ēm* component should perhaps be explained through certain usages of *ummatum* in Akkadian (see above), as well as through the earlier meaning of Hebrew *'ummāh*. This would yield the expression 'city and family (or rather, clan) in Israel'. This may be the case in other passages containing *'ēm*—Hosea 4: 5, Jeremiah 15: 8 and, perhaps, Genesis 37: 10 where it would be feasible (but not imperative) to revocalize the word as **'om*.[61] This phrase as now reinterpreted finds a striking parallel in Jeremiah's prophecy of the return of the tribes of the north (Jeremiah 3: 14): 'and I will take you one of a city and two of a "family", and I will bring you to Zion.' This would indicate that a *mišpāḥāh*, 'family', could be of considerable size, on occasion exceeding even the population of a single village or town.

Nawûm/nāweh[62]

We shall now proceed to forms of settlement, focusing on a specific mode of life best illustrated in the Mari texts by the concept of *nawûm*. In Standard Akkadian this word means 'desert, steppe, uncultivated field', as well as

[60] Already recognized by some of the medieval commentators; see Kimchi 1847, p. 19, stating 'and the family is called *'wm* and *'wmh*.' Compare his commentary on the verses Hosea 4: 5 and Jeremiah 15: 8, below.

[61] See above, n. 60; for the passage in Hosea, see Rudolph 1966, p. 97; for MT *'immeḵā* read *'ummeḵā*; similarly Genesis 37: 10; see Seebass 1978, pp. 76–77, n. 56; and cf. also, perhaps, the obscure phrase in 2 Samuel 8: 1—*meteg hā'ammāh*; see Frick 1977, p. 57. Note also the Arabic toponyms of the type: 'Umm el-Faḥm, 'Umm Rashrash, 'Umm Ğindi, etc., which seem to be indicative of urban centres (i.e. with surrounding villages?). Further note the unique biblical expression *'ēm hadderek̲* (Ezekiel 21: 26), NJPS: 'fork of the road'; RSV: 'parting of the way'—which actually may designate the main road to and from a city, which branches out at some point into smaller paths leading to the villages in the vicinity.

[62] See Malamat 1988a, pp. 168–172 as well as Artzi 1968, 1984; Rowton 1974; Matthews 1978, pp. 58–63; Anbar 1985, pp. 136–139; Ringgren 1986.

'ruin' and 'deserted region'; in its specialized West Semitic usage, however, it signifies semi-fertile pasturage and, by association, encampment there. Such a meaning can be seen both at Mari and in its Biblical Hebrew cognate, *nāweh*. It is this latter collective meaning that yields the concept of a migratory group or, similarly, transhumance.[63] Another possible meaning would be 'frontier country'.[64]

The term *nawûm* at Mari encompasses the various Biblical Hebrew expressions: tent, shepherds (*n^e^wēh rō'īm*), livestock (*n^e^wēh ṣō'n*) and pasturage (*n^e'^ōt deše* and *n^e^wēh midbār*, the latter not meaning 'oasis', as often rendered, but rather grazing lands).[65] In short, this term portrays the pastoralist way of life, embracing man, animals and camping area. The *nawûm* was the very antithesis of the city or village, the close interaction with which formed the dimorphic structure of the tribal society at Mari, dwelling partly in urban centres and partly in the hinterland of the encampments.

At Mari this term appears frequently in connection with the tribal organization of the Ḫaneans and the Yaminites; and there is one mention of a *nawûm* of the Simalites (*ARMT* II 33: 21). We also find the expression *Ḫana ša nawêm*, 'Ḫaneans of the pasturage, or frontier' (*ARMT* I 6: 26–28; 42: 5–7), and *Ḫana ḫibrum ša nawêm* (noted above, p. 40 n. 50), the as yet nomadic segments of this tribal organization, which was already predominantly settled. On one occasion, 2000 men of this particular non-sedentary group were to be recruited for a military expedition (*ARMT* I 42: 5–11), for the *nawûm*s generally served as a major source of recruits. Several times we also read of Suteans,[66] and particularly of Yaminites, attacking *nawûm*s of other tribes. On the other hand, a *nawûm* of the Yaminites at Ḫen (*Ḫi-en*) was seized by Yaḫdun-Lim, a fact attested in one of his year formulae.[67] An interesting possibility arises if we consider the word Ḫen not as a toponym at all but rather as the West Semitic term *'ayīn*, 'spring, water source', and it thus perhaps refers to Rās al-'Ayīn, situated on one of the tributaries of the Habur.

In the Bible *nāweh* (like other terms with Mari parallels) generally appears in exalted, poetic or archaic language. Accordingly, it is not found in prosaic portions of the Bible, and is most conspicuously absent from the Patriarchal narratives—although it would best portray the Patriarchal

[63] For the various meanings of *nawûm*, see above, n. 62; and *CAD* N/1, pp. 249 ff., s.v. *namû* A; Kraus 1976, pp. 172 ff., 'Sommerung, Sommerweidegebiet'.

[64] As elaborated by Thompson & Lamar 1981; see their foreword, pp. 3–13. Cf. Chaney 1983.

[65] Whereas *midbār* in the Bible often signifies 'desert', in certain contexts it cannot but mean 'grazing area'; *midbār* Gibeon (*midbār* Dothan), *midbār* Beer-sheba, *midbār* Tekoa, *midbār* Ziph, *midbār* Maon, *midbār* Jeruel, *midbār* En-Gedi, *midbār* Kadesh and, finally, *midbār* Judah—all of them pastures adjacent to villages or districts. See also Talmon 1984 and the extensive bibliography there.

[66] For this tribe see Heltzer 1981.

[67] See Dossin 1950, p. 52, year formula 6; and cf. Klengel 1972, p. 55. The toponym is usually interpreted as Ḫana; cf. *ARMT* XV/1, p. 15. Charpin & Durand 1985, p. 307, n. 70, reject this identification, but still consider the word as an actual toponym.

mode of life.[68] It is, however, found in such passages as Psalms 69:7 and Jeremiah 10:25 (and cf. Lamentations 2:2), in retrospective use, as in the expression *n^e^wēh Ya'^a^qob̲*, 'habitation of Jacob'. Such exalted language is also found in connection with David, whom God took 'from the pasture, from following the sheep' (*min hannāweh*; 2 Samuel 7:8).

At Mari the *nawûm* was an economic, sociological, political and even paramilitary factor. Such mobile units of the tribal society were occasionally the concern of official policy, for Mariote flocks (even royal flocks) were entrusted to the *nawûms* for pasturage. Note such expressions as: *nawûm ša abīya, 'nawûm* of my father' (*ARMT* II 45: 10); *nawûm ša belīya*, '*nawûm* of my lord', and *nawûm ša ḫalṣim*, '*nawûm* of the district'.[69]

Occasionally a *nawûm* is mentioned in Old Babylonian texts as being attached to a city, as is implied in such phrases as 'the *nawûm* of Carchemish', '*nawûm* of Larsa', Sippar and its *nawûm* (*Sippar u nawēšu*), and even 'the *nawûm* of Babylon'.[70] This is quite reminiscent of the depictions of the Patriarchs as dwelling on the outskirts of Canaanite towns. As previously noted (see p. 37), this closely conforms with the archaeological picture in Palestine during the Middle Bronze Age II, conjuring up a dimorphic society and involving 'enclosed nomadism'. An example alluded to in the Saul–David narrative, much later than the Patriarchs, is revealed in the obscure Biblical Hebrew expression *nwyt* (K^e^tib; Q^e^re: *nāyōt*; referred to several times in 1 Samuel 19: 18–20: 1), the dwelling place of a band of prophets. This is surely not a toponym or a specific locality in or near Ramah of Benjamin, as generally held, but rather the common term *nāweh* (pl. *nā'ōt*)—in Mari terms, '*Ramah u nawēšu*'.[71]

On the other hand, the relationship between a village base and an outlying *nawûm*, as seen in a Mari text (*ARMT* II 48: 8 ff.) is reflected in the biblical narrative of Jacob's sons, who ranged from their base encampment near Hebron, 'in the valley of the city', to distant pasturages, as far as Shechem and beyond, near Dothan (Genesis 37: 12 ff.). Here, too, as at Mari, we see a grazing cycle evolving during the spring and summer seasons, as can be inferred from the biblical reference to the 'pit' containing no water, in the midst of the pasture land of Dothan, into which Joseph was cast (Genesis 37: 12 ff.). In the Book of Job we find a similar illustration of what was surely the typical institution of *nawûm/nāweh* although, as in Genesis, the actual term does not appear in the prose framework. Job himself dwelled at a base encampment, while his sons ranged over the pasturage with their oxen, asses, sheep and camels—the same basic picture obtained with Jacob and his sons. In the Book of Job (1: 14–19), the outlying

[68] See Worschech 1983, pp. 50 ff., where Abraham's life-style as in the Book of Genesis is analysed. Cf, Gottwald 1979, pp. 451 ff.

[69] See Artzi 1968.

[70] See *CAD* N/1, p. 250, 2: 'pasture land ... around a city'; and cf. Frankena 1966, No. 66: 5 (*Sippar-Amnānum u nawēšu*).

[71] Cf. Malamat 1962, p. 146b; Stoebe 1973, pp. 365 ff.; and see McCarter 1980a, p. 328.

camp is devastated by man and by nature ('God'), the flocks are plundered and stricken, and the servants are killed.

Both in the Bible and at Mari we see that the transient nature of the *nawûm* exposed it to marauders, as is so in any frontier country. At Mari, the aggressive, nomadic Suteans preyed upon the '*nawûm* in the land of Qatna' in Middle Syria (*ARMT* V 23) and on the *nawûm* of the Yaminites.[72]

In a poetic passage in the Book of Job (5:3) the term *nāweh* is actually used with reference to a surprise raid. This contrasts markedly with the reference to the security of the divinely protected fold (*nāweh*) in Job 5:24: 'You shall know that your tent is safe, and you shall inspect your fold (*nāwᵉḵa*) and miss nothing' (RSV). The last phrase (*wᵉlō teḥᵉṭā'*), better translated 'and shall not be amiss',[73] finds its idiomatic parallel at Mari, though antithetically (*ARMT* III 15:15 ff.). When the *nawûm* of the Ḫaneans grazed on the eastern bank of the Euphrates, hostile elements could surprise it and cause 'damage' (*ḫīṭum*, literally 'neglect, failing'—cognate with the very Biblical Hebrew word, *teḥᵉṭā'*, used above),[74] but in contrast to the biblical passage, where God protects the *nāweh*. The protected encampment may have been referred to as *nᵉwēh 'ētān* (Jeremiah 49:19; 50:44), that is, a strong, secure *nāweh*.

An interesting set of values emerges from the study of *nawûm*/*nāweh*, in its Mesopotamian–Syrian–Palestinian context. The attitude toward the *nawûm* in the standard, urban-oriented Assyro-Babylonian culture was negative, regarding it as disruptive to civilization. The Bible, too, refers several times to the *nāweh* as counter-productive, where fertile lands have been devastated, but this negative attitude mainly concerns the *nāweh* of foreign peoples (cf. Isaiah 34:13; 35:7; 27:11; Ezekiel 25:5; Zephaniah 2:6, etc.). In general, both the Bible and Mari are positive in their approach to the *nawûm*/*nāweh*. At Mari, at the confluence of Mesopotamian and West Semitic cultures, the general attitude was practical and sympathetic, taking the *nawûm* as a fact of life. In the Bible we see a sort of internal self-view of the *nāweh*, fully identifying with it and its way of life. Perhaps the most idyllic picture of the biblical *nāweh* is found in Ezekiel 34:14: 'I will feed them on a good pasture (*bᵉnāweh ṭōḇ*) and upon the high mountains shall their fold be (*nᵉwēhem*); there shall they be in a good fold (*mir'eh*) and in a fat pasture shall they feed upon the mountain of Israel.'[75]

[72] See Dossin 1939b, pp. 987–988.

[73] Horst 1969, p. 88, points out that *ḥṭ'* is employed here in an archaic usage, meaning 'vermissen'; similarly Pope 1973, p. 46, emphasizes the sense 'to miss', rather than the common meaning 'to sin'.

[74] For an additional Hebrew–Akkadian correlation of *ḥṭ'*-*ḫiṭum*, again in the context of herding, see Finkelstein 1968. The Hebrew verb in question here is in the *pi'ēl*: *'ᵃḥaṭṭennāh* (cf. Genesis 31:39), translated by Finkelstein as: 'make good the loss' of the flock, which is parallelled by the obligation stipulated by the Old Babylonian contract.

[75] For this passage see Willmes 1984, passim. The *nāwehs* of *hārē mᵉrōm yiśrā'ēl*, 'high mountains of Israel', may actually refer to pasturages on lofty terraced fields; cf., in different contexts, Stager 1985, pp. 5 ff.

The *nāweh* concept in the Bible is value-laden and led to such idioms as 'a peaceful habitation' (Isaiah 32: 18), 'a quiet habitation' (Isaiah 33: 20), 'habitation of righteousness' (Jeremiah 31: 23), and 'holy abode' (Exodus 15: 13). Among the Israelites, the *nāweh* even assumed a theological dimension, as is clearly seen in the most familiar of all the Psalms—Psalm 23 (vss. 1-2): 'The Lord is my shepherd, I shall not want; he makes me lie down in green *nāwehs*—green pastures.'[76]

Ḫaṣārum/ḥāṣēr[77]

The meaning of *ḫaṣārum* in the Mari documents has not yet been properly clarified. This West Semitic word occurs in just a few documents, as in one passage where the enemies of the king of Mari plot 'to assault the *ḫaṣārum*' (*ana ḫaṣārim šaḫāṭim*) in the vicinity of the city of Razama (*ARMT* II 43: 7–8); and once in a description of the destruction of the *haṣirātum* (plural) of nomadic tribes.[78] In these and other cases the editors have translated the word as 'parc à moutons'[79] which is, of course, possible *per se*. However, in the case of the Biblical Hebrew term, it must be considered that two separate roots have merged into *ḥāṣēr*:[80] first, proto-Semitic **ḤẒR*; Arabic *ḥaẓīra(t)*; probably Aramaic *ḥuṭrā*—'enclosure (for sheep), court'; and second, proto-Semitic **ḤḌR*; Arabic *ḥaḍara*; South Arabian *ḥḍr*—'dwell(ing), settle(ment)', primarily for humans, not animals. It is this latter root which yields the Hebrew plural *ḥaṣērīm* (in contrast to *ḥaṣērōt*), a special type of unwalled village as defined expressly in Leviticus 25: 31: 'and the houses of the *ḥaṣērīm*, which have no walls around them, shall be reckoned as belonging to the country field.' In the Bible *ḥaṣērīm* are frequently mentioned as settlements in the vicinity of a city (Joshua 19: 8; 21: 12; 1 Chronicles 6: 41; and cf. Nehemiah 12: 29; and see above, n. 36) as in *ARMT* II 43: 7, mentioned above. Except for the *ḥaṣērīm*, of the Israelite tribes, reference to this kind of settlement occurs only in connection with the habitations of nomadic or semi-nomadic tribes—Ishmaelites (Genesis 25: 16); Avvites (Deuteronomy 2: 23); and sons of Kedar

[76] And cf. the divine epithet *ne'ōt 'elōhīm*, in Psalms 83: 13.

[77] For an early treatment, see Malamat 1962, p. 147. The etymology of this lexeme remains doubtful and the concept vague, for it is not certain whether the /ṣ/ in *ḥāṣēr* derives from Semitic *ḍ*, as the present author assumes (that is, the word represents a hamlet, open settlement), or *ẓ* (yielding 'sheepfold'), as commonly understood.

[78] See Dossin 1939b, p. 989. For additional instances, see the damaged passage in *ARMT* IX 43: 5: *ḫa-ṣa-*[*ra* ?]*-ti*, and in *ARMT* XIV 81: 8: *ḫa-ṣi-ra-tum*; as well as the form *ḫiṣrum*, in *ARMT* XXIV 5: 6.

[79] And thus in addition the two Assyrian dictionaries, *CAD* Ḫ, p. 130b; *AHw*, p. 331, s.v. *ḫaṣārum*, 'Hürde'; and cf. Anbar 1985, p. 140.

[80] For a linguistic analysis of Hebrew *ḥāṣēr*, see Orlinsky 1939. For the complex Ugaritic evidence, cf. inter alia, Loewenstamm 1958.

(Isaiah 42: 11).[81] Unwalled settlements of this type were particularly numerous on the fringes of the Negeb, as is attested by such place-names as Ḥaṣar-addar, Ḥaṣar-gaddah, Ḥaṣar-shual, Ḥaṣar-susah in the territory of Simeon and southern Judah. To these we can add Ḥaṣar-asam (*'sm*), mentioned in the Hebrew ostracon from Meṣad Ḥashavyahu (*ll.* 3–4), of the late 7th century BC.

Though we cannot *a priori* rule out the 'enclosure' interpretation, the term *ḫaṣārum* at Mari is to be understood, at least in some of the cases, in the above discussed, biblical sense: as a special type of unfortified settlement which originated with nomadic or semi-nomadic tribes.

Patrimony as a tribal institution[82]

A basic facet of West Semitic social institutions—as revealed at Mari and, especially, in the Bible—is reflected in the practice of land transfer not by means of formal sale but exclusively through an inheritance framework. The relevant terminology is identical in both the Mari idiom and Biblical Hebrew: the Mari verb *naḫālum*, Biblical Hebrew *nḥl*, 'apportion, assign, inherit', and the nominal derivative *niḫlatum/naḥ^{a}lāh*, designating the hereditary share, inheritance portion or, simply, patrimony. These expressions are unknown in other Mesopotamian contexts, but do occur in the West Semitic languages. In the Akkadian texts at Ugarit, the noun *naḫālum* is attested once, and is considered a West Semitic loan, but the root appears quite commonly in the alphabetic texts there (*nḥl*, 'heir'; *nḥlt*, 'inheritance').[83]

At Mari, even in the context of an actual land transfer—not an inheritance—the purchaser would receive the property in the guise of a hereditary portion; that is, the transfer was effected by fictitious means. Thus, in one document (*ARMT* VIII 11) Yarim-Addu, a palace official, received (*inḫil*) a large field from the Awin clan of the Rabbean tribe; to do so, he had to be adopted into the circle of co-heirs within the extended family or clan. He symbolically became a 'brother' of the thirteen sons of Awin. In another document (*ARMT* VIII 12), the transfer of land to the same Yarim-Addu is effected without payment, but in two further transactions

[81] In Jeremiah 49: 28–33, the tribe Kedar is associated with the 'kingdoms of Hazor (*ḥāṣōr*)' and the 'inhabitants of Hazor'. It is possible that *ḥāṣōr* here is not a toponym but rather a collective form for *ḥ^{a}ṣērīm*, 'tent villages'. Cf. Rudolph 1968, p. 271. However, it may well be that the homonym Hazor, referring to the well-known city in Gaililee, derives from the root *ḥẓr*, 'enclosure', in reference to its surrounding ramparts.

[82] Cf. Malamat 1962, pp. 147 ff.; and now Lipiński 1986. Recently, however, B. Batto has contested the supposed meaning of patrimony at Mari, suggesting the original sense of a royal land grant; see Batto 1980, pp. 225 ff.

[83] For *eqlāt*^{meš}*naḫali*, cf. Nougayrol 1955, p. 109, No. 251.16: 7. For alphabetic *nḥl*, *nḥlt* in the sense of 'heir', etc., see van Selms 1954, pp. 137 ff.

(*ARMT* VIII 13, 14), payment *per se* is made. The remarkable feature here is that even the remuneration is referred to by the verb *naḫālum*, and thus was considered a sort of inherited property. Furthermore, such payment was made *ina ṭūbi libbim*, 'of (his) own free will'—a legalistic formula also known from much later times (Neo-Assyrian and Elephantine documents).[84] Such transactions were thus effected under the guise of reciprocal inheritance, a kind of mutual sharing of patrimonies. These instances are drawn from the corpus of legal documents from Mari (*ARMT* VIII). There are further instances of the actual inheritance procedure at Mari, as in the case of a daughter of Zimri-Lim, who complained that her royal parents did not bequeath to her (*inḫilunini*) a field and a garden—that is, she was provided with no patrimony (*ARMT* X 90: 3 ff.; and cf. also *ARMT* I 91: 6′).

Significantly, the transfer procedure for hereditary portions is always described by the verb *naḫālum* in the *qal* or base stem.[85] In such transitive contexts in Biblical Hebrew, the causative *hiph'īl* form is generally applied, though the *pi'ēl* form, or even the *qal* form, is occasionally found. The Mari usage of the base stem now shows that there is no justification for emending the *qal* forms of *nḥl* in Numbers 34: 17, 18 and Joshua 19: 49, into the *pi'ēl*, as was usually done since the meaning was certainly transitive.[86]

In Israel the apportionment of land was initially effected by casting lots (*gōrāl*), as is reflected in the biblical description of the allotting of the tribal domains (Joshua 13: 6; 14: 1–2; 18: 10; and see Numbers 26: 52–56; 34: 13; 36: 2, as well as the idealized picture in Ezekiel 46: 1; 47: 22, etc.).

[84] Cf. Muffs 1969, pp. 137 ff.

[85] It has been argued, however, that *inḫil*, in the *qal*, may have been contracted from a West Semitic causative form **yanḫil*. Cf. Lipiński 1986, col. 346. See now also the *Gt* form *ittaḫlu*, for the transfer of property (*ARMT* XXV 96: tr. 1). The 'property' here consists of silver as royal tax, a use of *naḫālum* similar to that in *ARMT* XIII 13, 14 (see above).

[86] Thus *HAT*, p. 496a, and already, in contrast, *HAL*, p. 648a. A careful examination of the biblical passages in question proves, in the present author's opinion, that the use of either the *qal* or the *pi'ēl* depends, as with several other verbs, solely on the grammatical subject or especially object: if the object is singular (as in Mari), the verb is in the *qal*; if it is plural, the verb is in the *pi'ēl* (the so-called extensive *pi'ēl*). Compare the passages in which the *qal* is employed, yet transitively: 'who are to apportion (*yinḥ^{a}lū*) the *land* (singular) to you . . you must also take one leader . . . to apportion (*linḥōl*) the *land* (singular)' (Numbers 34: 17, 18); and possibly: 'when they had finished apportioning (*linḥōl*) the *land* (singular) by the borders thereof' (Joshua 19: 49). This as against the verses which use *pi'ēl* forms: '*these* ('*ēlleh*; plural) were (the heritages) whom the Lord commanded to apportion (*l^{e}naḥḥel*) to the Israelites' (Numbers 24: 29); '*these* ('*ēlleh*; plural) were (the inheritances) which Moses apportioned (*niḥḥel*) in the plains of Moab' (Joshua 13: 32); *these were* ('*ēlleh*; plural) (the inheritances) which the people of Israel received (here *naḥ^{a}lū*, intransitive!) in the land of Canaan, which Eleazer the priest and Joshua the son of Nun . . . apportioned (*niḥḥ^{a}lū*) to them' (Joshua 19: 51). The same phenomenon in other verbs has already been noted by the grammarians; cf. Gesenius & Kautzsch 1909, p. 148; Joüon 1947, p. 117. It was noted already by the 8th century Arab grammarian Sibawayhi 1889, ch. 445, pp. 251/52.

In any event, these traditions[87] may reflect actual, early procedures for distribution of land (cf. especially Micah 2: 5).

Like Biblical Hebrew *naḥ^{a}lāh*, the verb at Mari yields a substantive, *ni/eḫlatum*, in the sense of hereditary portion, patrimony, but also property or estate *per se*. Thus, in *ARMT* I 91: 6′, the phrase *niḫlatam inaḫḫil* should be translated 'he will inherit a patrimony.' One prophetic document (A 1121, now joined with A 2731; see below) is very illuminating in this respect: *āpilū*-diviners, speaking on behalf of the god Adad of Kallassu (at or near Aleppo), demand from Zimri-Lim a *niḫlatum* (line 15), perhaps best translated here as property, estate.[88] The cultic personnel or temple functionaries seem to have sought control over a specific piece of land (at Alaḫtum; line 27, presumably in the border region between Mari and Yamḫad). The diviners remind Zimri-Lim that it was Adad who made him king over Mari, and they threaten that, should he not adhere to the god's demand, he would be deprived of his entire possessions. However, should Zimri-Lim provide the *niḫlatum*, Adad would give him 'throne upon throne, palace upon palace, territory upon territory, city upon city' (lines 19–21; and see below, p. 82 and n. 50).

The relationship here is in decided contrast to that of the biblical concept, where it is Yahwe who promises an inheritance to the Patriarchs (Exodus 32: 13; Psalms 105: 8–11; Ezekiel 47: 14; 1 Chronicles 16: 15–18), and later, to the Israelite king (Psalms 2: 8; 89: 28—where the inheritance comprises the nations of the earth and their rulers). Indeed, the land of Canaan (and by metaphor, also, the people of Israel) is designated by the appellative *naḥ^{a}lat Yahwe* or *naḥ^{a}lat ’^{e}lōhīm* (Deuteronomy 4: 20; 9: 26, 29; 1 Kings 8: 51, 53)—a theological imagery[89] and, in contrast, by the more realistic *naḥ^{a}lat Yiśrā’ēl* (Judges 20: 6) and *naḥ^{a}lat Ya‘^{a}qoḇ* (Isaiah 58: 14). There is, however, at least one distinct occurrence in the Bible where *naḥ^{a}lat Yahwe* is confined to a specific domain, just as at Mari: the city of Abel-Beth-Maacah in Upper Galilee is designated *naḥ^{a}lat Yahwe* (2 Samuel 20: 19), presumably because of its conquest by David's army and its subsequent incorporation within his realm; that is, within the collective *naḥ^{a}lāh* of God. Similarly, the 'Song of the Sea' refers to the sanctuary on Mount Zion as *har naḥ^{a}lat^{e}ḵā* (Exodus 15: 17),[90] which might approximate the *niḫlatum* for Adad in the Mari document. Despite the supportive statement

[87] They are ascribed mainly to the P source, which is usually considered as the latest of the Hexateuchal sources. See, e.g., Levine 1983, for the lateness of the P source, claiming that, while *naḥ^{a}lāh* is early, the verb (which, according to him, is a denominative) is late. Yet many scholars would agree today that the P source contains early material and notions; cf. especially the Israeli 'school', represented by Y. Kaufmann, M. Haran, A. Hurvitz, M. Weinfeld and others.

[88] Malamat 1980. The lines of the tablet are given here in its 'pre-joint' form.

[89] Cf. Forshey 1975; and Loewenstamm 1986.

[90] For reference to a sanctuary on Mount Zion, see, e.g., Jeremias 1971, p. 166; Loewenstamm 1986, pp. 166–167.

in Psalms 79: 1, the *naḥ^{a}lāh* in the Song of the Sea could refer to the entire land of Canaan, or at least to the western hill-country. This very same motif—of a god possessing his *naḥ^{a}lāh* on a mountain—appears at Ugarit in the Baal myth, in the expression *ǵr nḥlty*, that is, Baal's patrimony on Mount Zaphon.

In other cases the Mari documents offer an even closer parallel to the biblical conceptualization of the *naḥ^{a}lāh* (and the Hebrew verb *nḥl*). In both Mari and Israel the patrimony was taken to be an essentially inalienable piece of land, possessed solely by a gentilic unit. Its transfer could thus be effected, as stated above, only within an inheritance framework. Such a mechanism served to perpetuate the stability of the patriarchal-tribal organization over the generations. At Mari we can observe several means devised to evade this restriction (see above), but such evasions are actually significant indicators of the very rule. In the Bible there are very strict rules against the transfer of a *naḥ^{a}lāh* from one clan to another. These, whether explicit or implied, are found in legalistic passages, narrative and poetry alike. The most explicit expression of the prevention of a patrimony from passing to another tribe can be seen in the case of the daughters of Zelophehad, and in the laws specifically appended to the episode: 'The inheritance portion (*naḥ^{a}lāh*) of the people of Israel shall not be transferred from one tribe to another, for every one of the people of Israel shall cleave to the inheritance portion of the tribe of his fathers' (Numbers 36: 7; and cf. Numbers 27: 1–11; Joshua 17: 3–6). This refers to a situation where there were only daughters to inherit the patrimony.[91] There are only two exceptions to this rule in the biblical narratives: first, Rachel and Leah complain 'Is there any portion or inheritance (*ḥēleq w^{e}naḥ^{a}lāh*) left to us in our father's house?' (Genesis 31 :14), although they have brothers; and second, the three daughters of Job inherit a *naḥ^{a}lāh*, together with their seven brothers (Job 42: 13–15).[92]

In the legal corpus of the Bible, there is provision for the redemption of all inheritance portions to their original owners in the Jubilee year, terminating all 'long-term leases' (Leviticus 25: 13, 25–28). This is also found in Ezekiel's vision concerning the inheritance of the future ruler of Israel. Whereas the land which he leaves to his sons remains in their permanent possession, 'if he makes a gift out of his hereditary portion (*naḥ^{a}lātō*) to one of his servants, it shall be his to the year of liberty (*yōḇēl*, 'jubilee'); then it shall revert to the ruler (*nāśī'*)' (Ezekiel 46: 17). The tenacity with which individual Israelites actually clung to their ancestral plots, still in monarchic times, is amply demonstrated by the incident of Naboth's

[91] Ben Barak 1980, pp. 22–23, dealing with the various customs concerning transfer of a patrimony to daughters. And cf. now Grosz 1987.

[92] Lipiński 1986, col. 348.

vineyard, which was part of his *naḥ^a^lat āḇōt*, 'patrimony of his forefathers' (cf. 1 Kings 21).[93]

In the final analysis, the entire concept of the institution of patrimony was a product of the semi-nomadic environment of Mari and of the patriarchal-tribal structure of the Israelites. In the urban society of Mesopotamia, organized on an entirely different pattern, such an institution was less able to gain a foothold. There, greater importance was attached to freedom of the individual, especially in the realm of real estate, and a liberal policy evolved regarding purchase and sale of lands—modes diametrically opposed to the ideals implicit in the biblical institution of the patrimony.

E. THE GEOGRAPHICAL SCENE

Turning now to the geographical aspect of our subject, we find that the Mari documents are of value on several planes. First and foremost, they encompass the region known in the Bible as Aram-Naharaim—the present-day Jezirah in north-eastern Syria.[94] This was the land from which the Patriarchs traditionally came to Canaan. In this context, it is most significant that the two cities which were erstwhile habitats of the Patriarchal clan—Haran and Nahor—find frequent mention in the Mari letters, specifically as focal points of nomadic tribal activity. Haran,[95] in the Upper Balikh valley, was a central station on the itinerary of the Hebrews on their way to Canaan. Abraham's father, Terah, remained there while Abraham himself continued on westward and southward. Nahor is noted as the residence of Laban (Genesis 24: 10), a relative of the Patriarchal clan, from whose family both Isaac and Jacob took their wives. In the new Ebla documents, too, Haran is frequently mentioned as an important economic centre; while the earliest mention of Nahor is in the Cappadocian Texts—records of merchants who traded between Assyria and Anatolia two or three generations earlier than the Mari archives.

[93] For Naboth's ancestral patrimony, see, e.g., Bohlen 1980.

[94] The term Aram Naharaim occurs only in the Bible, where it is based on the second element, which appears as *Naḫrima*, *Nārima* or *Naḫarin*(*a*) in the el-Amarna and Egyptian documents. The full biblical name seems to be an Israelite coinage, used anachronistically for the Patriarchs (like their alleged Aramaic affinity). The term most likely reflects the large Aramean influx into Upper Mesopotamia and Syria in the 12th–11th centuries BC; see Malamat 1952, 1973a, especially pp. 140–141.

[95] Haran is located at present-day Eski-Harran, just over the border in Turkey. While the site is well documented at Ebla and during the 1st millennium BC, at Mari it is mentioned but a few times; cf. *ARMT* XVI/1, p. 14, to which we may add *ARMT* XXIII 241: 20, where a messenger from Haran to Mari is referred to. The most important instance of Haran at Mari occurs in an unpublished document concerning an alliance, concluded in the Sin temple at Haran, between a tribal organization (the Yaminites) and the kingdoms of Haran and Zalmaqum. At this time, Haran was a kingdom and the centre of Sin, the moon god (Dossin 1939b, p. 986). Significantly, as in the biblical tradition, Haran is mentioned as a staging-post on an important caravan route crossing Mesopotamia; see in the Old Babylonian itineraries, Goetze 1953; Hallo 1964, pp. 81 and 86.

The precise site of Nahor is still disputed,[96] but it is probably to be located somewhere on the western arm of the Upper Habur river, east of Haran. Though most of the material on Nahor has yet to be published (in the forthcoming *ARMT* XX), the fifteen-odd instances published so far reveal something of that city's geographic and political status in the Mari period, especially during the reign of Zimri-Lim.[97] Nahor appears to have been the seat of a district (in the land of Idamaraṣ) subject to Mari and governed by a high Mariote official rather than by a vassal king. At one period, the post of governor was held by Itur-Asdu, the statesman whom we quoted above (see pp. 4 ff.).

No less significant than the appearance of the early Patriarchal habitat in the Mari archives is the light shed on the dynamic dimension of mobility in the entire region. The comings and goings of the Patriarchs between Aram-Naharaim and Canaan are thus brought into comprehensible perspective. The numerous references in the Mari documents to merchant caravans, official missions and, especially significant, the movements of tribal groups—making their way from the Middle Euphrates region to as far away as northern Canaan (see below p. 62)—provide a much more convincing and reliable backdrop for the simple, almost naive picture reflected in Genesis. The obsolete view, of a centrifugal flow from the Arabian Desert into the surrounding areas, must now give way to another model of tribal movements which, metaphorically, we can grasp as a sort of 'alternating current'—or perhaps, windscreen wipers—back and forth . A good example of these movements in the Mari evidence is provided by the Yaminites (see e.g., p. 44), some of whom were centred on the area of Haran and Nahor, but at times migrated westward with their flocks, to the regions of Yamḫad, Qatna and Amurru—and perhaps even further southward (see p. 2, n. 3). And such a model also exactly fits the tribal descriptions of the Patriarchal migrations between Aram-Naharaim and Canaan. Parts of the Patriarchal clan settled at Haran or Nahor, while some of their kinsmen moved south to Canaan, other elements shuttling back and forth between them.

Actually, there appears to be in the Bible itself an internal parallel to the 'wanderings' of the Patriarchs from Aram-Naharaim to the Land of

[96] Initially this city was thought to have been located in the Baliḫ valley (cf. Dossin 1948, p. 125, etc., followed by several scholars). Presently, however, there is clear evidence for a location in the land of Idamaraṣ, at the western edge of the Habur triangle (cf. *ARMT* XVI/1, p. 24). The precise location is on the Upper Habur, north of the city of Amaz, which is mentioned several times at Mari, and modern Ras al-'Ain. See in detail, and with bibliographical references, Beitzel 1976, pp. 236–237, 377.

[97] Add now to *ARMT* XVI/1, p. 24 (s.v. Naḫur): XXIII 594: 4 (a contingent of 100 soldiers from Nahor sent to the aid of the king of the Turukkeans); XXV 682 (two men from Nahor, arms smiths); XXV 756: 5 ff. The city was a centre for nomadic tribes, including the Ḫabiru, who were rampant in the vicinity and endangered caravan trade. The rulers of Mari took steps to suppress such activity.

Canaan. Genesis 22: 20–24—the genealogical list of the sons of Nahor,[98] Abraham's brother—a somewhat perplexing genealogy interpolated into the Abraham cycle—seems to reflect an early situation, as if certain West Semitic elements had radiated out from centres at Haran and Nahor. The biblical view of the antiquity of the tribal confederation of Nahor's twelve sons is evident in the fact that this genealogy is grafted onto Abraham's brother. In other words, it is attributed to the first generation of the Patriarchs, in contrast to the confederations of the Ishmaelites (Genesis 25: 13–15) and of the Israelites, who are related to the second and third generations of the Patriarchs, respectively.

The attribution of the Nahorites to a wife (Milcah), on the one hand, and to a concubine (Reumah), on the other hand, clearly has a geographical basis.[99] Nahor himself, together with his eight 'legitimate' sons, represent tribal entities or localities in Aram-Naharaim and the Middle Euphrates region, whereas the four sons by the concubine represent such entities in the Valley of the Lebanon and in the Upper Jordan valley, far to the southwest. Bible scholars have long considered that in genealogies, concubines and their progeny represent 'hangers-on' who at some point joined the main tribal confederation. To my mind, however, the Bible seeks to convey just the opposite—that is, that lineage through a concubine or secondary wife generally implies the migration of clan elements from an ancestral habitat to far-off, outlying areas. Thus, of Abraham's sons by concubines, it is explicitely stated (in Genesis 25: 6) that '. . . he sent them away from his son Isaac, eastward to the east country.' This is precisely the biblical view of the origins and subsequent locales of the Hagarites, Ishmaelites and Amalekites (for the latter, see Genesis 36: 2), who are similarly traced back to concubines or maidservants. In other words, all the tribes regarded in biblical tradition as deriving from the Patriarchal clan through secondary unions had migrated, or were forced to do so, from their erstwhile home to marginal areas—that is, to the desert fringes.

Similarly, Nahor's descendants through his concubine can be seen as having broken off from the ancestral clan in the Upper Habur region, eventually settling far off to the west, in Northern Canaan. If our reasoning is correct, the genealogical scheme of the Nahorites may serve as an enlightening inner-biblical analogue for distant, westward migrations, such as those of the Patriarchs themselves.

Mari had close ties not only with North Syria—particularly Yamḫad and, further south, Qatna, but also with the coastal cities of Ugarit and Byblos, as is becoming increasingly evident.[100] Mari also paved a way further south-

[98] For a new attempt to analyse Nahor's genealogy, see Malamat 1967, pp. 129 ff. See also Westermann 1981, pp. 448 ff; and see above, p. 40, and n. 51.

[99] Maisler 1946.

[100] For the West in the Mari documents, see in general Kupper 1973, chapter 1 (pp. 1–41) and the bibliography there; Malamat 1970. For more recent studies see Sasson 1984; Finet 1985a; Limet 1985, and also the references there to Ugarit and Byblos; cf. Villard 1986.

ward, into Canaan. This name, Canaan, seems to appear in a
in the form LÚ *Ki-na-aḫ-num*^{MEŠ}—that is, in a normal cuneifor
for 'Canaanites'.[101] It occurs at Mari in connection with the term *ḫu*
'marauders', a synonym of Ḫabiru, the better known name for
disfranchised, outlawed elements. The intention, in any event, was
person from Canaan', and the context of the word shows that the region involved was probably the northernmost part of the land of Canaan, south of Qatna (rather than Palestine proper). This, then, is the earliest attestation of Canaan or Canaanites—pushing the documentation back some three centuries farther than the hitherto known earliest reference to this name.[102] Thus, the term 'Canaan' is no longer to be considered anachronistic with respect to the first half of the 2nd millennium BC.

Hazor[103]

One of the most important cities of Canaan was Hazor, the farthest centre noted on Mari's economic horizon to the southwest (see p. 2). Indeed, it was precisely in the Mari period that Hazor grew to greatness. In Palestinological terms, this was the transitional period from the Middle Bronze Age II A to the subsequent Middle Bronze Age II B or, very possibly, an early phase within the latter.[104] At this time, a huge lower city of some sixty hectares was founded, below and to the north of the mound proper (which was of some ten hectares in area). The ramparts surrounding the lower city were about three km long, making it of a size and form comparable to other centres of this period to the north, such as Qatna (100 hectares), Ebla (fifty-six hectares) and even Mari itself (fifty-four hectares).

It is significant that several cuneiform tablets from Old Babylonian times have been discovered in the excavations at Hazor.[105] These include (1) a jar inscribed with a personal name containing a theophoric element, most likely Adad (see below) and an initial element, *išme-*, of Akkadian form (rather than West Semitic); (2) fragments of clay model livers, display-

[101] The single reference at Mari so far mentioning Canaan or Canaanites was published in Dossin 1973; and cf. Rainey 1979, p. 161.

[102] Until the Mari discoveries, the earliest known reference to the land of Canaan had been in the Idrimi Inscription from Alalaḫ, of the early 15th century BC—some 300 years later than Mari; the next oldest reference appears in an Egyptian inscription of Amenhotep II, of the end of the 15th century BC.

[103] Cf. my series of articles on Hazor in the Mari documents: Malamat 1960, 1970, 1971b, 1982; forthcoming.

[104] For the archaeological discoveries at Hazor see the excavation reports—well summarized in Yadin 1972 and 1976. The Mari period would correspond with Level XVII (Upper City) and Level 4 (Lower City) there, ascribed to the 18th–17th centuries BC.

[105] (1) A personal name (correct reading to: Išme-Adad, as suggested by A. Shaffer, *Iraq* 49 [1983], p. 115, n. 28), incised on a jar; Artzi & Malamat 1960; (2) Fragments of clay model livers; Landsberger & Tadmor 1964; (3) A lawsuit by three persons against a woman; Hallo & Tadmor 1977; and (4) A fragment of a lexicographical text; Tadmor 1977. These texts are but a faint echo of the cultural, economic and administrative significance of Hazor at that time.

ing affinities with those from Mari; (3) a tablet recording a lawsuit brought before the king against a woman, concerning a house and an orchard and expressly mentioning the city of Hazor; and (4) a fragment of the ḪAR-*ra* = *ḫubullu* lexical series, the *vademecum* of every cuneiform scribe. Thus, the cuneiform scribal craft seems to have spread to Hazor already by this time, possibly even from Mari itself, as might also be hinted at, inter alia, by a text (*ARMT* I 66: 5–8) mentioning the despatch of a liver model via Mari to Qatna, Hazor's not too distant neighbour to the north.

A last vestige of the greatness of Hazor in the Old Babylonian period is found in the pre-eminence accorded the city during the Israelite conquest, many centuries later. The biblical historiographer notes: 'For Hazor beforetime was the head of all those kingdoms' (Joshua 11: 10). He was not referring to Hazor on the eve of the Israelite conquest, but rather to the large city founded in the Middle Bronze Age and which prospered during the Amarna Age. Moreover, the title 'King of Canaan' (Judges 4: 2, 24), uniquely atributed to Jabin of Hazor, was apparently also reminiscent of much earlier times, when the king of Hazor was *the* king of Canaan, or at least one of its principal kings.

There are now some fourteen Mari documents—a not inconsiderable number—attesting ties between Mari and Hazor of one sort or another, and several more are apparently soon to be published. Of these, a partial translation of one tablet has appeared and it seems to be the earliest mention of Hazor, harking back to the period of the Assyrian inter-regnum at Mari.[106] It is a letter from Šamši-Adad giving instructions to Yasmaḫ-Adad, his son and viceroy at Mari, concerning messengers from the West on a stop-over at Mari on their way home. The messenger of Išḫi-Adad, king of Qatna, was to take care of the group, at least as far as Qatna. The group included envoys from Hazor and from four kings of the land of Amurru (4 *šarrāni*^{meš} *A-[mu]-ur-ri-i*). It is particularly unfortunate that this extraordinary letter has not so far been published in full. Hazor or Hazorites are mentioned in three other letters, and in some ten administrative and economic texts (including those in *ARMT* XXV). An administrative document (*ARMT* XII 747) lists eighteen persons from various localities (including Mari): messengers, artisans, singers and even a priest—all receiving choice cuts of mutton during their sojourn in the palace of Zimri-Lim. The messengers were from many scattered parts: Babylon and Ešnunna

[106] A. 2760; see Dossin 1957, pp. 37–38. This document is of importance for the chronological correlation between Mari and Hazor; the relationship between them would be comprehensible only at the time when, at the beginning of the Middle Bronze Age II B, the huge lower city at Hazor was founded and flourishing. It would have been this bustling city which attracted the attention of Mari and the other Mesopotamian kingdoms. On the basis of the Middle Chronology, utilized here throughout, Šamši-Adad died in 1783 (or 1781) BC, more or less the latest date possible for the establishment of Greater Hazor (and thus of the beginning of the Middle Bronze Age II B in Palestine). Basing on the Low Chronology, the relevant date would be ca. 1720 BC. (For the several chronological systems, see above, p. 1, n. 2). And see Mazar 1968 and now Dever 1987.

to the south; Carchemish, Emar and Yamḫad, to the northwest; and Hazor (*Ḫaṣurayu*ki) to the southwest.[107]

Two economic texts deal with a 'strategic' commodity—tin, a metal commonly alloyed with copper (usually at a ratio of 1 to 7–10), to obtain bronze, a stronger, more practical alloy than pure copper, particularly for the manufacture of tools and weapons. The tin trade was brisk in this period, and Mari was a major tin emporium, serving especially as a channel for the metal to the West.[108] In Syria and Palestine, copper was readily available, but tin—like crude-oil in modern times—was a raw material which had to be brought from afar. The origin of the tin handled by Mari is still enigmatic, but recent studies have shown that it probably derived from Afghanistan via Iran.[109] In one of these documents (*ARMT* VII 236), Hazor is mentioned with Yamḫad as the destination of a shipment of about five kg of tin—a quantity sufficient to yield thirty-five to forty-five kg of bronze. The other document (A 1270), of considerable significance in several respects,[110] deals with consignments of tin sent from Mari to several destinations in the West. The reverse of the tablet has recently been collated, and certain parts of the original reading (by Dossin) have been corrected (cf. now esp. *ARMT* XXIII 556: 18–32). After recording consignments to Aleppo, the text lists: '10 minas of tin (for) Sumu-Eraḫ at Muzunnim; 8⅓ minas of tin (for) Ewri-Talma (!) at Layašim (or Layišim); 30 minas of tin (for) Ibni-Adad, king of Hazor, responsible: Addi-Addu at Ḫazazar on first registration. 20 minas of tin for Amud-pi-El (king of Qatna); 20 minas of tin for Ibni-Adad on second registration; 1[+] minas of tin for the Caphtorite (i.e. man of Crete); ⅓ mina of tin to the dragoman, chief [merch]ant among the Caphtorites in Ugarit; [20 (?) minas of tin for Ib]ni-Adad on third registration.'

The tin consignments to Hazor represent a considerable amount: some unknown quantity over 50 minas (this quantity alone would suffice for some 400 kg of bronze alloy). The name of the king of Hazor is mentioned

[107] For a similar list, but containing, besides Hazor, various other localities; see *ARMT* XXIII 243.

[108] See the basic study on tin, in Muhly 1973 and 1976. On the tin trade at Mari, see the brief remarks in Dalley 1984, pp. 63–65; see also below, nn. 109, 110. A problem is raised by the fact that in the Cappadocian Texts, of half a century or so earlier, tin was shipped in huge quantities from Ashur to Anatolia (Kaniš), whereas the kings of Mari directed their trade southwards, to Syria and Palestine. Could ethnic affinity (i.e. Amorite origins) have been a factor here? Further, it seems likely that Mari might have been responsible for the intensification of bronze manufacture as it is encountered in the Canaanite sphere, particularly in the days of Zimri-Lim.

[109] See Cleuziou & Berthoud 1982 for an early report on sources of tin in Afghanistan; previously, even Thailand had been proposed as its origin (see Dalley 1984, p. 64). Work is currently being carried out in the Taurus range in southern Anatolia, and according to preliminary reports, sources of tin (numerous but minor) have been discovered. See Yenner & Özbal 1987. It is too early, however, to speculate whether the long-standing enigma has been resolved, for serious historical problems are involved.

[110] Published in Dossin 1970; and see Malamat 1971b, pp. 31–38; and remarks on certain toponyms and personal names, in Sasson 1971, p. 172; Astour 1973, pp. 73–75.

here for the first time—Ibni-Adad—the Akkadian form of the name, the West Semitic cognate of which, as probably used at Hazor proper, was Yabni-Addu.[111] Could this name possibly be connected with that of the (much later) biblical king of Hazor, Jabin (which is presumably a hypocoristicon of a full theophoric name)? The document mentions several kings contemporaneous with Ibni-Adad: Ḫammurabi of Babylon, Yarim-Lim of Aleppo and Amud-pi-El of Qatna—all reigning in the first 9 [+] years of Zimri-Lim's reign.[112]

One problem in this document is the placename Layaš/Layiš (*La*-PI-*iš*). With the initial publication, it seemed certain that this toponym referred to the biblical city of Laish (later Dan), only thirty km north of Hazor. Such an identification appeared to be supported by excavations on the site, which revealed a large, well-fortified city (twenty hectares) of the Mari period.[113] In another recently published document, however, a city named Layash is noted in a context which would locate it somewhere between Aleppo and Ugarit (*ARMT* XXIII 535: iv, 27)—hundreds of kilometres north of Palestine. If both references are to one and the same place, a location near Hazor would be ruled out; on the other hand, the seemingly close association of Layaš/Layiš with Hazor in the above document may point to the possibility that there were two cities of similar name, one in northern Palestine and the other far to the north, in Syria.

Between the second and third entries concerning Hazor in this document, there is a most interesting reference to tin consigned to persons at Ugarit. The *ta-ar-ga-ma-an-num*, 'dragoman', mentioned here is one of the earliest occurrences of this rare term, known already from the Cappadocian economic texts of the 19th century BC (where, for example, a 'supervisor of the dragomans' seems also to have received some metal). Our 'dragoman',[114] was apparently the spokesman of the commercial colony (*kārum*) of Cretans at Ugarit, a colony presumably existing there also in the 14th–13th centuries BC. The 'Caphtorite' (*Kap-ta-ra-i-im*) was undoubtedly a merchant from Crete or one of the Aegean islands, since that entire region seems to have been called Kaptara in Akkadian (see above, p. 57). Ugarit cultivated close ties with the Aegean throughout its history, and there is

[111] Akkadianized forms such as the king's name may have appeared in court circles of the West, a sort of assimilation of Babylonian culture. For the transition Yabni-Addu > Yabni > Jabin, see already the vague remark in Albright 1968, p. 43, n. 99. Since Jabin is mentioned as king in the 'time' of Joshua (Joshua 11: 1) and the Judges (Judges 4: 2, 24), the name may have been a dynastic one at Hazor going back to Old Babylonian times (i.e. the Middle Bronze Age II B).

[112] The complex problem of the length and year formulae of Zimri-Lim's reign is beyond the scope of the present context. It appears that he ruled for only some fourteen years (Middle Chronology: 1775–1761 BC); cf. Birot 1978; Anbar 1979; Veenhof 1985; Charpin & Durand 1985, and see chart there on p. 306. Yarim-Lim of Yamḫad died in Zimri-Lim's year 9′, denoted 'Adad of Maḫanum'; his successor, Ḫammurabi, ascended the throne of Aleppo in the same year.

[113] For the most recent excavation reports on Dan/Laish, see Biran 1975, 1980, 1984.

[114] For the Kulturwort *targamannum* see Gelb 1968, and now Lambert 1987, p. 410.

clear archaeological evidence at that site for commerce with the Aegean during the Mari period (i.e. 'Ugarit moyen 2'), particularly the Middle Minoan II pottery ('Kamares ware') found there.[115] Thus, we may assume that the 'Caphtorite' goods mentioned in Mari documents from the days of Zimri-Lim—which included luxury pottery, weapons and possibly even textiles[116]—reached Mari primarily through Ugarit. Ugarit's position as a mercantile intermediary between the Mediterranean lands and the Middle Euphrates region is thus brought into closer focus by this interesting document from Mari.

One of the texts mentioning Hazor (*ARMT* XXIII 541) is in a group of documents (*ARMT* XXIII 535–548) which seem to indicate that Zimri-Lim engaged in a journey far beyond his realm, a visit to his father-in-law, Yarim-Lim, king of Yamḫad. Zimri-Lim, his wife, Atar-Aya, and his entourage continued beyond Aleppo to Ugarit, and gifts were exchanged at the numerous stop-overs on the way, in accord with the usual diplomatic procedures of that day.[117] In the brief part of a letter published long ago, we read that Zimri-Lim journeyed in person to Ugarit at some time or another, accompanied by select troops,[118] though it is not clear when this occurred, or whether it was a mere visit (like the pilgrimage Zimri-Lim once made to Aleppo), or an actual military campaign to the Mediterranean coast, like that of his predecessors, Yaḫdun-Lim and Šamši-Adad (see below, pp. 107 ff.). In any event Zimri-Lim, like his father, was faced by an insurrection in one of his territories upon his return home.

Atar-Aya, one of Zimri-Lim's wives, may originally have come from Ugarit, or from some adjacent town, and thus she may have been 'taking home leave', just as Zimri-Lim's own daughters—married off to various rulers allied to Mari—would occasionally return home to the Mari palace, for a visit. However, it has been surmised on the basis of as yet unpublished material on Hazor,[119] that Atar-Aya was a princess from Hazor. If so,

115 See Schaeffer 1939, pp. 22 ff., 53 ff.; Schaeffer 1949, pp. 51, 256, Fig. 109A and Pl. 38.

116 In the recent volumes of *ARMT*, references to Kaptara and goods dispatched to Mari from there are as follows: *ARMT* XXII 324: ii 9′ (textile); *ARMT* XXIII 104: 30′ (weapon); *ARMT* XXIV 98: 10 (ornamental weapon); *ARMT* XXV 393: 13 (*bur-zi*), 499: 21 (vase), 507: 2′ ([giš]*kur-sa-lu*), 511: 6′ and 526: 4 (vases), 601: 10 (weapon), 610: 8 (1 *marḫašu* UD.KA.BAR, a bronze object).

117 The dossier on the grand tour of Zimri-Lim to the west has been published and interpreted by P. Villard in *ARMT* XXIII, pp. 457–521; Villard 1988. And see the reconstruction of the journey in Sasson 1984. Zimri-Lim may even have been accompanied to the Mediterranean by his father-in-law, the king of Aleppo, an exceptional diplomatic courtesy; cf. Charpin & Durand 1986, pp. 173 ff.

118 Jean 1939, p. 67. According to *CAD* B, p. 211b (s.v. *bēru*), the army unit accompanying Zimri-Lim was conscripted in the land of Idamaraṣ (emending *i-da-ku-uk* to *I-da-ma-<ra>-aṣ*). If so, it would appear that both journeys (or was there only a single journey ?) took the same route.

119 Durand, in *ARMT* XXIII, p. 475, n. 52.

this would reveal familial ties between the dynasties of Mari and northern Palestine, an unanticipated 'windfall' for the historian.

Various other economic texts from Mari are quite revealing of the two-way commerce between Mari and Hazor. In one case, a messenger from Hazor (the name is damaged) was at the Mari palace when a three-jar shipment of wine was received there (*ARMT* XXIV 75); the king of Hazor (among other rulers) received a consignment of clothing from the king of Mari (perhaps on the occasion of his journey through Syria; and see *ARMT* XXIII 541: 4–5); precious objects—gold and silver vessels, as well as gold jewellery—were sent to Zimri-Lim by the king of Hazor (*ARMT* XXV 43, 103; 119),[120] and so forth. On a more earthly plane, we read in one text (*ARMT* XXIII 505) of trade in the other direction— of a shipment of eighty-four head of cattle received at Hazor, along with (?) six mules or onagers (*parûm*). The editor of this text[121] has noted an interesting feature of the script, which is somewhat peculiar and 'provincial', particularly in the writing of the numeral '84'. Could the scribe himself have been a Hazorite who had been trained locally (i.e. in Canaan) in the cuneiform scribal craft?

In contrast to the rather humdrum tenor of these economic and administrative texts, there are three actual letters mentioning the city of Hazor or Hazorites. One of them provides an especially vivid picture of intrigue and crime (see below). In the other two, Baḫdi-Lim, prefect of the Mari palace, reports to Zimri-Lim on groups of messengers arriving at Mari from various directions. In *ARMT* VI 78, missions from Mari and Babylon have returned from Hazor and Qatna. The passage on Hazor reads: '[T]o my lord speak. [Thus] speaks Baḫdi-Lim [your servant:] (5) A group of messengers (*ṭēḫītum*) from Haz[or and Qatna have arri]ved here . . . (10) [and a man of Ha]zor [as their] escort (*ālik idim*) have come to my lord. Two messengers from Babylon, who have long since resided at Hazor, (15) with one man from Hazor as their escort, are crossing to Babylon. . . .'

In this period, deputations between the larger centres of the Near East were constantly on the move, engaging in various political and economic

[120] The texts are mainly in the recent volume of H. Limet, *ARMT* XXV: No. 43, a gold ring or necklace and three silver vases sent as a gift by Ibni-Adad to Zimri-Lim at Ugarit (this coastal city is frequently mentioned as a depot for Mari goods, and the gifts may have been sent there during Zimri-Lim's visit to the West); No. 103, a gold vase, gift from the king of Hazor sent to the depot of Zimri-Lim at Mahra[ ]; No. 119, a necklace for the king of Karana at the city of Shuna. From this text it would appear that this piece of jewellery was originally sent to Mari, but was later transferred by Dariš-libur, a Mari official, to the king of Karana. It is also known from other texts that there was a sort of safe or deposit box belonging to Zimri-Lim at Shuna. And see now Malamat 1989.

[121] Soubeyran, in *ARMT* XXIII, pp. 434–435. For Hazor as a centre of scribal craft, probably even with a scribal school, see above, pp. 55f. and n. 105, noting the cuneiform inscriptions found there. The above mentioned numeral '84' is written with eight oblique *Winkelhaken* and two vertical pairs of wedges. This same system seems to appear on a tablet of about the same period, recently discovered at Hebron (see Anbar & Na'aman 1986/87, pp. 4 and 6)—both cases possibly reflecting a practice current in the West.

undertakings. In the relevant texts, precise details are occasionally given concerning the make-up of deputations,[122] and we learn that the rank of those participating varied according to the importance of the mission and the degree of responsibility required for its fulfilment. This letter, like others from Mari, illustrates the then current diplomatic practice of attaching to each mission a local representative of the people to whom the mission had been sent. This person acted as an escort and accompanied the delegation on its way home. Thus, a Hazorite accompanied the missions returning from Hazor to Mari and Babylon. The fact that the delegation from Babylon had sojourned at Hazor for some time shows that the relations between these kingdoms were enduring and no mere passing contact.

Whereas this letter is concerned with the movements of emissaries from the West to Mari, another letter (*ARMT* VI 23) describes a mission in the opposite direction—from southern Mesopotamia to Syria and Hazor. Among other matters, Baḫdi-Lim reports to his lord that emissaries from six lands—three east of the Tigris—have arrived (or are about to arrive) at Mari on their way west (*ll.* 19–34): 'Further, a group of travellers in transit (*ētiqtum*)[123] from Babylon, Ešnunna, Ekallatum, Karana, Qabra and Arrapḫa, on the way to Yamḫad, Qatna, Hazor and [. . .] have arrived (or are to arrive) here. Shall I let them go on or detain them?' Mari's key position on the way from Mesopotamia west made her a prime station for convoys and missions of every sort. Right of passage was not a matter of course, but was subject to the will of the Mari authorities, and hence Baḫdi-Lim's request for instructions from the king.[124] This list of western destinations in the letter follows a strict geographical order from north to south: Yamḫad (Aleppo); Qatna; Hazor. Another placename is mentioned after Hazor, but unfortunately the tablet is damaged at this point and the traces are too fragmentary to enable restoration. In accord with the route outlined, the city mentioned here was apparently south of Hazor, in Palestine or, less likely, in Egypt (or could it have been Egypt itself—a

[122] For diplomatic and commercial missions at Mari, see Pack 1981, pp. 128 ff. The various types of messengers include: *mār šiprim*, a general term for a messenger, frequently of higher status, but also a commercial agent or a resident ambassador; *lāsimum ša sikkim* and *kallûm*, express couriers (of the *mārū šipri*); *ālik idim*, escort; *mubassirum*, messenger. And cf. Munn-Rankin 1956, pp. 99–108.

[123] For the term *ētiqtum*, appearing several times in *ARMT* VI, cf. *CAD* E, pp. 395b–396a. There may be a connection with the Hebrew verb (in the causative) *haʿᵃtēq*, as used in Genesis 12: 8 and 26: 22; the Patriarchs roam about Canaan and travel from place to place as if 'in transit'. Might the causative form indicate that not they alone but the entire entourage was transferred by them?

[124] In another case, Bahdi-Lim ordered the temporary detention of messengers on their way to Qatna till instructions were received from the king; see *ARMT* VI 19: 4–11.

land otherwise not mentioned at all in the Mari archives).[125] Various suggestions have been made as to the illegible placename: Megiddo (Malamat); Laish (Yadin); and such non-Palestinian sites as Gubla/Byblos (Landsberger, orally) and Carchemish (Na'aman)—and even Gaza or Egypt (Alt, Albright). The letter also depicts the historical reality which may have served as the setting for such pseudo-historical episodes as the biblical account of four eastern kings joining in a campaign to the far West (Genesis 14).[126]

A parallel to this list of localities has come to light in another document—part of a Babylonian 'Dream Book' containing, inter alia, a collection of dreams about journeys to various places. This fragment, from the Kassite period and found at Babylon, gives what may well have been a detailed itinerary from southern Mesopotamia to the West. In the salient passage, the following towns are listed: Mari; Emar; Aleppo; Qatna; Hazor.[127] The 'Dream Book', though of a slightly later time, still reflects the geographical and political circumstances of the Mari period. The fact that Hazor is the terminal point on the 'dreamer's' journey west further demonstrates that it was the last centre in the West—at least in the Mesopotamian geographical consciousness.

A similar route is outlined in a Mari document describing the wanderings of a tribe of Yaminites from the Euphrates region to Yamḫad, and the lands of Qatna and Amurru.[128] Thus, Amurru seems to have extended to the south of Qatna, which would well correlate with Amurru's geographical position in the Amarna Letters. The occurrence of Amurru here is parallel to that of Hazor in the lists cited above, implying that the two locales were adjacent to one another, but not identical.

Entanglement of the quadrilateral: Mari, Aleppo, Emar and Hazor

The most intriguing of the Mari documents pertaining to relations between Mari and Hazor is probably a copy of a letter sent by Zimri-Lim

[125] See above, p. 2, n. 3. In Malamat 1970, p. 173, n. 6, it was suggested that *ll.* 27–30 are parallel to the construction of the previous paragraph (*ll.* 19–24); the last destination in *l.* 29 should be restored [*Ar-ra-*]*ap-ḫi-im*, Arrapḫa, across the Tigris—parallelling the last city in the list of messengers who had arrived at Mari (*l.* 22). On the basis of our conclusions, Na'aman 1981, pp. 171–172, sought to restore the above lacuna as *Kar-ka-mi-iš*, Carchemish, by regarding the two passages in question as absolutely identical; his restoration, however, remains doubtful. He further points out 'that Baḫdi-Lim does not refer to a specific diplomatic mission but asks his lord for instructions regarding the potential arrival of messengers at Mari.'

[126] Speiser 1964 surmised that Genesis 14 was translated into Hebrew from an original Akkadian source—which would bring our two sources even closer.

[127] Oppenheim 1956, p. 313; the last three placenames also occur in a late copy found in the library of Ashurbanipal.

[128] The text is unpublished; the contents have been announced by G. Dossin; cf. Parrot 1950a, p. 7, followed by Kupper 1957, p. 49.

to his father-in-law Yarim-Lim, king of Aleppo.[129] It concerns events surrounding the dispatch of an official (?) from Mari, commissioned to purchase precious materials for use at the palace:

> To Yarim-Lim, say, thus Zimri-Lim, your son: (5) Concerning the cupbearer (?—or was he a smith of some sort?), you have written me as follows: Thus you (say): 'This man took away from Hazor silver, gold and precious stone(s) and made off to you. And (hence) the Hazorites (10) have detained the asses and the persons who come up for trade, saying as follows: "The cupbearer (?) took away the silver, gold and precious stone(s) and made off to Zimri-Lim."' This is what you have written to me. (15) Certainly this man has not brought to me any silver, gold or precious stone(s). (Rev.) As to that man, they seized him (2) at Emar and made undue demands of him, nay, they robbed all that he was carrying. The sealed document (attesting) that this man had bought (the goods) for money was taken from him. Verily, this man fled to (25) me for his life. Now, my father, concerning that man ... [about a dozen lines missing] ... May he (someone in Yamḫad ?) send a message to Emar, and may the belongings of that man be taken to my father.

Thus, the letter seems to be dealing with a mishap of trade between Mari and Hazor. We have seen that relations between these two centres, both commercial and diplomatic, appear to have been correct and cordial—but then comes this exceptional incident, complicated by the 'mugging' at Emar, in the territory of Yamḫad.

The goods from Hazor destined for Zimri-Lim were this time precious materials—the metal either as raw material or as finished products (see above p. 57). This is a significant indicator of the presence of these materials as commodities *per se* in the cities of Canaan in the Middle Bronze Age II. They are otherwise attested only rarely by such evidence as a legal document in Akkadian, found at Hazor ('200 [shekels ?] of silver'), mentioned above (see p. 56), and by sporadic finds of gold and silver objects in contexts of this period, mainly in tombs at such sites as Gezer and Megiddo.[130] And several centuries later, large quantities of gold and silver (both ingots and finished products) were listed among the booty seized by Thutmose III in northern Palestine. But surely neither Hazor nor any other site within Canaan was the ultimate source of these materials, and we must assume that the gold, at least, was brought from Egypt, the major supplier of that metal in antiquity.[131]

[129] The document was briefly outlined in Birot 1973, pp. 10–11; it carries the sigla S. 115 72–16. I am obliged to M. Birot for providing me with a transliteration of the text (the cuneiform of the actual tablet, now in the Aleppo Museum, has not been published), and for kindly granting me permission to present it; see Malamat 1982.

[130] For the legal document from Hazor, see Hallo & Tadmor 1977, n. 105. For the finds at Gezer, see Macalister 1911–12, I, pp. 125ff.; III, Pls. XXXI, XXXV and XXXVI; at Megiddo, see Guy & Engberg 1938, p, 172, Fig. 176: 3, Pl. 107: 19; p. 173, Fig. 178: 1, Pl. 115: 10; and Loud 1948, Pl. 227: 1.

[131] See Helck 1971, pp. 379ff., where Egypt is also noted as a prime exporter of gold. And see Störk 1977.

The letter well reflects certain practices and contingencies in the current caravan trade.[132] Thus, we learn of the Hazorites' detaining a caravan—a phenomenon far from unknown in antiquity. In our text the verb employed is *kalûm*, 'to detain, hold back, stop', frequent at Mari especially in the correspondence of Baḫdi-Lim.[133] Usually this verb refers to messengers, as in a case noted above, but in this instance it includes merchants and their asses. Another interesting point concerns the term *kunukku* in line 22, the usual meaning of which is 'seal', but it can also mean a 'sealed document',[134] as in our case, apparently referring to the 'bill of sale' for the purchase of the precious goods. Seals and sealed documents played an important role within the commercial apparatus of antiquity in general, and in caravan trade, in particular. The specific mention that the 'sealed document' was also stolen indicates that the 'cupbearer' was left bare of documentation concerning the legal conclusion of the transaction at Hazor. In other words, he had no proof that he had come into possession of the goods legally (and one suspects that this may indeed have been the case!).

Finally, in sending this letter it was not Zimri-Lim's intention merely to draw Yarim-Lim's attention to the full extent of the episode; rather, he seems to have regarded Yarim-Lim as liable for his loss and, seeking redress, urged him to investigate at Emar. We can presume that this is what the damaged section on the reverse contained, as can be inferred from the passages immediately before and after the break.

In reconstructing the specific circumstances of this letter, we must also take into consideration the power play between the entities directly involved within the political configuration of the day in Syria. The Mari archives have been relatively generous in this regard, regarding relations between Mari and Yamḫad. Less is known of Mari–Emar and Yamḫad–Emar relations, and nothing (except this letter) is known of contacts between either Yamḫad or Emar and Hazor. Zimri-Lim was far from being an iron-bound vassal of Yarim-Lim's, and he was sufficiently independent to dare to bring pressure to bear upon his father-in-law in order to obtain assistance in a real time of need. Emar was a vital link in Mari's trade to the north, especially with Yamḫad and its capital, Aleppo, only some fifty miles west

[132] See, e.g., Leemans 1960, 1968; for caravans several decades earlier, see Larsen 1967; Veenhof 1972.

[133] See, e.g., *ARMT* VI 18: 13′, 16′; 19: 9–10; 23: 25, 32; 31: 29—in all of which only messengers are mentioned, whereas in our document merchants as well as asses are referred to—a true caravan (cf. *ARMT* X 18: 10). For the verb, see *CAD* K, pp. 95 ff., s.v. *kalû*; *RLA* 5, pp. 419–420, s.v. Karawane.

[134] On *kunukku* in the sense of 'sealed document', see *CAD* K, p. 547, s.v. *kunukku* 3; and Leemans 1982.

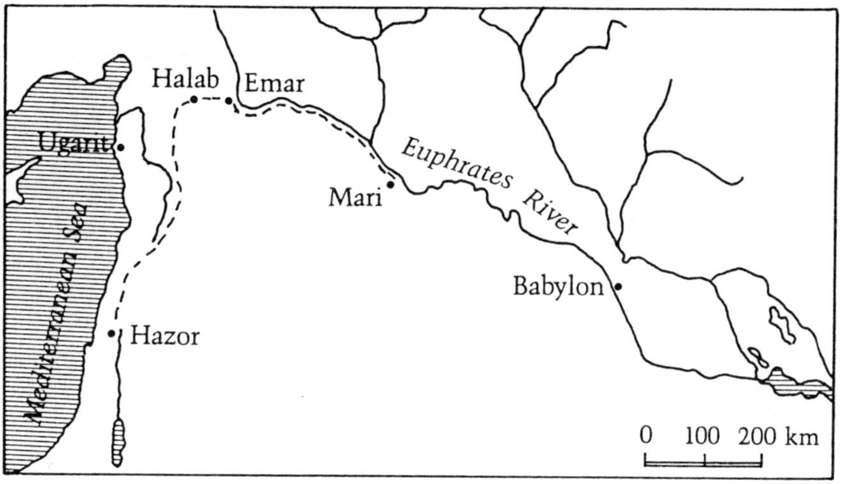

6. The route between Mari and Hazor.

of Emar.[135] Mari, at the peak of its power under Yaḫdun-Lim (Zimri-Lim's father), had controlled Emar for a time.[136] But the Assyrian conquest of Mari broke his hold, and eventually Yamḫad stepped into the vacuum and took control of Emar.

Reviewing the chain of events, we can see two separate but related episodes: in the initial episode, the 'cupbearer' seems to have departed Hazor without having finalized his purchase of the precious materials. The Hazorites, seeking to protect their interests, detained a caravan from Mari. In the meantime, in the second episode, the 'cupbearer' was robbed at Emar, on the last leg of his journey home. He was not only deprived of the goods from Hazor but also of his bill of sale—the only proof that he had paid for the goods. He escaped 'by the skin of his teeth', and finally reached Zimri-Lim to relate his sad tale.

In this letter, Zimri-Lim was clearly seeking to prod his father-in-law into recovering his stolen property. In such a context it is interesting to note that the Code of Ḫammurabi orders compensation for stolen property by the authorities at the venue of the crime, in cases where the thief was not caught. The Code places an obligation upon the responsible party to

[135] Emar, a riperian emporium on the great bend of the Euphrates, is fairly well documented in the Mari texts (cf. *ARMT* XVI/1, pp. 7–8, s.v. Imar, and the indices of the more recent volumes, beginning with *ARMT* XXI). It is even more frequently noted in the Ebla texts, for the latter is relatively closer. Various Mari texts indicate that Emar's relations with Mari were often strained, disrupting smooth communications between Mari and Yamḫad (see, e.g., *ARMT* XIV 33: 1′ ff.). At Meskene, the site of Emar, excavated by Margueron, however, no Early or Middle Bronze Age levels have so far been located, possibly because they have been eroded away by the Euphrates river. On Emar in general, see Klengel 1965a, pp. 275–279.

[136] As attested by the year formula 'The year when Yaḫdun-Lim defeated Emar'; see Dossin 1950, p. 52, n. 4.

search for the stolen property.[137] But the major theme underlying this entire story is one of international law—of merchants or agents in trouble on foreign soil. It was no doubt just this sort of incident that led to the conclusion of interstate agreements giving protection to merchants abroad, as exemplified at Ugarit in the 13th century BC.[138] In this light we can also comprehend the claims of Kadašman-Enlil II of Babylon against the Hittite king Ḫattušili III, following the murder of Babylonian merchants in northern Syria.[139] Since the crime was committed in a locale subject to Hittite control, the Hittites were held liable and therefore were sued for damages. Two other instances of a ruler invoking the obligations of a second party to treaties, to protect messengers and caravans, are found in the Amarna archive, both letters addressed by Burnaburiaš II of Babylonia to Amenhotep IV (Ikhnaton).[140] One letter (EA 7: 73–82) relates that a single Babylonian caravan was twice plundered in regions under Egyptian jurisdiction, and the Babylonian monarch demands compensation from Egypt. Burnaburiaš admonished Amenhotep: 'Canaan (*Kinaḫḫi*) is thy land and (its) kings are (thy servants). In thy land have I been violently dealt with. Bind (your vassals, and) the money which they have stolen make good.' He then warns and advises the Egyptian king that the roads must be kept secure lest communications break down and Egypt thereby lose control over its vassals. In our letter, Zimri-Lim too would have done well to advise Yarim-Lim of a similar message.

In the lacuna on the reverse of our letter, Zimri-Lim presumably sought Yarim-Lim's aid in obtaining release of the Mariote caravan detained at Hazor. The outcome of these events is, of course, entirely unknown, and the break in the text—as so often occurs in ancient documents—leaves a very broad range of possibilities. Indeed, much of the 'stuff of history' is bolstered by reconstructions of just this very sort of lacuna. Be what may, the episode does provide a fascinating glimpse into the trials and tribulations of international trade at that time, especially in the West.

Conceptions of space and time

On his way to and from Hazor, our errant official of the last document travelled in all four cardinal directions. Though the ancients did not possess the compass, they did have certain very interesting conceptualizations of

[137] Codex Ḫammurabi, para. 23; and cf. para. 7: 'If a man buys silver or gold ... or has received (them) for safe custody without witnesses or contract, that man is a thief; he shall be put to death'; see Driver & Miles 1955, pp. 14–15. This may explain the eagerness of our messenger to emphasize that he indeed had had a 'bill of sale' in his hand.

[138] See Nougayrol 1956, e.g. RS 17.146 and 17.230; RS 17.130 and 17.316. And cf. Yaron 1969.

[139] See Klengel 1980.

[140] The relevant documents are EA 7: 73–82; 8: 13–34. For the most recent authoritative and annotated translation, see Moran 1987, pp. 73 ff. For the English translation quoted below, see Mercer 1939, p. 27.

space and direction, and some of them were closely related to temporal concepts, as well. Generally, the cardinal directions were conceived in reference to the winds, or to other major factors of nature, geography or demography.[141] In Biblical Hebrew, of the four common terms for the cardinal directions, two relate directly to the sun, referring respectively to the sunrise and the sunset (*mizrāḥ*, 'east', and *ma' ᵃrāḇ*, 'west').[142] However, in archaic biblical contexts, in poetic passages but occasionally also in prose, these two directions appear as *qedem*, 'fore', and *'āḥōr*, 'hind', respectively—indications of true *orient*ation. The early Israelite ego faced east.[143] In keeping with this, south and north were referred to as *yāmīn*, 'right', and *śᵉmō'l*, 'left', respectively. Indeed, all four of these archaic designations are to be found in a single passage in Job (23: 8–9): 'Behold, I go *fore*ward (*qedem*, that is, east), but he is not there; and *back*ward (*'āḥōr*, that is, west), but I cannot perceive him; on the *left* hand (*śᵉmō'l*, that is, north) I seek him, but I cannot behold him; I turn to the *right* hand (*yāmīn*, that is, south), but I cannot see him.'[144]

In Standard Akkadian, too, there is more than one set of terms for the four winds, based either on the names of various peoples living toward the four cardinal directions or by other specific terms.[145] At Mari, however, we find certain West Semitic terms for the cardinal points in specific usages, terms which are identical with those in archaic Hebrew. These are *aqdamātum*, 'fore (eastern) side' and *aḫarātum*, 'hind (western) side'—both referring especially to banks of the river Euphrates;[146] **yamīna*, 'right' (that is, south), and **sim'al*, 'left'' (that is, north). The two latter examples, south and north, are deduced from the designation, known only from Mari, of certain tribes as DUMU.MEŠ-*yamīna* and DUMU.MEŠ-*sim'al*,: 'sons of the right' and 'sons of the left', respectively (and see above, pp. 35, 42, n. 57). This same viewpoint has left its imprint, to this very day, in the names of several Near Eastern lands, such as the Yemen in the south. Thus, we clearly see a general eastward orientation among the Semitic peoples, just as today we are 'orientated' northward, by convention.

141 See Tallqvist 1926, with emphasis on the cardinal directions of the Semites. And see Harel 1983/84.

142 *Mizrāḥ*, 'east', from the root *zrḥ*, 'to shine'; *maᵃrāḇ*, 'west', from *'rb*, 'to set, to enter'; and cf. the Akkadian verb *erēbu*, of the same meaning.

143 See Tallqvist 1926, pp. 123 ff; Harel 1983/84, p. 157; Cassin 1969.

144 Occasionally it is only through an awareness of this archaic geographical usage that we are able to understand the true meaning underlying a passage, as in Ezekiel 16: 46: 'And your elder sister is Samaria, who lived with her daughters to the *left* of you; and your younger sister, who lived to the *right* of you in Sodom with her daughters' (the RSV has already translated 'north' and 'south' for left and right here, respectively). Cf. also *śᵉmō'l* in Genesis 14: 15, referring to the *north* rather than to the west.

145 Most common is the denotation of direction according to surrounding peoples. Thus, in Akkadian: *Subartu*, i.e. north; *Akkad*, i.e. south; *Elam*, i.e. east; and *Amurru*, i.e. west; other designations are *ištānu* (*iltēnu*), north; *šūtu*, south; *šadû*, east.

146 On *aqdamātum* and *aḫarātum*, cf. von Soden 1949; and Lewy 1952, and the view there that the terms refer simply to the near and far banks of the Euphrates.

This geographical usage brings us to a further conceptualization held in common by Mari and Israel—on the temporal plane. Here, the Akkadian word *aqdamātum* and the Hebrew words, *qedem* and *'āḥōr*, are not spatially applied but are used temporally.[147] *Qedem* has a dual meaning just as does the English word 'before', while *'āḥōr*, spatially 'behind', is also temporal 'after', or 'future'. *Qedem*, meaning past, is so common in Biblical Hebrew that no examples are necessary. The temporal aspect of *'āḥōr* can be demonstrated by the sober phrase *'aḥ^a^rīt hayyāmīm*, literally 'the afterwards of the days', in other words, 'the end of days'. And we may note other examples, such as Isaiah 41: 23: 'Tell us what is to come hereafter (*l^e^'āḥōr*, literally 'backwards'), that we may know that you are gods'; and Isaiah 46: 10: 'declaring the end (*'aḥ^a^rīt*) from the beginning and from ancient times (*qedem*) things not yet done'; in other words, *'aḥ^a^rīt* parallels the future, something which has not yet happened. Something similar is seen in the related word *'aḥ^a^rōn* which, besides its usual meaning of 'last', has a nuance of 'future', and even 'west' (as in *hayyām yām 'aḥ^a^rōn*, 'the western sea' [Joel 2: 20; Zachariah 14: 8], that is, the Mediterranean). Its reference to 'future' can be seen in Proverbs 31: 25: 'Strength and dignity are her clothing, and she laughs at the time to come' (RSV; Hebrew *yōm 'aḥ^a^rōn*; NJPS: 'to her future' or 'future day'); as well as in Isaiah 30: 8: '. . . inscribe it [an oracle] in a book, that it may be for the time to come (*yōm aḥ^a^rōn*) as a witness for ever' (RSV; NJPS 'for future days').

This dual spatial–temporal usage is also significantly seen in two recently published Mari texts, in which the West Semitic term *aqdamātum*, 'east', is clearly used in the temporal sense of 'the past'. This is in contrast to Standard Akkadian, in which the expression would be *ina panītim*. In one of these instances, a 'prophetic' text reads: *ša ištu aqdami*, speaking of a treasure 'which is from before-times' (*ARMT* X 80: 18). Another text, a letter dealing with a river ordeal, includes the phrase *ištu aqdami*: '(the city) since beforehand (had been given to PN).'[148]

In summary, the ancient concept of the flow of time is, outwardly, the very opposite of the modern, western one, in which we look forward into the future and walk into it, while the past remains behind us. The expression 'March of Time' aptly exemplifies this western view. The Mariotes and early Israelites—and probably the ancient Semites in general—regarded the past as revealed and spread out before them, while the future lay behind them, unseen and unknown. Thus, they progressed backwards into the future. This is not like Alice through the looking-glass, eating the cake and then cutting it: quite the opposite. It is like a rower in a boat who faces the stern and rows 'backwards' through the water. We are used to seeing this imagery in the many sculls racing along the Thames and many other rivers of the world. Such a temporal conceptualization was bound

[147] See Wolff 1974, p. 88. For *qedem*, see also Eph'al 1976; for *'aḥ^a^rīt*, see Seebass 1973.

[148] Published in Bottéro 1981, p. 1036, *l.* 25 (a letter addressed to Zimri-Lim).

to have serious repercussions—in both the historical and the religious outlook, but these are matters beyond our present scope.

This 'backside-forward' concept has never really left us. Several years ago, the late Gershom Scholem, then doyen of Jewish Studies, wrote an essay about his friend, the late Walter Benjamin, the German Jewish writer and philosopher, who had referred to a painting by Paul Klee entitled 'Angelus Novus'. This painting, now at the Israel Museum in Jerusalem, had attracted Benjamin's attention. To him it symbolized a concept of history: 'The angel of history', Benjamin stated, 'ought to look like this. His face is turned to the past . . . but a storm blowing from Paradise drives him unchecked into the future, to which his back is turned. . . .' It is the glaring expression in the eyes of Klee's angel which betrays the biblical awe of time—past and future.[149]

[149] See Scholem 1983, pp. 35–72, esp. pp. 64–65, quoting Benjamin 1974, pp. 697–698. And see Ebach 1982, pp. 61 ff., 89–90.

III

PROPHETS, ANCESTORS AND KINGS: ASPECTS OF WEST SEMITIC RITUAL

Another facet of Mari which can make a considerable contribution toward an understanding of the ancient Israelite experience is to be found in religious manifestations and ritual practices. Both at Mari and in the Bible, the main characteristic underlying this realm is, once again, the basic West Semitic tribal heritage. The author has studied certain specific aspects of this subject, such as the covenant-making ceremony, the controversial concept of census-taking and ritual expiation,[1] and enforcement of the ban (or taboo) as penalty for certain types of transgression.[2] It is to this last subject that we shall now turn.

A. THE BAN

The aspect of taboo or ban concerning an object utterly forbidden to human contact is a universal numinous phenomenon.[3] It is of a two-fold nature, deriving either from extreme uncleanness or from extreme holiness. Biblical Hebrew applies separate terms to these two aspects: *ḥērem* for an interdiction or an object under ban, and *qodeš* for a consecrated object.[4] Either term can appear in a positive or a negative sense: normally, *ḥērem* is an anathema (as, e.g., in Deuteronomy 7: 26), but can also be 'a most sacred thing' (Leviticus 27: 28); while *qodeš* is most often sacred but at least once its verbal form, *tiqdaš*, is applied to the forfeited or abhorred (Deuteronomy 22: 9). What these ostensibly opposite aspects hold in common is their absolute prohibition of human contact with, let alone any use of, the devoted object. Such contact was contagious, the transgressor becoming devoted in turn—and as such, foredoomed to death.

In the Bible, the exact nature of banned or consecrated property, and its religious and judicial corollaries, may now further be comprehended through the Mari documents. There, the Akkadian terms *asakkum* and

[1] See Speiser 1958; Held 1970, pp. 32–37; Malamat 1971a, pp. 18–21.

[2] See Malamat 1966b.

[3] For the taboo among the Semitic peoples, see Smith 1894, General Index, s.v. For taboo in general, see Steiner 1956; Radcliffe-Brown 1969, pp. 133–152.

[4] For the various facets of the *ḥērem*, see Brekelmans 1959a; and recently Lohfink 1982, with bibliography. For *qodeš*, see Müller 1976. Both words originally had the meaning of separateness, apartness, conveying taboo. For *qdš*, cf. Ullendorff 1977, pp. 63–64; and Milgrom 1976.

asakkam akālum (lit. 'to eat the *asakku*'),[5] used to denote the concept of taboo and its violation, are of frequent occurrence. The meaning of the word *asakku* was established even before the Mari discoveries, from Akkadian religious documents and lexical lists.[6] There, however, the word appears only as a stereotype, whereas the Mari documents display a dynamic use of the concept, closely resembling the several nuances attached to the Biblical Hebrew terms *ḥērem* and *qodeš*.[7]

In *ARMT* VIII,[8] containing the legal texts from Mari, the term *asakku* constitutes an important element in the sanctions to be invoked upon violation of a contract—a use unknown outside Mari (on Terqa, see below). In several contracts, a man who defaults from agreed terms is likened to 'one who has eaten the *asakku*' of a particular king or god. In one case the penalty exacted for failure to honour a contract for the sale of a field is likened to that for eating the *asakku* of the god Dagan, of king Šamši-Adad, and of the god Itur-Mer (*ARMT* VIII 6: 9′–11′). In another instance, the penalty is as that meted out for eating the *asakku* of the god Šamaš, of ... and of the king Šamši-Adad (*ARMT* VIII 7: 9′–10′); and in a third case, the violator is compared to one who has eaten the *asakku* of the god Itur-Mer, of the goddess Ḫanat, and of the king Zimri-Lim (*ARMT* VIII 85: 3′–5′).

In all these cases, the breach of contract is treated as a serious religious transgression equal to the eating of a taboo; or, in biblical terms, to the violation of a holy or banned object. The simile of eating the *asakkum* was probably founded on actual practice, as is clearly indicated by an alternate formula where the term *asakkum* is replaced by the sumerogram SAR, meaning 'plant' or 'herb'. In this particular instance, the violator's punishment is compared to that of 'one who has eaten the "herbs" of (the king) Šamši-Adad, of ... and of Awin the Rabbean' (the head of a clan of a semi-nomadic tribe called Rabbû) (*ARMT* VIII 11: 29–31). From this variant reading, the editor of the text concluded that *asakku* was originally some sort of plant thought to have magical influence over the health of its possessor (*ARMT* VIII, p. 167). Another formula frequently mentioned in contracts from Terqa in the Ḫana period (slightly later than the Mari per-

5 See *CAD* A/2, s.v. *asakku* B, pp. 326 f.

6 See Landsberger 1933, pp. 218–219; and *AHw* I, p. 73, which, following Landsberger, distinguishes between the word under discussion (s.v. *asakku* II) and its Akkadian homonym (*asakku* I), which denotes a demon, as well as an illness. Cf. also *CAD* A/1, p. 255, s.v. *akālu* 7a. The somewhat synonymous concepts *ikkibum* and *anzillum*, not occurring at Mari, lie outside the scope of the present discussion. For the three terms, see van der Toorn 1985, pp. 42–43.

7 In an unpublished lecture, Landsberger alluded to the possibility that the phrase *asakkam īkul* was an attempt to translate some Canaanite expression such as *hāyā lᵉḥērem*. Brekelmans 1959, pp. 138–139, also mentions the Mari reference in passing, without realising its import for our subject; cf. also Saggs 1960, p. 414. The comparison between Mari and the Bible has been rather weakly rejected by Milgrom 1976, pp. 241 f.; for a view in its favour, cf. Weinfeld 1983, pp. 189–190.

8 For the discussion of *asakkum*, cf. *ARMT* VIII, pp. 166 ff.

iod), reads: '*nīš* DN (an oath to or life of a deity such as Šamaš, Dagan or Itur-Mer) and king RN he has eaten'—that is, the violator of the contract (usually concerning the sale of a field) has committed a sacrilege and must pay a fine to the temple.[9]

Whatever the case, the *asakkum* of a god or king is not to be considered a mere figure of speech derived from archaic religious concepts, solely employed in penal clauses of contracts. At times it was plainly conceived as an actual, physical object. This is attested by the use of the term *asakkum* at Mari to designate consecrated property belonging exclusively to a divinity or to royalty. In one letter, Šamši-Adad mentions 'bronze, the *asakkum* of (the god) Adad' (*ARMT* I 101:6); an administrative document records a consignment of about 40 kg, apparently of some metal (the word is missing), constituting the '*asakkum* of Adad of the city Terqa' (*ARMT* VII 105: 1–3, and p. 342). And an unpublished letter sent to Zimri-Lim by an *āpilum* (diviner–prophet; see below, pp. 86–87) urges in the name of Šamaš of Sippar that an *asakkum* be sent to the temple of Adad of Aleppo (A.4260: 15–18).[10]

Such property in divine possession is also known in the Bible, in such analogous expressions as *qodeš lᵉYahwe* and *ḥērem . . . lᵉYahwe*. The ban of destruction decreed upon Jericho excluded all metal objects: 'But all silver and gold, and vessels of bronze and iron, are sacred (*qodeš*) to the Lord; they shall go into the treasury of the Lord' (Joshua 6: 19; cf. v. 24). In other words we have here an '*asakkum* of Yahwe', so to speak, and in Israel as in Mari consisting of metal objects.[11]

In the whole of Akkadian literature apart from Mari, there is no reference to the *asakkum* (or for that matter to the *ikkibum*)[12] of a king (*asak šarrim*) or other mortal, in contrast to the *asakkum* of a god. Thus, Mari was unique in its well established tradition of a taboo existing outside the divine sphere. The *asakkum* of a king could be used even to lend binding force to an oath, reflecting upon its religious significance. Thus, in place of the usual oath-formula by a king or a god, in one contract the two parties swear to observe the agreement by the *asakkum* of Yaḫdun-Lim and Zimri-Lim (*ARMT* VIII 16: 1′–8′). In the Bible, in comparison, it is God himself who makes the oath by his own *qodeš* (Amos 4: 2; Ps. 89: 36).

As Zimri-Lim ascended the throne of Mari many years after the death of Yaḫdun-Lim, his father, it is obvious that the name of the dead monarch

[9] See Rouault 1984; for references, cf. p. 9, *l*. 21.

[10] See Dossin 1966, p. 85. In another administrative text, a bronze consignment for a deity, or rather the artisans in his service, is termed: *asakkum ša Dagan ša Subatum* (*ARMT* XXII, 196).

[11] In this connection, we may note an entry in a lexical series, where *asakku* is defined as silver of the god: *a-sak-ku* = *kàs-pa ili* (for references, see above, n. 6); and cf. 2 Kings 12: 4: 'All the money (lit. 'silver') of the holy things (*haqqᵒdāšīm*) which is brought into the house of the Lord. . . .'

[12] For *ikkibu* see *CAD* I/J, pp. 55 ff., s.v. *ikkibu*, 'interdicted, forbidden thing, place or action'. And see van der Toorn 1985, pp. 43–44, also for its biblical equivalent, *tō'ēḇāh*.

was later added to the oath-formula (*ARMT* VIII, pp. 32f., n. 2). From this it would follow that the taboo associated with a king lost none of its force even after his death. However, the case of Yaḫdun-Lim (who fell victim to a court conspiracy or rather to a rebellion of his vassals),[13] may be exceptional and numinous powers may have been attributed to his name. A hint of this veneration is to be found in the demand of a diviner–prophet that Zimri-Lim offer sacrifices to his father's *manes* (*ARMT* III 40).

The king's *asakkum*, like that of a god, at times also assumed a tangible physical significance, as in instances of the infringement of palace goods (*ARMT* II 55: 35–37; III 22: 13–15). Thus, in certain cases royal property was conceived as being the king's taboo, a kind of banned or consecrated object, the disposal of which against his express wish was regarded as an act of desecration. The biblical concept of sacred objects mentioned in connection with the king is something quite different: these were simply gifts dedicated *by* the king *to* the deity.[14] Indeed, since the biblical notion of taboo functioned on a purely religious plane, banned objects (*ḥērem*) and consecrated gifts (*q^odāšīm*) were the exclusive property of God: 'every devoted thing (*ḥērem*) is most holy to the Lord' (Leviticus 27: 28), or of his representatives, the priests: 'Every devoted thing (*ḥērem*) in Israel shall be yours (i.e. the house of Aaron)' (Numbers 18: 14; Ezekiel 44: 29; and cf. Leviticus 23: 20; 27: 21).[15] But at Mari, the king probably also had a religious function and was thus regarded as representative of the deity, not unlike the priests in Israel.

So far we have discussed the *asakkum* proper of a god or king. However, the fuller significance of the comparison of the Mari evidence and the Bible lies in the implications inherent in the infringement of the taboo. The eating of the *asakkum* idiomatically expresses the biblical concept of the violation of the *qodeš* or the *ḥērem*, with all the consequences involved in such an act. Interestingly, the Bible applies the very same verb as the Akkadian to the infringement of the *qodeš*—*'kl*, 'to eat' (see Leviticus 22: 14; Jeremiah 2: 3). The transgressor of the biblical *ḥērem* himself becomes taboo, as classically attested by the terms of the ban on Jericho: 'But you keep yourselves from the things devoted to destruction (*ḥērem*), lest when you have devoted them (*taḥ^arimū*) you take any of the devoted things (*ḥērem*) and make the camp of Israel a thing for destruction (*l^eḥērem*; i.e. bring it under

[13] See above, p. 10; for a probable palace revolution, cf., e.g., Landsberger 1954, p. 35, n. 28.

[14] Votive gifts of the kings of Israel and Judah are mentioned in 1 Kings 7: 51 (cf. 2 Samuel 7: 11); 15: 15; 2 Kings 12: 19 (English version, v. 18); 1 Chronicles 26: 26. It is noteworthy that the Bible distinguishes between the 'treasuries of the house of God' and the 'treasuries of the dedicated gifts (*ōṣ^erōt haqq^odāšīm*)' (1 Chronicles 26: 20). For the several treasuries, see Delcor 1962, pp. 353 ff.

[15] Jars found at Hazor, Arad and Beer-sheba, from the Iron Age II and incised with the word *qdš*, 'holy' or, rather, 'consecrated', can be regarded as such priestly, consecrated objects. And note especially a small ivory pomegranate-shaped vessel of the late 8th century BC, inscribed: *lby̆[t yhw]h̆ qdš khnm*, 'Belonging to the Tem[ple of Yahw]e, consecrated (rather than "holy"—A.M.) for the priests'. See A. Lemaire 1981.

the ban), and bring trouble upon it'[16] (Joshua 6: 18); 'Israel has sinned; they have transgressed my covenant which I commanded them; they have taken some of the devoted things (*ḥērem*); ... Therefore the people of Israel cannot stand before their enemies; ... because they have become a thing for destruction (*hāyū lᵉḥērem*)' (Joshua 7: 11–12).

Anyone violating the ban must forfeit his life: thus the fate of Achan, who took from the *hērem* of Jericho, becoming taboo and consequently being put to death (Joshua 7). This is also clear from the Mosaic Law on the ban: 'No one devoted, who is to be utterly destroyed (*kol ḥērem 'ᵃšer yoḥᵒram*) from among men, shall be ransomed; he shall be put to death' (Leviticus 27: 29).

This same basic principal no doubt underlies the Mari attitude towards a man guilty of eating the *asakkum* of a god or king. In such a case, just as the violator of a biblical *ḥērem* became taboo and had to be destroyed, so too the 'eater' of the *asakkum* undoubtedly became taboo and had to suffer the consequences.[17] Admittedly, this last assumption appears at variance with the fact that the penalty in the Mari contracts is merely monetary. However, from a contract of adoption it is clear that such transgression was originally conceived as a capital offence. Of the man who fails to honour the terms of that particular contract it is stated: 'He has eaten the *asakkum* of (the gods) Šamaš and Itur-Mer, of (the king) Šamši-Adad and (the viceroy) Yasmaḫ-Adad, and he shall pay 3½ minas of silver, (the fine for) a capital offence (*dīn napištim*)' (*ARMT* VIII 1: 28–31). The wording of this clause strongly suggests that the original punishment for the crime in question was death but that it subsequently 'degenerated' into a fine (cf. *ARMT* VIII, p. 168).

Invocation of the *asakku* is not limited to breaches of contract but includes all forms of law-breaking and, in particular, the crime of *lèse majesté*. Thus, for example, the refusal to obey an order given by Šamši-Adad for the full mobilization of the Yaminites was considered a violation of the king's taboo: 'Any "mukhtar" (*sugāgum*) whose troops are not mustered in full, who leaves behind (even) a single man, will have eaten the king's *asakkum*' (*ARMT* I 6: 18–19; and cf. below, *ARMT* II 13). This is somewhat reminiscent of the biblical episode at Jabesh-Gilead, most of whose inhabitants fell under the ban following a public oath condemning to death any Israelite of the tribal federation who failed to join the holy war against the tribe of Benjamin (Judges 21: 5–11).[18] Another military application at Mari was the case of the stern order by the governor of Saggaratum to despatch elite troops to Mari, any delay in doing so constituting a violation of 'my

[16] For the meaning of *'kr* as 'to make taboo', see *HAL*, p. 779, s.v. *'kr*, 'zum Tabu machen'; and Mosis 1987, col. 76. As for the Hebrew expressions 'take' and 'steal' from the *ḥērem* (Joshua 7: 11), compare the Akkadian parallels *leqûm*, *šarāqum*, 'to appropriate' the *asakkum*; cf. *CAD* A/2, p. 327 (b 2').

[17] For the contagious nature of the taboo, see Smith 1894, pp. 446–454; and Steiner 1956, chapters 5 and 6.

[18] Cf. Greenberg 1971.

lord's *asakkum*' (*ARMT* XIV 67: 8; and cf. *ARMT* XIV 1: 22, for the same formula, concerning the safekeeping of a lion).

Spoils of war

Yet the greatest similarity between Mari and Israelite practice in the imposition of taboo concerns spoils of war. This was undoubtedly an important factor in ensuring the orderly distribution of booty.[19] Such a measure served as an alternative for proper military regulations on the matter. The taboo was imposed, first and foremost, to deter individuals from laying hands on spoils set aside for the god or, at Mari, the king and other mortals. This is evident from two instructive letters sent to Yasmaḫ-Adad, viceroy at Mari, by notables under his tutelage. In one letter (*ARMT* V 72), a tribal chief relates that he issued the following order to his officers: 'Whosoever takes of the booty[20] will have eaten the *asakkum* of the gods Adad and Šamaš' (*ll.* 12–13). The writer then goes on to accuse a certain man of appropriating two (bronze) kettles,[21] silver, gold and other articles. Unfortunately, the tablet is damaged and it is not clear whether later in the letter (*l.* 1′), the word *lidūkū* ('they shall kill') relates to the accused or not. Whatever the case, the writer ends by comparing the crime to an infringement of the god's taboo, to the desecration of the taboo of Šamši-Adad and of the viceroy, Yasmaḫ-Adad (*ll.* 10′–22′). From the last line of the letter it would appear that the accused had merely to pay a fine. The resemblance of this case to that of Achan at Jericho is striking (Joshua 7).[22] Despite variant details, the basic elements are the same in both: the enjoyment of spoils of war, considered in particular circumstances to be a violation of the taboo.

However, the classical use of the *asakkum* concept in connection with spoils of war is provided by the second letter, addressed to Yasmaḫ-Adad by one of his high-ranking commanders (*ARMT* II 13).[23] Let us quote it in full:

> To my lord say,
> Thus (speaks) Samadaḫum, your servant:
> When the men of [ ] took the city of Ṣibat
> I was told that my lord had departed for [the city of Q]abarā.
> Therefore I did not bring the slaves (captives) of Ṣibat
> to my lord. Thus did I (say to myself):
> 'When my lord shall have returned to his country

[19] This point has been stressed particularly by Schwally 1901, pp. 39 ff. But cf. Brekelmans 1959a, p. 148.

[20] The word *šuḫtum*, translated 'booty' in *ARMT* V 72: 12, is defined by von Soden 1953, p. 209, and *AHw*, p. 1262a, as 'Grünspan' (verdigris); cf. also Limet 1960, pp. 270 and 276. If so, the meaning is possibly 'whosoever takes (of the spoil, even) a piece of rusty copper.'

[21] For the exact meaning of *ruqqu(m)*, see Salonen 1966, pp. 255 ff.; and *AHw*, p. 995a.

[22] Cf. Brekelmans 1959a, p. 138, where the similarity is noted.

[23] This document was first published in Thureau-Dangin 1941, pp. 41–43; and see the partial studies of Glock 1968, pp. 78–79; and Marzal 1971, pp. 190–191.

I will bring my lord's share (of the booty).' Now,
behold, I send you four slaves, my lord's share.
Therefore far be it from my lord to say
as follows: 'My servant has taken profuse spoils.'
Thus did I [myself] say to the 'major(s)' and the 'captains'[24]
saying: 'My share, the portion (of the booty)[25]
[ ] give [me!]'
....
Three days, four days, I w[aited . . .]. The 'majors'
filled their hands full (of the booty)[26]
and to me they gave nothing.
On the fifth day they brought me
six slaves belonging to the soldiers.
To their owners (i.e. the soldiers)
I returned them.
I assembled the 'major(s)', the 'captain(s)', the 'lieutenant(s)' and the 'sergeant(s)'[27]
and thus did I proclaim my ordinance as follows:
'You have not given me my [share],
in addition to my lord's portion (of the booty).[28]
He who has deprived a soldier of his booty,
be he a 'general' (lit. the Great-of-Amurru), a military scribe (lit. the Scribe-of-Amurru),[29] a 'major' or a 'captain',
has eaten the *asakkum* of (the god) Dagan and (the god) Itur-Mer,
the *asakkum* of Šamši-Adad and Yasmaḫ-Adad.
In my mouth and (in that) of the 'major' I placed an oath by the king[30]

[24] The translations for the military titles here merely convey the relative rank involved; for the terms GAL.KUD and NU.BÀNDA, see *ARMT* VII, pp. 190–191 and 243–244. For the military hierarchy in the Old Babylonian period, cf. Landsberger 1955, pp. 122 ff.; as well as Landsberger 1967, p. 58, n. 212; and Salonen 1968, pp. 160–162. And cf. Deuteronomy 1: 15, for military ranks in the Bible.

[25] For *isqum*, 'lot, share', here translated 'portion (assigned by casting lots)', see *CAD* I/J, p. 199b, s.v. *isqu* A 2. In *l.* 26, *isiqtum* is either the feminine form or is derived from the verb *esēk/qum—esēḫum*, of a similar meaning; for the latter alternative, see *CAD* I/J, p. 191b, s.v. *isiḫtu*. Cf. the similar semantic development of Hebrew *gōrāl*, 'lot', also sometimes used for captives; cf. Joel 4: 3; Obadiah 1: 11; Nahum 3: 10.

[26] For the significance of the idiom *ana mīl qātišunu*, 'to fill their hands', as an expression taken over into the cultic terminology of the Bible, see Noth 1958, pp. 8 ff. and 28, n. 9. Following our conclusion (see below) that the booty in question was banned or consecrated, the Akkadian in this instance, too—and in contrast to the common use of *ana qāt X mullūm* (cf. *AHw*, p. 598)—possibly had a certain ritual nuance referring to the appropriation of such objects; cf., e.g., the expression *lemallē' 'et yādām* (Exodus 29: 33).

[27] See above, n. 24.

[28] See above, n. 25.

[29] For the designations GAL.MAR.TU (the Great-of-Amurru) and DUB.SAR.MAR.TU (the Scribe-of-Amurru)—the latter attested only at Mari—see Kupper 1957, pp. 190 ff. In the Mari period these are military titles of high rank, originally of commanders of troops mustered from amongst the Amurru (i.e. nomadic tribes). In the Bible, special functions of military scribes are evident in 2 Kings 25: 19 (=Jeremiah 52: 25) and 2 Chronicles 26: 22.

[30] I.e., I have committed myself and the 'major' through an oath by the king; cf. Thureau-Dangin 1941, p. 42, n. 9; al-Zeebari 1964, No. 8, *ll.* 43–44 and p. 28. For the expression *nīš šarrim* in the sense of an oath 'by the life of' the king, cf. *ARMT* III, p. 173; and *CAD* N/2, pp. 291–292, s.v. *nīšu* A.

that the booty of a soldier should not be taken.
After my ordinance the tenth day had not yet passed
(when) a letter from your father came (saying) as follows:
'Whoever of (my) servants who has seized the booty of a soldier
has eaten my *asakkum* (i.e. has committed a sacrilege against me).'
After this matter let my lord pursue.
Other (than of this) to my lord
I do not write.
All is well with my lord's army.

Thus the writer complains to his overlord of unjust distribution of spoils, in this case captives. He accuses the army officers of appropriating the shares of the booty rightly reserved for their soldiers—as well as those of the writer himself, in addition to their own shares. To prevent such wantonness, the writer invokes the taboo, the misdeed being in violation of the *asakkum* of the gods, the king and the viceroy.[31]

The document contains instructive details on the manner in which a taboo was imposed, through public proclamation—here called *šipṭum*, 'ordinance' or 'ruling' (*ll.* 24 and 33).[32] Of the two documents previously quoted, one employs this same term, referring to an order for mustering troops (*ARMT* I 6: 16–19), whereas the other uses the synonymous phrase *dannātim šakānum*, 'to issue a stern order' (*ARMT* V 72: 11; and cf. *ARMT* XIV 67: 3′). *Šipṭum* in this context is of particular interest, being derived from the West Semitic root *špṭ*, which also yields verbal *šapāṭum*, participial *šāpiṭum* (the counterpart of the *šōpeṭ* in the Book of Judges) and abstract *šāpiṭūtum*, all characteristic of the Mari idiom (see above, p. 34, n. 24).[33] The expression *šipṭam nadānum/šakānum* corresponds to the biblical *śīm mišpāṭ*, 'making an ordinance', 'making a ruling' by a duly authorized person —which is employed in connection with the authoritative acts of a Moses, a Joshua or a David (Exodus 15: 25; Joshua 24: 25; 1 Samuel 30: 25). The last instance is in a context similar to that of the Mari document: After the defeat of the Amalekites, David promulgated regulations for the just distribution of the booty among the combat troops and those of the reserve

[31] A division of war spoils in the Bible, among the king (both Saul and David) and his senior officers, is inferred from the reference to the consecration of spoils to 'the house of God' in 1 Chronicles 26: 26–28. See also Genesis 14: 24, where the 'boys' (*n*^{e}*ʿārīm*) and 'men' (*ʾ*^{a}*nāšīm*) who participated in Abraham's raid are to receive their share (*ḥelqām*) of the booty. The verb *ʾkl*, used in connection with the *n*^{e}*ʿārīm*, does not mean 'to eat' but 'to appropriate' what is due to them, like one Akkadian usage of *akālum*; cf. *CAD* A/1, col. 251b, s.v. *akālu* 2a. As for the setting aside of captives and cattle from the spoils, note the biblical institution of *meḵes*, 'excise' (occurring only in connection with the war against Midian; Numbers 31: 28 ff., discussed above, p. 2, n. 6; and cf. Haran 1962, cols. 964–965, s.v. *meḵes*.

[32] The term *šipṭum* was initially studied by Thureau-Dangin 1943, pp. 110–112. Yet his translation (and others following him), 'reprimand, rebuke', does not adequately convey its basic meaning, which rather connotes the making of a definite command or decree, a ruling by a high authority. See Malamat 1970, p. 19; and cf. Marzal 1971.

[33] For a reappraisal of the biblical concepts contained in the root *špṭ*, in the light of Mari (and other external) evidence, see above, p. 34 and n. 24.

guard (cf. similarly, Numbers 31: 27). On this ruling, the text comments: 'He made it a statute and an ordinance (*ḥōq u-mišpāṭ*; 1 Samuel 30: 25).

From our document it may further be inferred that at Mari the invocation of a taboo was not the sole prerogative of the king, though its imposition apparently did require royal assent. It is in this sense that we may understand the letter of Šamši-Adad (of which *ll.* 34–36 represent a quotation). In Israel as at Mari, the ban did not become operative in battle automatically, nor was it an established element even of the 'holy war' (as maintained by von Rad).[34] Here, too, it was imposed by special decision taken for the particular occasion, *ad hoc*, as is evident from the traditions on the enforcement of the *ḥērem* preserved in the Bible. Prior to the fall of Jericho, Joshua proclaimed the city an anathema before the entire people and he reinforced this decree with a stern warning against touching anything included under the ban (Joshua 6: 16–19). Similarly, the banning of Amalek was decreed by Samuel, at God's command (1 Samuel 15: 3), while that of the Canaanites in the vicinity of Hormah (Numbers 21: 1–3) was by means of a special vow made to the Lord.[35]

Thus we see that in the military sphere, too, the institution of the *ḥērem* was essentially the same in both Mari and Israel, though in Israel it had a purely religious function. This is stressed explicitly in various passages, such as Joshua 6: 17: 'And the city (Jericho) and all that is within it shall be devoted to the Lord for destruction' (and cf. Deuteronomy 13: 16–17).

Under the Hebrew Monarchy, when the institution of the *ḥērem* fell into neglect, it was the prophets, the instruments of God, who tended its preservation.[36] Cf., e.g., Micah 4: 13: 'You shall beat in pieces many peoples, and shall devote (LXX; MT: I shall devote) their gain to the Lord.' It is in such terms as these that we can comprehend the clash between Saul and Samuel over the banning of Amalek (1 Samuel 15), the king having 'spared Agag, and the best of the sheep . . . and would not utterly destroy them' (v. 9), whereas the prophet absolutely condemned such a violation of the *ḥērem*.[37] In essence, this is parallel to the clash between an anonymous prophet and king Ahab over the sparing of the vanquished Aramean king, Ben-Hadad, concluding: 'Thus says the Lord: "Because you have let go out of your hand the man whom I had devoted to destruction (*'īš ḥermī*), therefore your life shall go for his life, and your people for

[34] Von Rad 1951, p. 13.

[35] For these three instances as the only reliable historical traditions in the Bible to have been transmitted on the enforcement of the *ḥērem*, see Brekelmans 1959a, pp. 153 ff. However, the etiological motifs in these, such as the derivation of the placename Hormah from the root *ḥrm*, have also played an important role in the formation of these traditions. For the *ḥērem* in Saul's war against the Amalekites, see Yonick 1970, pp. 41 ff.

[36] Cf. Brekelmans 1959b; and von Rad 1951.

[37] Since the *ḥērem* is not to be regarded as a sacrifice or votive gift to the Lord, as some scholars have argued, but as a doomed thing and entirely taboo (cf. Eichrodt 1957, pp. 82 f.), the offering up of the 'best of the *ḥērem*' (1 Samuel 15: 21) from the spoils of Amalek to the Lord is expressly treated as a grave violation of the ban.

his people"' (1 Kings 20:42). Another illuminating instance the Mesha inscription, where the king of Moab boasts: 'An said to me, "Go take Nebo from Israel." So I ... slayed a had devoted them (*hḥrmth*) to (the deity) Ashtar-Chemosh' (Just as the Israelites here came under the ban of the Moabite Edomites are considered in Isaiah 34:5, as *'am ḥermī*, 'the people I have doomed', i.e. a ban of Yahwe. Significantly, Israel is denoted *'am qodeš*, 'the holy people', i.e. consecrated (Isaiah 62:12; 63:18), a sort of mirror image of *'am ḥērem*.

All the foregoing instances conform with the Akkadian concept of '*asakkum* (or *ikkibum*) of a particular god', though at Mari the taboo could also be imposed for the benefit of mortals—first and foremost the king, but even common soldiers, as seen above. Despite such a fundamental difference, the Mari documents facilitate a fuller historical and legal appreciation of those passages of the Bible dealing with *qodeš* and *ḥērem* and their implementation. This is particularly so of the story of Achan, whatever its true historical context. This peculiar episode can now be reconciled with the very old legal and ritual practices current among the West Semitic tribes hundreds of years prior to the Israelite conquest of Canaan.[39]

B. INTUITIVE PROPHECY

A phenomenon attested only at Mari and in the Bible is intuitive prophecy—that is, prophetic revelation without resort to mantic or oracular devices and techniques. This is not 'run-of-the-mill' haruspicy, or any similar variation of examining the entrails of sacrifices, which was in the province of the formal cult priests and sorcerers, and which generally served the royal courts throughout most of the ancient Near East. Indeed, one of the most remarkable disclosures at Mari is this informal type of divination, which existed alongside the more 'academic' mantic practices. These Mariote diviner–prophets were spontaneously imbued with a certain consciousness of mission, and of a divine initiative.

In the religion of Israel, of course, prophecy held—and holds—a far greater significance than the somewhat ephemeral role evident at Mari. The prophetic utterances at Mari have almost nothing comparable to the socio-ethical or religious ideology of biblical prophecy (but see below, p. 83). Generally the Mari oracles are limited to a very mundane plane, placing before the king or his delegates divine demands of a most material nature and reflecting a clear *Lokalpatriotismus*, concern solely for the king's personal well-being.

The corpus of known prophetic texts from Mari—that is, documents

[38] Donner & Röllig 1962, p. 31. For the passage in point, see also van Zyl 1960, pp. 201–202 and Greenberg 1971, col. 384.

[39] The ancient legal character of the Achan episode *per se* has been stressed by Kaufmann 1963, pp. 110–122.

conveying prophecies—presently numbers twenty-eight.[40] Several works have appeared which discuss this material (save one document, published in 1975; and see below),[41] and we can now summarise our understanding of this topic as follows.

Two types of diviners at Mari

A Mari letter not directly related to our subject can serve as a key for understanding the reality behind prophecy at Mari. Baḫdi-Lim, the palace prefect, advised Zimri-Lim: '[Verily] you are the king of the Ḫaneans, [but s]econdly you are the king of the Akkadians! [My lord] should not ride a horse. Let my [lord] ride in a chariot or on a mule and he will thereby honour his royal head!' (*ARMT* VI 76: 20–25). This is a clear reflection of the two strata comprising the population of Mari: West Semites (Ḫaneans, the dominant tribal federation of the kingdom), on the one hand; and a veteran Akkadian component, on the other hand.[42] As we have seen, the symbiosis between these two elements left a general imprint on every walk of life at Mari, including religion and cult.

It is in this context that we can understand at Mari (and for the present, with one late exception,[43] only at Mari) the coexistence of the two patterns noted above of predicting the future and revealing the divine word. As at every other Mesopotamian centre, we find here the typical Akkadian divination as practised by specially trained experts, above all the *bārûm* or haruspex. We are familiar with several such experts at Mari, the best known of whom was Asqudum, whose spacious mansion has recently been uncovered not far from Zimri-Lim's palace.[44] The activities of these 'professionals' was usually confined to such crucial matters as omens for the security of the city.[45] Alongside this academic, supposedly 'rational' system, we are confronted at Mari with an atypical phenomenon in Mesopota-

[40] See Malamat 1956, 1958, 1966a, 1980 and 1987 (the latter including all the material published to about 1986).

[41] We cite here only general works on the entire corpus of 'prophetic' materials and not studies of individual Mari documents: Ellermeier 1968; Moran 1969a; Moran, in *ANET*, pp. 623–625, 629–632; Huffmon 1970; Craghan 1974; Noort 1977; Wilson 1980; Schmitt 1982; Nakata 1982a; Dietrich 1986; and van der Toorn 1987.

[42] Charpin & Durand 1986 now suggest that the duality in the above text refers to two geographical components of Zimri-Lim's kingdom: Terqa and the Land of the Ḫaneans, and the land of Akkad.

[43] I.e. neo-Assyrian prophecy; see Weippert 1981, 1985; Hecker 1986; and see below, nn. 47, 64.

[44] See Margueron 1982b, 1983, 1984a (and above, p. 8). On the archive of Asqudum discovered on the site, see Charpin 1985. Asqudum's wife, Yamama, was either the daughter or the sister of Yaḫdun-Lim.

[45] The texts have recently been collected in Parpola 1983. For extispicy in Mesopotamia in general, and at Mari in particular, see Starr 1983, pp. 107 f. and Index, s.v. *Mari* (p. 141); and cf. the comprehensive Bottéro 1974.

mia—intuitive divination or prophecy, the informal acquiring
of god. Indeed, this is the earliest such manifestation known to
in the ancient Near East. This type of prophecy should properly
as one of a chain of social and religious practices exclusive to
in part, similar to those found in the Bible.

This informal type of divination at Mari places biblical prophecy in a new perspective. Both phenomena bypass mantic or magic mechanisms, which require professional expertise; rather, they are the product of psychic, non-rational experience. The essential nature of prophecy of this type entails certain dominant characteristics, the three most significant of which, in my opinion, are delineated as follows:[46]

(a) Spontaneous prophetic manifestations resulting from inspiration or divine initiative (in contrast to mechanical, inductive divination, which was usually initiated by the king's request for signs from the deity). In this connection we may compare the utterance of Isaiah, communicating the word of God: 'I was ready to be sought by those who didn't ask for me; I was ready to be found by those who didn't seek me. I said, "Here am I, here am I . . ."' (Isaiah 65: 1).

(b) A consciousness of mission, the prophets taking a stand before the authorities to present divinely inspired messages.

(c) An ecstatic component in prophecy, a somewhat problematic and complex characteristic. This concept should be allowed a broad, liberal definition, enabling it to apply to a wide range of phenomena from autosuggestion to the divinely infused dream. Only in rare instances did this quality appear as extreme frenzy, and even then it is not clear whether it was accompanied by loss of senses—for the prophets always appear sober and purposeful in thought, and far from spouting mere gibberish.

These particular characteristics—not necessarily found in conjunction—link the diviner–prophet at Mari with the Israelite prophet more than with any other divinatory type known in the ancient Near East.[47] Nevertheless, comparing Mari and the Bible, one cannot ignore the great differences between the two types of source-material: respectively first-hand documents, as against compositions which had undergone lengthy, complex literary processes. Furthermore, the documentation concerning prophecy at Mari is mostly restricted to a very short span of time, perhaps only to the final decade (or less) of Zimri-Lim's reign. In comparison, the activity

[46] Noort 1977, pp. 24 ff., rejects the characteristics mentioned below as typical of prophesying at Mari and accordingly denies any relationship to biblical prophecy. But his approach is too extreme in requiring every single characteristic to appear in each and every 'prophetic' text. He has justifiably been criticized, for example, by Nakata 1982b, pp. 166–168.

[47] Except for the *rāgimu* (fem. *rāgintu*), 'the pronouncer', 'speaker' of the neo-Assyrian period, addressing Esarhaddon and Ashurbanipal. See Weippert 1981. And see below, n. 64.

of the Israelite prophets extended over a period of centuries.[48] In other words, here too, Mari represents a synchronous picture, a cross-section at one particular point in time, while the Bible gives a diachronous view, tracing the development of the prophetic phenomenon over a period of time (and see lecture II, p. 35).

Prophecy at Mari and in the Bible—similarities and differences

Despite the external, formal similarity between the diviner–prophets at Mari and the Israelite prophets, there is an obvious discrepancy in content between the divine messages and in the function they assumed, as well as, apparently, in the status of the prophets within the respective societies and kingdoms. In Israelite society, the prophet seems usually to have enjoyed a more or less central position, though certain types of prophet were peripheral. At Mari, however, the prophets apparently played only a marginal role.[49] Admittedly, this distinction might merely be illusory, deriving from the nature of the respective source materials. In both societies many of the prophets, basing on their place of origin and locale of activity, came from rural communities: in Mari, from such towns as Terqa and Tuttul, and in Judah, from Tekoa (Amos), Moreshet (Micah), Anathot (Jeremiah) and Gibeon (Hananiah); but others resided in the respective capitals.

As for contents, the prophecies at Mari are limited to material demands on the king, such as the construction of a building or a city gate in some provincial town (*ARMT* III 78; XIII 112), the offering of funerary sacrifices (*ARMT* II 90; III 40; and see below, p. 96), the despatch of valuable objects to various temples (A 4260), or the request of property (*niḫlatum*) for a god (A 1121; the reference is surely to a landed estate sought by a sanctuary and its priestly staff).[50] Many of the more recently published Mari prophecies refer to military and political affairs, above all the welfare of the king

[48] The lengthy span of prophecy in Israel is especially evident if we include, for our present purposes, both the early, 'primitive' prophets as well as the late, 'classical' ones, who were not so decidedly distinct from one another. This distinction has gained currency ever since the over-emphasis of the Canaanite origin of the early Israelite prophecy; cf. Hölscher 1914, and Lindblom 1962, pp. 47 and 105 ff. In contrast, subsequent scholars occasionally pointed out the continuity of certain early elements through the period of classical prophecy; see e.g. Haran 1977 (with earlier literature).

[49] The question of centre and periphery in the status of the prophets has been raised only in recent years, under the influence of sociology. See Wilson 1980, where the peripheral role of all Mari prophets is emphasised, when compared with the central role of the *bārûm*; and see most recently Petersen 1981. The author considers the *nāḇī'* and the *ḥōzeh* to be 'central' in both Israel and Judah, while the *rō'eh* and the *'îš hā'ᵉlōhîm*, as well as the *bᵉnē nᵉḇî'îm* ('sons' of the prophets) are regarded as peripheral. For the latter see also Porter 1981.

[50] Interestingly, the divine threat of Adad hanging over Zimri-Lim should he refuse to donate the estate—'What I have given, I shall take away . . .' (A 1121, *l.* 18)—closely mirrors Job's words: 'The lord gave and the Lord has taken away . . .' (Job 1: 27).

and his personal safety. He is warned against conspirators at home and enemies abroad (*ARMT* X 7, 8, 50, 80), especially Ḫammurabi, king of Babylon (see below), who was soon to conquer Mari. This sort of message is very distinct from biblical prophecy, expressing a full-fledged religious ideology, a socio-ethical manifesto and a national purpose. But this glaring contrast might actually be something of a distortion. At Mari nearly all the 'prophetic' texts were discovered in the royal-diplomatic archives of the palace (Room 115), which would serve to explain their tendency to concentrate on the king. Prophecies directed at other persons presumably did exist but, on account of their nature, have not been preserved. In comparison, had the historiographic books of the Bible (Samuel, Kings and Chronicles) alone survived, we would be faced with a picture closely resembling that at Mari, in which Israelite prophecy, too, was oriented primarily toward the king and his politico-military enterprises.

A glimmer of social-moral concern can, however, be seen at Mari, in a prophetic message which is contained in two recently joined fragments (A 1121 + A 2731):[51] A diviner–prophet urges Zimri-Lim, in the name of the god Adad of Aleppo: 'When a wronged man or woman cries out to you, stand and let his/her case be judged.' This command has an exact parallel in Jeremiah's sermon to kings: 'Execute justice in the morning, and deliver from the hand of the oppressor him who has been robbed' (Jeremiah 21: 12; and cf. 22: 3).

A tangible example of the imposition of obligations on the king at Mari is found in one letter (*ARMT* X 100), in which a divinely imbued woman writes to the king directly, with no intervention of a third party (although a scribe may have been employed). The woman (whose name is apparently to be read Yanana) addressed Zimri-Lim in the name of Dagan concerning a young lady (her own daughter, or perhaps a companion) who had been abducted when the two of them were on a journey. Dagan appeared to the woman in a dream and decreed that only Zimri-Lim could save and return the girl. Thus, a woman who was wronged turned to the king in seeking redress, in the spirit of the prophetic commands adduced above.

All told, the analogy between prophecy at Mari and that in Israel is presently still vague, the two being set apart by a gap of more than six centuries. Furthermore, all the intervening links are 'missing'. It would thus be premature to regard Mari as the prototype of prophecy in Israel.[52] But the earliest manifestation of intuitive prophecy among West Semitic tribes at Mari should not be belittled, notwithstanding its still enigmatic aspects. In this regard we can put forward two assumptions (which are not mutually exclusive):

[51] For the join (initially proposed by J.-M. Durand) of A 1121, published long ago, and a fragment previously published only in translation, see Lafont 1984. For earlier treatments of the following passage, see, inter alia, Anbar 1975, and Malamat 1980, p. 73 and n. 6.

[52] Here I fully agree with Noort 1977; see his summary on p. 109; I do reject, however, the remarks such as those of Schmitt 1982, p. 13.

…itive prophecy was basically the outcome of a specific social situa- … erstwhile non-urban, semi-nomadic, tribal society. Urban sophisti- … matter how primitive, naturally engenders institutionalized cult … s, such as the *bārû* (haruspex), the foremost of the diviner types in Mesopotamia and part and parcel of the cult personnel of any self-respecting town or ruler.

(b) The phenomenon of intuitive prophecy was a characteristic of a particular *Kulturkreis* which extended across the West, from Palestine and Syria to Anatolia, and as far as Mari in the east. This assumption is based mainly on the ecstatic element in prophecy, attested throughout this region (albeit rather sporadically). It is found outside the Bible in such cases as the prophets of the Hittite sources, at Byblos (as mentioned in the Egyptian Tale of Wen-Amon), in Syria (in the Aramaic inscription of Zakkur, king of Hamath), and in notations in classical literature.[53]

Let us now delve deeper into the data at hand concerning prophecy at Mari. Since 1948, twenty-eight letters addressed to the king and containing reports on prophecies and divine revelations have been published. The senders were high ranking officials and bureaucrats from all over the kingdom. About half were women, mostly ladies of the palace, headed by Šibtu, Zimri-Lim's principal queen. Several of the letters contain two individual visions and thus the total number of prophecies is some thirty-five. In several cases the correspondent was the prophet himself (though the letters *per se* may well have been written by scribes; one is reminded of Baruch son of Neriah, Jeremiah's anamuensis). Thus, a prophet acting in the name of Šamaš of Sippar (A 4260); the court lady Addu-Duri (*ARMT* X 50); and a woman named Yanana (mentioned above; *ARMT* X 100). As already noted, the words of the diviner–prophets, whether transmitted through intermediaries or dispatched directly to the king, were generally formulated with utmost lucidity. This was perhaps due to the slight interval between the actual prophetic experience and the committing of the vision to writing. How much more is this so in connection with biblical prophecy, which generally has undergone repeated editing (though certain prophecies may well have been preserved in their pristine form).

This raises the possible conclusion (not usually considered),[54] that the messages of the diviner–prophets at Mari may originally have been pronounced in the West Semitic dialect conventionally designated 'Amorite'. Should this be the case in the documents before us, the original words

[53] The West as a separate *Kulturkreis* from the East (Southern Mesopotamia) with regard to certain basic religious elements has been appreciated by Oppenheim 1964, pp. 221 ff. Several scholars assume that prophecy in both Mari and Israel originated in the Arabian-Syrian desert; see, e.g., Rendtorff 1962, p. 146. For the ecstatic prophet in Hittite sources, see *ANET*, p. 395a; for the prophet from Byblos, see Cody 1979, pp. 99–106. The author derives the Egyptian word *'ḏd* from the West Semitic *'dd*, which in the Aramaic inscription of Zakkur (see below) designates a type of diviner–prophet; and see Malamat 1966a, p. 209 and n. 2.

[54] An exception in Sasson 1980.

of the prophecies (or at least some of them) would have already been rendered into the language of the chancery, Akkadian—either by the officials writing or by their scribes. Such an assumption could also serve to explain why the 'prophetic' texts at Mari display a relatively greater number of West Semitic idioms and linguistic forms than do the other Mari documents. If these assumptions are correct, the transmission of the prophetic word, *ipsissima verba*, to the king's ear, was considerably more complex than outwardly appears.

The diviner–prophets at Mari were of two types: professional or 'accredited'—recognisable by distinctive titles (as were the biblical *rō'eh*, *ḥōzeh*, *nāḇī'* and *'īš 'ᵉlōhīm*); and casual—lay persons who held no formal title (see below). Thus far, five different titles are known at Mari designating 'cult' prophets (if we may use a term current in Bible studies):

(1) A priest (*šangûm*) is mentioned once as a prophet (*ARMT* X 51), imbued with a prophetic dream containing a warning; in the Bible, too, Ezekiel was originally a priest, and so was Pashhur, son of Immer (Jeremiah 20: 1, 6).

(2) There are three references to the prophetic *assinnum* (*ARMT* X 6, 7, 80),[55] though this term is not entirely clear in meaning. Basing on later sources, it might refer to a eunuch, a male prostitute or a cult musician. One such functionary served in a temple at Mari and prophesied in the name of Annunītum (a goddess normally associated with women), apparently while disguised as a woman (perhaps in the manner of present-day transvestites).

(3) In one solitary instance (*ARMT* X 8), a prophetess bears the title *qabbātum* (or possibly *qamatum*),[56] a term undoubtedly derived from the Akkadian verb *qabûm*, 'to speak, proclaim'.[57]

(4) One of the best known of the 'accredited' prophets at Mari is the *muḫḫûm* (fem. *muḫḫūtum*) who, as etymology would indicate, was some sort of ecstatic or frenetic.[58] The peculiar behaviour of this type of prophet led him to be perceived as a madman, similar to the biblical *mᵉšugga'*, a term occasionally used as a synonym for *nāḇī'* (2 Kings 9: 11; Jeremiah 29: 26; Hosea 9: 7).[59] We may also mention instances of the Akkadian verb *immaḫu* (3rd person preterite), derived from the same root as *muḫ-*

[55] For this prophet, see Wilson 1980, pp. 106–107, with bibliography.

[56] For this term, and additional bibliographical references, see *CAD* Q, p. 2b. It is tempting to link this term with the Hebrew root *qbb*, 'to curse', frequently applied in connection with the prophecy of Balaam, who announced: *mah eqqoḇ lō' qabboh 'ēl* . . . (the form *qabboh* is irregular and resembles a possible root **qbh*), Numbers 23: 8: 'How can I curse whom God has not cursed?'

[57] Cf. Renger 1969, pp. 219 ff.; and *CAD* M/1, p. 90a, which includes Old Babylonian references outside Mari.

[58] The *purrusum* form of the noun is peculiar to Mari (in other Akkadian sources we find the form *maḫḫûm*). This nominal form designates bodily defects and functionally resembles the Hebrew *qittēl* form used in such words as *'iwwēr*, 'blind', *pissēᵃḥ*, 'lame', and *gibbēn*, 'hunchback'. See Holma 1914 and Landsberger 1915, pp. 363–366.

[59] Malamat 1966a, pp. 210–211 and n. 4, for additional references and earlier bibliography on *muḫḫûm*.

ḫ̮ûm, and used in the N-stem, resembling Biblical Hebrew *nibbā'* (cf. also *hitnabbē'*). This word, *immaḫ̮u*, means 'became insane', 'went into a trance' (*ARMT* X 7: 5–7; 8: 5–8). Besides the five unnamed *muḫ̮ḫ̮ûms* mentioned in the 'prophetic' documents, the recently published volumes of Mari documents[60] include new administrative material naming five *muḫ̮ḫ̮ûms*, along with the deities they served. These documents are lists of personnel receiving clothes from the palace. In a previously published list, there is a reference to an *āpilum* (*ARMT* IX 22: 14; and see below). This would imply that the *muḫ̮ḫ̮ûm* (as well as the *āpilum*) received material support from the royal court. A surprising feature here is that four of the named *muḫ̮ḫ̮ûms* have strictly Akkadian (rather than West Semitic) names: Irra-gamil, *muḫ̮ḫ̮ûm* of Nergal; Ea-maṣi, *muḫ̮ḫ̮ûm* of Itur-Mer (*ARMT* XXI 333: 33′/34′; XXIII 446: 9′, 19′); Ea-mudammiq, *muḫ̮ḫ̮ûm* of Ninhursag; and Anu-tabni, *muḫ̮ḫ̮ūtum* of the goddess Annunītum (*ARMT* XXII 167: 8′ and 326: 8–10); 326: 8–10); the fifth was a *muḫ̮ḫ̮ûm* of Adad, mentioned with the intriguing notation that he received a silver ring 'when (he) delivered an oracle for the king' (*ARMT* XXV 142: 3′). Another *muḫ̮ḫ̮ūtum* with court connections was named Ribatum; she sent an oracle to Zimri-Lim concerning the two tribal groups, the Simalites and the Yaminites.[61]

It is possible that on the whole these prophets, who were dependent on the royal court of Mari, had already been assimilated into Akkadian culture to a great extent, hence their Akkadian names. In any case, the direct contact with the royal court calls to mind the court prophets in Israel, such as Nathan the *nāḇī'* and Gad the *ḥōzeh*, who served David and Solomon, or the Baal and Ashera prophets functioning at the court of Ahab and Jezebel.

(5) Finally, there was the *āpilum* (fem. *āpiltum*), a prophetic title exclusive to Mari and meaning 'answerer, respondent' (derived from the verb *apālum*, 'to answer').[62] Unlike the other types of prophets, *āpilums* on occasion acted in consort, in groups similar to the bands of prophets in the Bible (*ḥēḇel* or *lahᵃqat nᵉḇī'īm*). The *āpilum* is attested in documents covering a broad geographical expanse, with a wider distribution than any other type of prophet—from Aleppo in northern Syria to Sippar near Babylon. Thus, an *āpilum* of Šamaš of Sippar, addressing the king of Mari directly, demanded a throne for Šamaš, as well as one of the king's daughters (?) for service in his temple.[63] He also demanded objects for other deities (including an *asakku* or consecrated object; see above, p. 72): Adad of

[60] *ARMT* XXI; *ARMT* XXII; *ARMT* XXIII; *ARMT* XXV (1986).

[61] Charpin & Durand 1986, p. 151 and n. 7.

[62] Malamat 1966a, pp. 212–213 and n. 2, for the various spellings *apillû*, *aplûm*, *āpilum*; and see *CAD* A/2, p. 170a; Malamat 1980, pp. 68 ff.; Anbar 1981, p. 91.

[63] Interestingly, compliance with this prophetic demand seems to be alluded to in the female correspondence. Further on in our document the name of Zimri-Lim's daughter is given as Erišti-Aya. Indeed, a woman by this name sent several doleful letters to her royal parents from the temple at Sippar; see *ARMT* X 37: 15; 43: 16, etc. Cf. Kraus 1984, p. 98 and n. 224; and Charpin & Durand 1985, pp. 332, 340.

Aleppo, Dagan of Terqa and Nergal of Ḫubšalum (A 4260). Another *āpilum* was in the Dagan temple at Tuttul (near the confluence of the Baliḫ and the Euphrates rivers) and there was an *āpiltum* in the Annunitum temple in the city of Mari itself. And an *āpilum* of Dagan, bearing the strictly Akkadian name Qišatum, received bronze objects from the palace, like the 'gifts' from the king noted above (*ARMT* XX 5: 2′–3′).[64] It is noteworthy that the *muḫḫûm* and the *muḫḫūtum* functioned in these very same sanctuaries as well, indicating that two different types of diviner–prophets could be found side by side. Indeed, in the Dagan temple at Terqa, three types of prophet were at work simultaneously: a *muḫḫûm*, a *qabbātum* and a dreamer of dreams.

Affinities in terminology and contents—Mari and Israel

The terms *āpilum* and *muḫḫûm* would appear to have counterparts in Biblical Hebrew. The terms *'ānāh* and *'ōneh*, 'answer' and 'answerer', respectively, can refer to divine revelation.[65] Most significantly, the very verb *'ānāh* is used at times to describe the prophet's function as God's mouthpiece, whether actually responding to a query put to the deity or not. This is clearly seen, for instance, in 1 Samuel 9: 17: 'When Samuel saw Saul, the Lord answered him; "Here is the man of whom I spoke to you! He is it who shall rule over my people."' This is also indicated by Jeremiah's condemnation (23: 33 ff.) of one Hebrew term for prophetic utterance, *maśśā'* (cf., e.g., Lamentations 2: 14 and 2 Kings 9: 25), and his commendation of the more 'legitimate' *'ānāh* in its stead: 'What has the Lord answered and what has the Lord said?' (Jeremiah 23: 37). The term *ma'ᵃnēh 'ᵉlōhīm* (lit. 'God's answer'), meaning the word of the Lord, occurs once in the Bible, in Micah 3: 7, which also elucidates the use of *'nh* in connection with the oracles of Balaam: 'Remember now, O my people, remember what Balak king of Moab devised and what Balaam the son of Beor *answered* him' (Micah 6: 5). The verb *'ānāh* here does not indicate response to a specific question put forth to Balaam but, rather, the prophetic oracle which Balaam was compelled to deliver in Israel's favour. It is possible that this non-Israelite diviner, who is never designated *nāḇī'*, was a prophet of the *āpilum* ('answerer') type. The analogy might be strengthened by the cultic acts performed by Balaam, on the one hand (Numbers 23: 3,

[64] Another *āpilum*, of Marduk (!), is mentioned in an unpublished Mari letter addressed to Išme-Dagan, king of Assyria, urging him to deliver a handsome ransom to the king of Elam (A 428: 21–28); see Charpin 1987b, p. 133. 'Prophetic' documents of this same period have been discovered also at Ishchali, on the Lower Diyala river, seat of the goddess Kititum; her oracles, addressed to Ibal-pi-El, king of Ešnunna, a contemporary of the Mari kings, are similar in tone and message to those from Mari, but they are quite different in their mode of transmission, for they appear in the form of letters from the deity herself, with no prophetic intermediary involved. See Ellis 1987, pp. 251–257.

[65] Malamat 1958, pp. 72–73.

14–15, 29), and by the band of *āpilums*, on the other hand (A 1121, esp. *ll.* 24–25)—both soliciting the divine word.[66]

It is of interest that the recently discovered 'Balaam Inscription' from Tell Deir 'Alla in Transjordan, from the late 8th or early 7th century BC and written in either an Ammonite or 'Israelite–Gileadite' dialect, enumerates various types of sorcerers, including a woman designated *'nyh*. The latter term most likely means '(female) respondent', that is, a semantic equivalent of the Mari term *āpiltum*.[67] This interpretation gains cogency through the phrase following the reference to the woman: *rqḥt mr wkhnh*, 'a perfumer of myrrh and priestess'. Even more significant is the Aramaic inscription of Zakkur, king of Hamath, from about 800 BC. In his hour of peril, Zakkur turned to his gods, 'and Baalšamayn responded to me (*wy'nny*) and Baalšamayn [spoke to me] through seers and diviners' (*'ddn*; *ll.* 11–12).[68]

A probable overlap of the prophetic activity of the *āpilum* and that of the *muḫḫûm* is indicated in a letter containing the message of a *muḫḫūtum*, imploring the king of Mari not to leave the capital to wage war at that time; it declares: 'I will *answer* you constantly' (*attanapal*; *ARMT* X: 22–26). In other words, there are cases where a *muḫḫûm* would be involved in the act of 'answering' (*apālum*).

Before turning to the matter of lay prophets at Mari, let us examine two prophecies of similar content, reminiscent of the biblical oracles 'against the nations': one of an *āpilum* (curiously spelled here *aplûm*); and the other of 'the wife of a man', that is, a lay woman. Both reports were transmitted through Kibri-Dagan, Zimri-Lim's governor at Terqa. The *āpilum*/*aplûm* 'arose' in the name of Dagan of Tuttul, 'and so he said as follows: "O Babylon! Why doest thou ever (evil)? I will gather thee into

[66] Balaam was certainly not a prophet of the *bārûm* type, as was long ago suggested in Daiches 1909, pp. 60–70. This claim has often been refuted, correctly; see Rofé 1979, p. 32, n. 53. Offering sacrifices in preparation for deriving the word of the deity as is found in the Balaam pericope is similarly alluded to at the beginning of Mari texts *ARMT* XIII 23 and A 1221; it is explicitly mentioned in a 'prophetic' document which has so far been published only in French translation—A 455: '. . . One head of cattle and six sheep I will sacrifice . . .', that is, seven sacrificial animals. In what follows, a *muḫḫûm* 'arises' and prophesies in the name of Dagan. Compare the seven altars, seven bulls and seven rams which Balaam had Balak prepare before delivering his oracle (Numbers 23: 29–30).

[67] See the Deir 'Alla inscription, first combination, *l.* 11; Hoftijzer & van der Kooij 1976, pp. 180, 212. The editors interpreted *'nyh* as a female answerer, indicating a prophetess, following our conclusion concerning the title *āpilum* at Mari and its relationship to biblical terminology. This opinion has been accepted by Rofé 1979, p. 67 and n. 33, among others. Indeed, in the dialect of this inscription verbs with a third weak radical are spelled preserving the *yod* before the final *he*, like Hebrew *bōḵiyāh* (I must thank B. Levine for this information; and see his forthcoming study on this text). This term has nothing to do with 'poor woman', despite the Hebrew homograph *'nyh*, as various scholars contend; see, e.g., Caquot & Lemaire 1977, p. 200; McCarter 1980b, p. 58; Weippert 1982, p. 98; and Hackett 1984, p. 133, s.v. *'nyh*.

[68] See Gibson 1975, pp. 8 ff. The author there translates the word *'ddn* as '(prophetic?) messengers' on the basis of *'dd* in Ugaritic (p. 15), and cf. above, n. 53. For a possible connection between prophecy at Mari and that at Hamath, see Ross 1970.

a net! . . . The houses of the seven confederates and all their possessions I shall deliver into Zimri-Lim's hand!"' (*ARMT* XIII 23: 6–15). This prophecy, which contains several motifs well known in the biblical prophecies of doom,[69] reflects the deteriorating relations between Mari and Babylon, brought about by Ḫammurabi's expansionist aspirations. The other prophecy explicitly mentions Ḫammurabi as an enemy of Mari (*ARMT* XIII 114). A divinely inspired woman approached Kibri-Dagan late one afternoon with the following words of consolation: 'The god Dagan sent me. Send your lord; he shall not worry [. . .], he shall not worry. Ḫammurabi [king] of Babylon . . . [continuation broken].' The urgency of the matter is indicated by the fact that the letter bearing this encouraging message was dispatched the very day it was uttered.

From these two prophecies—and possibly from most of the visions concerning the king's safety—it is apparent that they were recorded at a time of political and military distress at Mari. This, too, would be analogous to Israelite prophecy, which thrived particularly in times of national emergency—such as during the Philistine threat in the days of Samuel and Saul, during Sennacherib's campaign against Jerusalem, and especially at the time of Nebuchadnezzar's moves against Judah. The crisis factor was certainly one of the principal forces engendering prophetic manifestations in both Mari and Israel.[70] However, in contrast to the Bible with its prophecies of doom and words of admonition against king and people, the messages at Mari were usually optimistic and sought to placate the king rather than rebuke or alert him. Such prophecies of success and salvation (see *ARMT* X 4, 9, 10, 51, 80), coloured by a touch of nationalism, liken the Mari prophets to the 'false prophets' of the Bible. Surely, the corresponding prophecies are quite similar. Indeed, one of the prominent 'false prophets' in the Bible, Hananiah of Gibeon, Jeremiah's rival, rashly proclaimed in the name of the Lord (and not in the name of a foreign god) the impending return of the Judean exiles from Babylonia: 'for I will break the yoke of the king of Babylon' (Jeremiah 28: 4). How reminiscent is this of the *āpilum*'s prediction against Babylon (see above, *ARMT* XIII 23). In both instances the message is a whitewashing of the critical situation, for such prophets of peace served the 'establishment' and expressed its interests (compare the four hundred prophets at Ahab's court, who prophesy 'with one accord'; 1 Kings 22: 13).[71]

In contrast to Mari, the Bible is replete with prophecies unfavourable

[69] Especially the motifs of gathering into a net and delivering into the hand, which are found frequently in both ancient Near Eastern and biblical literature in connection with vanquishing an enemy; Malamat 1980, pp. 217 f. and cf. Heintz 1969, who relates these motifs to the 'Holy War' in the ancient Near East and the Bible.

[70] This has been indicated by, among others, Uffenheimer 1973, pp. 27, 37; Noort 1977, pp. 93, 109; and Blenkinsopp 1983, p. 45. Remarkably, just prior to Ḫammurabi's conquest of Mari there is a noticeable rise in future-telling activities of the *bārûm*; see Starr 1983, p. 107.

[71] For the 'false' prophets and their dependence on the Israelite establishment, see, among others, Buber 1950, pp. 253 ff.; Hossfeld & Meyer 1973; de Vries 1978.

to king and country; their heralds, the so-called prophets of doom (or 'true' prophets), were constantly harrassed by the authorities. One well-known case is that of Amos who, at the royal sanctuary at Bethel, foretold of King Jeroboam's death and the exile of the people (Amos 7: 10–13). In reaction, the priest Amaziah, by order of the king, expelled the prophet to Judah in disgrace. Jeremiah provoked an even more violent response, in the days of both Jehoiakim and Zedekiah. Pashhur (the priest in charge of the temple in Jerusalem), when confronted by the prophet's words of wrath, 'beat Jeremiah the prophet, and put him in the stocks that were in the house of the Lord' (Jeremiah 20: 2).

At certain times, however, we do find close cooperation between king, priest and prophet. A priest occasionally officiated as an intermediary between the king and the prophet, as when Hezekiah sent emissaries to Isaiah (2 Kings 19: 20 ff. = Isaiah 37: 2 ff.) and Zekediah to Jeremiah (Jeremiah 21: 1 ff.; 37: 3 ff.). Similarly, Hilkiahu, the high-priest, headed the royal delegation which Josiah sent to Huldah the prophetess (2 Kings 22: 12ff.). The roles are inverted at Mari, where a prophet's report could be conveyed to the king via a priest. According to two documents (*ARMT* VI 45 and X 8), prophetesses appeared before Aḫum the priest, who served in the temple of Annunītum in Mari proper. Once Aḫum reported the message to Baḫdi-Lim, palace prefect, who passed it on to the king; at another time he transmitted the prophetic words to the queen, Šibtu.[72] In the latter case, a new element appears, to which we have alluded only briefly above—the frenetic here was a mere maidservant named Aḫatum and had no prophetic title—that is, she was a simple lay-person.

Lay prophets and message dreams

More than half the 'prophetic' documents from Mari deal with lay-persons, 'prophets' not 'accredited' to any sanctuary. Among these we find such designations as 'a man', 'a woman', 'a man's wife', 'a youth' and 'a young woman (or 'maidservant')', as well as several instances of persons who are merely mentioned by name. In one case a prophetic message was elicited from 'a man and a woman' (lit. 'male and female'), who prophesied jointly (*ARMT* X 4). Because this manner of prophecy was uncommon and surprising at Mari, it should be examined briefly.

Queen Šibtu wrote to her husband that she had asked a man and a woman to foretell the fortunes of Zimri-Lim's forthcoming military venture against Išme-Dagan, king of Ashur. As noted, the mode of divination here

[72] Moran 1969, p. 20, holds that *ARMT* VI 45 deals with the same event as *ARMT* X 50, while Sasson 1980, p. 131b, associates it with *ARMT* X 8. Neither suggestion is compelling. *ARMT* X 50 does not mention a priest by the name of Aḫum, but someone else, while *ARMT* X 8 mentions a prophetess by name but without title, and *ARMT* VI 45 speaks of an anonymous *muḫḫūtum*. It may be assumed, therefore, that both professional and lay prophets would occasionally appear before Aḫum, a priest in Mari.

is exceptional, and has led to various scholarly interpretations.[73] The key sentence at the opening of Šibtu's letter reads (according to a recent collation): 'Concerning the report on the military campaign which my lord undertakes, I have asked a man and a woman about the signs (*ittātim*) when I plied (them with drink) and the oracle (*egerrûm*) for my lord is very favourable' (*ARMT* X 4: 3–37). Šibtu immediately inquired of the fate of Išme-Dagan, and the oracle 'was unfavourable'. This query concerning the fate of the enemy recalls how king Ahab consulted the four-hundred prophets, prior to his battle against the Arameans (1 Kings 22: 6 ff.). Further on, Šibtu cited the full prophecy proclaimed by the two persons, which contains several motifs found in biblical prophecies.[74] How are we to perceive this kind of divination? It has been suggested that the man and woman themselves served as a sign and portent, partly on the basis of the words of Isaiah (8: 18): 'Behold, I and the children the Lord has given me are signs and portents in Israel'—but such an interpretation seems forced. Rather, the queen seems to have selected a couple at random, offering them drink (perhaps wine) to loosen their tongues and thus obtained an *egerrûm*-oracle, based on 'chance utterances'. This type of divining, known as cledomancy, has been likened to the divinatory method known in Hebrew as *bat qōl* (literally 'a trace of a voice', usually translated 'echo'). The same Hebrew term is found in Talmudic sources, where it serves as an ersatz for prophecy *per se*.[75]

Among lay prophets as well as transmitters of prophetic reports, there was an unusually large proportion of women, mostly from Zimri-Lim's court. Indeed, one of the king's daughters explicitly stated to her father: 'Now, though I am a (mere) woman, may my father the lord harken unto my words. I will constantly send the word of the gods to my father' (*ARMT* X 31: 7′–10′). Some prophetesses and female dreamers of dreams sent their prophecies directly to the king, without a mediator (*ARMT* X 50, 100). Šibtu, more than anyone else, served as an intermediary for conveying prophetic messages to her husband. This would call to mind rather bizarre episodes throughout history, where a 'prophet' or mystic used or exploited a queen so as to bring his visions and message to the attention of her husband, the king. Among the 'accredited' prophets, too—as as we have

[73] On *ARMT* X 4, and the mode of prophesying, see the recent studies: Finet 1982, Durand 1982; Durand 1984a, pp. 150 ff.; and Wilcke 1983b, p. 93.

[74] Note, above all, the motif of the gods marching alongside the king in time of war and saving him from his enemies, a motif resembling the intervention of the Lord in the wars of Israel. This involves also driving the enemy into flight; cf.: 'Arise, O Lord, and let they enemies be scattered...' (Numbers 10: 35; and see also Psalms 68: 2) [in relation to the above-mentioned biblical parallel, note the utterance of the prophet Micaiah the son of Imlah concerning the dispersion of the Israelite army (1 Kings 22: 17)], and eventually decapitating the foe who would be trampled under the foot of the king of Mari (see, e.g., Joshua 24: 25). And see Weinfeld 1977.

[75] For this type of oracle, see *CAD* E, s.v. *egirrû*, p. 45: '... oracular utterances ... which are either accidental in origin (comp. with Greek *kledon*) or hallucinatory in nature....' For the parallel with Hebrew *bat qōl*, see Sperling 1972.

seen—there were many women, as there were in the Bible. The outstanding of these were Deborah, wife of Lapidoth (Judges 4: 4) and Huldah, wife of Shallum (2 Kings 22: 14). In both instances the Bible specifically notes that they were married women, probably to stress their stability and reliability—as in the case of the 'wife of a man', one of the Mari prophetesses (*ARMT* XIII 114: 8).

Are there any characteristics which distinguish the 'accredited' prophets from the lay ones? Two prominent features have been noticed by scholars: (a) Only in the case of the 'accredited' are the actual messages preceded by the verb *tebû*, 'to arise' (e.g. 'he/she arose and . . .'), somehow alluding to prophetic stimulation in the temple.[76] Synonymous expressions are used in connection with the biblical prophets, as well (Deuteronomy 13: 2; 18: 15, 18; 34: 10; Jeremiah 1: 17; etc.); note in particular Ezekiel: 'And set me upon my feet' (Ezekiel 2: 2; and cf. Ezekiel 3: 22–24; Daniel 8: 17–18; 10: 10–11; 2 Chronicles 24: 2). (b) Among the lay prophets, dreaming is prevalent as the prophetic means, while this medium is totally absent among the 'accredited' prophets.

Almost half the published prophecies from Mari were revealed in dreams. Phenomenologically, we thus find two distinct categories of acquiring the divine word. 'Accredited' prophets enjoyed direct revelation while fully conscious; whereas lay prophets often received revelations through dreams. The latter was a widespread phenomenon throughout the ancient Near East, including Israel.[77] At Mari, as in the Bible, we find a specific subcategory of 'message dream' alongside ordinary revelatory dreams—that is, dreams in which the message was not intended for the dreamer himself, but rather for a third party (in the Bible, see Numbers 12: 6; Jeremiah 23: 25 ff.; 29: 8; Zachariah 10: 2; etc.).

The two above categories of prophecy now clarify a parallel distinction made in the Bible, especially in legal contexts: 'If a prophet arises among you, or a dreamer of a dream, and gives you a sign or a wonder . . .' (Deuteronomy 13: 1 ff.). In an incident involving Saul, the Bible is explicit in differentiating between three distinct divinatory methods: 'The Lord did not answer him, either by dreams or by Urim or by prophets' (1 Samuel 28: 6; and see v. 15).[78] Even Jeremiah regarded the dreamer as a distinct type of prophet (Jeremiah 27: 9), though he belittled this medium, contrasting it with 'the word of God' and associating it with false prophets: 'Let the prophet who has a dream tell the dream, but let him who has my word speak my word faithfully. What has straw in common with wheat?' (Jeremiah 23: 28). This deflated status of the dream as a source of prophetic

[76] See, in particular, Moran 1969, pp. 25–26; and Weinfeld 1977, pp. 181–182.

[77] Malamat 1966a, pp. 221 f. and n. 1 on p. 222, for literature on the dream in the Bible. for the ancient Near East, see the basic study of Oppenheim 1956.

[78] An exact parallel to these three alternative means of inquiring of the deity may be found in the Plague Prayers of the Hittite king Muršili II; see *ANET*, pp. 394b–395a; and Herrmann 1965, pp. 54 f.

inspiration also finds clear expression in the Rabbinic dictum comparing sleep to death, just as 'a dream is a withered prophecy' (*nōḇelet n^eḇū'āh ḥ^alōm*; Genesis Rabba 44: 17).

The Mari letters reporting dream-revelations are usually structured on a regular scheme: (1) the male or female dreamer; (2) the opening formula of the dream—'(I saw) in my dream' (*ina šuttīya*—an obviously West Semitic form identical with Biblical Hebrew *baḥ^alōmī*; cf. Genesis 40: 9, 16; 41: 17);[79] (3) the content of the dream, based on a visual or, more often, an auditory 'experience'; and finally, (4) the communicator's comments, in many cases including a statement that a lock of the prophet/prophetess's hair and a piece of the hem of his/her garment are being sent to the king as well.

In one illuminating incident at Mari, where the same dream recurred on two successive nights, the dreamer was a mere youth (*ṣuḫārum*), to whom a god appeared in a nocturnal vision. The dream was eventually reported to the king by Kibri-Dagan: 'Thus he saw (a vision) as follows: "Build not this house . . .; if that house will be built I will make it collapse into the river!" On the day he saw that dream he did not tell (it) to anyone. On the second day he saw again the dream as follows: "It was a god (saying): 'Build not this house; if you will build it, I will make it collapse into the river!'" Now, herewith the hem of his garment and a lock of hair of his head I have sent to my lord . . .' (*ARMT* XIII 112: 1′–15′). The boy, who apparently had no previous prophetic experience, did not at first realize the source of his dream; only when it recurred the next night did he become aware of its divine origin and of the mission imposed upon him. This immediately calls to mind young Samuel's initial prophetic experience, while reposing in the temple at Shiloh (1 Samuel 3: 3 ff.). The Lord informed him, in a nocturnal vision, of the impending demise of the Elide clan. In Samuel's case, it was only after the fourth beckoning (but on the same night) that he comprehended the divine nature of the vision.[80]

In general, novice and inexperienced prophets were unable to identify divine revelations when first encountered (as in the case of Samuel; see 1 Samuel 3: 7). Hence we find the repetition of the manifestation, both at Mari and in the Bible. Jeremiah's initial call is also most illuminating: he too was reluctant to accept his prophetic calling, pleading youthfulness (Jeremiah 1: 6–7). After bolstering the youth's confidence, God tested him by a vision: 'And the word of the Lord came to me saying: "Jeremiah, what do you see?", and I said: "I see a rod of almond (Hebrew: *šāqēd*)."

[79] The West Semitic form was pointed out by M. Held, apud Craghan 1974, p. 43, n. 32. The standard Akkadian form would be *ina šuttim ša āmuru/aṭṭulu*; compare a similar West Semitic usage in one of the first prophecies published: *ina pānīya*, lit. 'in front of me', meaning 'on my way'; see Malamat 1956, p. 81.

[80] See Malamat 1980, pp. 223 ff.; and Gnuse 1984, esp. pp. 119 ff. The phenomenon of an identical dream recurring several times is known especially from the Classical world; see Hanson 1978, p. 1411, and the passages from Cicero, *De divinatione*, cited there.

Then the Lord said to me: "You have seen well for I am watching (*šōqēd*) over my word to perform it"' (Jeremiah 1: 11–12). God, in his response, expressly confirmed the reliability of the prophet's perception—a totally unique event in the realm of prophetic vision in the Bible—and thus proving Jeremiah's fitness to undertake his prophetic mission.[81]

Prophetic credibility

In the most recently published 'prophetic' text from Mari (A 222),[82] the name of the writer has been lost, as has been the name of the recipient (who was probably Zimri-Lim, recipient of the other letters). We read:

> The woman Ayala saw (*iṭṭul*) in her dream as follows:
>
> > A woman from Šeḫrum (and) a woman from Mari in the gate of (the temple of) Annunītum . . . /line missing/ which is at the edge of the city—quarrelled among themselves. Thus (said) the woman from Šeḫrum to the woman from Mari: 'Return to me my *position as high priestess* (*enūtum* may refer instead to 'equipment'); either you sit or I myself shall sit.
>
> By the *ḫurru*-bird I have examined this matter and she could see (*naṭlat*) (the dream). Now her hair and the hem of the garment I am sending along. May my lord investigate the matter!'

The nature of the dispute between these two women is not entirely clear although it may involve rivalry over the office of the high priestess. The penultimate passage relates that the writer confirmed the validity of the vision by means of augury. This divinatory device, well known in the classical world, appeared at a very early period in Hither Asia.[83] In this instance, the examination 'proved' that the woman actually did see (*naṭlat*), that is, she actually did see the vision she claimed to have seen. Inasmuch as the verb *amāru*, 'to see (a dream)', is synonymous and interchangeable with *naṭālu*, the intention here seems to be that the woman was indeed competent and experienced in the art of dream oracles.[84] Thus, the meaning is precisely as the editor of the text translated: 'Elle a bien eu ce songe!'—just like God's words to Jeremiah: 'You have seen well' (*hēṭaḇtā lir'ōt*)! The writer did not suffice with his own examination of the dream, and

[81] See Malamat 1954, esp. pp. 39–40.

[82] The document was published by Dossin 1975 (attributed by him to King Yaḫdun-Lim!); and see the comments in Sasson 1983, p. 291. His interpretation of *enūtum* (see below) as 'utensils' rather than 'priesthood' is possible.

[83] Divination by bird behaviour is a typically western practice; cf. Oppenheim 1964, pp. 209–210. This practice was especially widespread among the Hittites; see Kammenhuber 1976, which deals only briefly (p. 11) with the kind of bird mentioned in our text: *MUŠEN ḪURRI*; for this bird, see Salonen 1973, pp. 143–146; and cf. McEwan 1980.

[84] See *CAD* A/2, s.v. *amāru* A 2, p. 13: to learn by experience (especially stative . . .). The stative form with the meaning 'experienced, trained' is particularly prevalent in the Mari idiom, and we may therefore assume a similar nuance for the stative of *naṭālu*: *naṭlat* in our document.

sent the woman's hair and the hem of her garment to the king—for his examination. This unique and somewhat puzzling practice, attested only in connection with the Mari prophets, is mentioned on nine different occasions; that is, in a third of all the 'prophetic' letters. Several scholarly interpretations have been offered, all of which remain in the realm of speculation. This procedure was clearly related in some manner to the reliability of the diviner and of his message. In most of the cases, the prophet's words were presented to the king only as recommendations, the final decision to act upon them remaining in his hands: 'Let my lord do what pleases him'; 'Let my lord do what, in accordance with his deliberation, pleases him.' (In this matter, these prophecies decidedly differ from biblical prophecy, which is absolute and 'non-negotiable'.) Several points should be noted in this context.

The lock of hair and the hem of the garment are unequivocally personal objects,[85] specific to their individual owners, and seem to have served as a sort of 'identity card'. In the Bible, we read how David took the fringe of Saul's robe in the cave near En-Gedi (1 Samuel 24), in order to show him that Saul had been entirely at his mercy. In other words, the Mari procedure may primarily have had a legal significance, more than a religio-magic meaning, as often suggested. These personal items may also have been sent to the king in order to serve as evidence for the very existence of a diviner, and that the message was not simply a fabrication of the reporting official, who may have had some particular motive for promoting a false report.[86] Surely *fraus pia*, 'pious fraud', was no rarer in that period than it was later. This aspect also emerges from a long text (A 15) in which the writer specifically states of a dreamer–prophet: 'since this man was trustworthy, I did not take any of his hair or the fringe of his garment.'[87]

The credibility of prophetic revelation was obviously a sensitive matter, not to be taken for granted. Thus it was often verified and confirmed by the accepted mantic devices, considered more reliable means than intuitive prophecy *per se*.[88] Alongside the obscure practice of sending the hem

[85] For the hair (or lock of hair—*šārtum*) and the hem of a garment (*sissiktum*) see Liverani 1977; Malul 1986; the latter suggests that not merely the hem but the entire garment (or rather, undergarment, covering the private parts) was involved; and see n. 86, below.

[86] Malamat 1956, pp. 81, 84; Malamat 1966a, pp. 225 ff. and notes. For other explanations, see Uffenheimer 1973, pp. 29–33; Ellermeier 1968; Moran 1969, pp. 19–22; Noort 1977, p. 83–86; and Craghan 1974, pp. 53 ff. Note in two documents (A 455: 25; and *ARMT* X 81: 18), the illuminating but problematic addition appearing after the despatch of the hair and the hem; in the latter: 'let them declare (me) clean (*lizakkû*)'; according to Moran 1969a, pp. 22–23: '. . . it is the haruspex who "tries the case" and it is his response that will in effect declare the prophetess clean.' And cf. *ARMT* X, p. 267, ad loc.; Noort 1977, pp. 85–86. See Dalley *et al.* 1976, pp. 64–65, No. 65—for initial evidence for an identical procedure outside Mari (at Tell al-Rimaḥ).

[87] Dossin 1948, p. 132; in *l.* 53 we read (with Oppenheim 1956, p. 195, and 1952, p. 134): *tâk-lu*, 'trustworthy' (rather than Dossin's *kal-lu*, a kind of official).

[88] Moran 1969a, pp. 22–23; Craghan 1974, pp. 41–42; and Saggs 1978, p. 141.

of a garment and a lock of the dreamer–prophet, we encounter the following features: Šibtu wrote to Zimri-Lim that she personally examined a prophet's message, prior to sending it on to him, and found the report to be trustworthy (*ARMT* X 6). In another letter, a lady of the royal household reported a vision, and advised the king: 'Let my lord have the haruspex look into the matter . . .' (*ARMT* X 94). In a third letter, a woman implores the king to verify the vision of an *āpiltum* by divinatory means (*ARMT* X 81); the same woman advises the king, following the prophecy of a *qabbātum* (see above, p. 85), to be alert and not to enter the city without inquiring of the omens (*ARMT* X 80).

In contrast, in Israel the prophetic word—whether accepted or rejected by the king or the people—was never subjected to corroboration by mantic means, but was vindicated by the test of fulfilment (cf. Deuteronomy 18: 21–22; Ezekiel 33: 33).

In sum, the problem of reliability existed wherever intuitive prophecy flourished. It concerned the Mari authorities no less than the biblical law-makers and 'true' prophets, from Moses to Jeremiah—all of whom sought a yardstick for measuring prophetic authenticity. In the words of one expert: 'The prophets who preceded you and me from ancient times prophesied war, famine and pestilence against many countries and great kingdoms. As for the prophet who prophesies peace, when the word of that prophet comes to pass, then it will be known that the Lord has truly sent the prophet' (Jeremiah 28: 8–9).

C. THE ROYAL ANCESTOR CULT

Afterlife has always been a universal concern of man, in one manifestation or another, and bridging the chasm between the living and the dead has been one of man's principal concerns. The Mari archives are a prime source of information on an early stage of the Mesopotamian ancestor cult as represented by the Akkadian term *kispum*.[89] Two of the Mari 'prophetic' texts (see above, p. 82) touch upon the royal ancestor cult. One mentions the sacrifices to be made for Zimri-Lim's deceased father (*ARMT* III 40): a *muḫḫûm* at Terqa, speaking in the name of Dagan, urged the local governor, 'Hurry, write to the king that they are to offer the *kispum* sacrifices for the shade (*eṭemmum*) of Yaḫdun-Lim.'[90] In the other document (*ARMT* II 90), perhaps related to the same event, another diviner–prophet also urges the governor, 'Write to your lord that in the coming month, on the

[89] Cf. *CAD* K, pp. 425 ff., s.v. *kispu*, and the literature cited below. On the cult of the dead in general in Mesopotamia, and in Mari in particular, see Tsukimoto 1985; and see Bayliss 1973; Bottéro 1987.

[90] This possibly indicates that Terqa may have been the ancestral home of the Lim dynasty. It was certainly the religious centre of the Mari kingdom, and after the kingdom's destruction at the hands of Ḫammurabi, Terqa became the capital of the kingdom of Ḫana; see Charpin & Durand 1986, pp. 142–143.

14th day, the funerary sacrifices (*pagrā'ī*)[91] is to be performed. Under no circumstances are they to omit this sacrifice.' Such *kispum* ceremonies in honour of the dead are attested only from Old Babylonian times on, that is, they first appear roughly in the Mari Age, though there may well have been parallel rites earlier on.[92] Although not particularly West- Semitic in origin, this ritual was certainly well developed throughout the Amorite sphere, and had specific West Semitic nuances, adaptations and appendages.[93] Underlying these offerings of food and drink was the belief that the dead could influence the living and guide them—benevolently when cared for and malevolently when neglected and unappeased.

Though the bulk of the textual evidence on the early *kispum* ritual comes from Mari, there is important evidence from other Old Babylonian sources as well. A *kispum* offering is certainly intended in the ritual text of Takil-ilišśu, king of Malgium: 'At the New Moon and Full Moon, I regularly placed before him his pure bread and precious water.' In an appeal to Sin, the moon god, we read: 'Release them [the ghosts of members of the family of a certain Sin-Naṣir] in order to let them eat his bread and drink his water';[94] and: 'What shall I bring your family [lit. 'your father's house] throughout the year for *kispum* on the New Moon?'[95] All these examples, and others, however, are of a private nature.

At Mari, the rich material concerns mainly the royal ancestor cult, *kispum ša šarrāni*, 'funerary sacrifices for the [dead] kings'. Most of these texts derive from the administrative records of foodstuffs for the king's meals (see above, p. 21), some of which specifically note the dates and quantities for the royal *kispum* meals. The texts clearly show that sacrifices were held at the New Moon and at the Full Moon—in other words, at the start

[91] The lexeme *pagrā'um* (plural *pagrā'ī*), a *niṣbe* formation from *pagrûm*, 'corpse, carcass', remains enigmatic, despite there being cognates in both Ugaritic and Biblical Hebrew, perhaps having different connotations. In Malamat 1956, p. 5 (commenting on *ARMT* II 90: 22), I pointed out the two rival (but possibly not mutually exclusive) meanings: (a) a funerary stele or statue (i.e. the 'corpse' of a god or king, a meaning possibly attested, e.g., by Leviticus 26: 30; Ezekiel 43: 7–9; see below, n. 121), as initially proposed in Neiman 1948; accepted by Albright 1957; but more feasible (b) a funerary offering or sacrifice (see, e.g., Moran 1969a, p. 43, n. 1, where it is speculated that *pagrā'um* is the West Semitic equivalent of Akkadian *kispum*; and cf. *AHw*, p. 809, s.v. *pagrā'um*). Here, as in the previous prophecy, Dagan, is 'initiator' of the ceremony, and thus bears the epithet *bēl pagrē*, 'Lord of *pagrā'ī*' (*ARMT* X 63: 15); thus he has been linked to the underworld (cf. Roberts 1972, p. 19). For the more recently published instances of *pagrā'um* at Mari, see *ARMT* XIV 12, and p. 217; XVIII 38: 5; XXI 62: 1, 4, 43; 76: 2′; 147: 4 and n. 20; XXIII 561: 15.

[92] For the Sumerian cult at Lagaš, see Bauer 1969; for the Sumerian tradition in general, see Tsukimoto 1985, pp. 26 ff. For the Ur III period and the funeral rites for King Šu-Sîn at various places, see Sigrist (forthcoming).

[93] Finkelstein 1966 stresses the fact that *kispum*, *per se*, is not a West Semitic custom, but assumed especial significance in that sphere.

[94] Kutscher & Wilcke 1978, p. 114, *ll*. 14–17; Wilcke 1983a, pp. 49 ff.; and cf. Greenfield & Shaffer 1985, pp. 51–52, and the literature cited there concerning the 1st millennium BC.

[95] Kraus 1964, No. 106: 17–19.

of each lunar month (on the 1st) and at its middle (around the 15th).[96]

We have noted much earlier (pp. 24f.) a Mari text (12803) from the days of Šamši-Adad which describes for the first time the actual mechanism of the *kispum* ritual. To quote again the first column of the text, somewhat more fully: 'At the going-out of the first day of Adạr [around February], the *kispum* (shall be offered) in the city and in its environs: The "meal" is to be taken (from) the palace. A sheep shall be sacrificed in the hall of the thrones for the statues (*lamassātum*) of Sargon and Naram-Sin [two kings of Akkad who ruled hundreds of years earlier]. . . . Before the arrival of the king [i.e. Šamši-Adad], the sacrifice in the hall of the thrones is to be performed; the meats are to be cooked, and the best meats shall be presented to Šamaš; so long as they have not been presented to Šamaš, the *kispum* (to the statues of the two dead kings) shall not be offered. Only after they have been presented to Šamaš, the *kispum* (shall be offered) to (the statues of) Sargon and Naram-Sin, to the *yaradu* Ḫaneans and to those of the (tribe of) Numḫa. . . .'[97] The text then goes on to mention other matters, including various royal sacrifices at temples.

Thus, this *kispum* ceremony took place on the second day of Adar, but it was most likely held on some special occasion[98] and did not represent the regular monthly *kispum* ritual. What is unusual here is that while two long-dead kings of Akkad are honoured, Šamši-Adad's own father, Ila-kabkabu, is not even mentioned. This ceremony took place in the 'hall of the thrones', with the king himself present at least for part of it. (It may well have taken place in the throne room of the Mari palace; see above, p. 25). The term 'hall of the thrones' used here may be of specific significance. Birot took it to refer to the thrones of the statues of gods in the temple of Šamaš.[99] But it may have been that (putative or real) ancestor figures were placed on these chairs; or that such chairs were reserved for the ghosts of the deceased at the *kispum* ritual, for indeed, we find in the lexical lists the expression *kussû eṭemmē*, 'chair for the ghosts'.[100] And much later, in a Standard Babylonian text,[101] we read: 'You place a chair for the spirits of his family to the left of the cult installation, you place chairs to the left for the spirits of his family, you make a food offering (*kispa takassip*) for the spirits of the family, you give them presents, you praise them, you honour them.'

Thus, offerings were made to several sorts of ancestral spirits, some of them much earlier kings grafted on to the dynastic genealogy of Šamši-Adad. The inclusion of the two most famous kings of Akkad, Sargon and

96 For full bibliography till 1978, see Talon 1978; and cf. the calendric tables there. For more recent material, see Charpin 1984.

97 Birot 1980; and cf. Tsukimoto 1985, pp. 73 ff.; Charpin & Durand 1986, pp. 165 ff.

98 Perhaps for legitimising the Assyrian domination of Mari, actually a usurpation.

99 Birot 1980, p. 146.

100 ḪAR-*ra* = *ḫubullu* IV, *I*. 93; Landsberger 1957, p. 157; *CAD* E, p. 397, s.v. *eṭemmu*.

101 Zimmern 1901, No. 52, esp. *II*. 12–13, pp. 164–167; cf. *CAD* E, p. 399, s.v. *eṭemmu*..

Naram-Sin, was entirely putative but derived from the compulsion to gain prestige and legitimacy. This immediately brings to mind two well-known genealogical texts—the Assyrian King List (or 'AKL') and, in particular, the so-called Genealogy of the Ḫammurabi Dynasty (or 'GHD'), preserved on a clay tablet long gathering dust at the British Museum (BM 80328) and published only some 20 years ago.[102] The latter text contains 31 names, real and fictitious, tribal eponyms and historical personages—all in descending order till Ammi-ṣaduqa, the great-grandson of Ḫammurabi. The final dozen or so lines of the text reveal that it was clearly intended for use at a *kispum* ceremony. Here we find a list of other 'shades': soldiers who fell in battle (something like the 'Unknown Soldier'), reminiscent of those 'fallen or slain by the sword'; *(ha-)nop^{e}līm baḥereb*, *ḥal^{e}lē ḥereb*, mentioned especially in Ezekiel (32: 20, 21, 22, 24, 28, 30, 32); princes and princesses; and 'all "persons" from East to West'—a catch-all phrase for those dead who had no one to look out for their interests. All these were invited to eat and drink of the offerings—and to bless the incumbent king of Babylon.

Fairly high up the GHD list, in the part which could be denoted the 'genealogical stock',[103] we find Ḫeana (or Ḫana), Ditanu and Namḫu—all three eponyms of known tribal groupings of West Semites. These three ancestral names also appear in slightly variant order and spelling in the upper part of the Assyrian King List (where the form Nuabu appears instead of Namḫu). Significantly, this Assyrian list records the forebears of Šamši-Adad, real and putative, and it should not be forgotten that the *yaradu* of both the Ḫaneans and the Numḫa also appear in Šamši-Adad's *kispum* ritual text from Mari. Shades of the third eponym, Ditanu, have to be sought elsewhere (see below, pp. 100f.).

The *yaradu* of the two groups represent the tribal ancestries of Šamši-Adad's line: the Ḫaneans, who comprised (as we have seen) the major element on the Middle Euphrates; and the Numḫeans, another well-known Amorite group in the Upper Habur region, perhaps even the very ancestral tribe of Šamši-Adad.[104] We have already mentioned this duality of Akkadian and tribal 'affiliations', concerning Zimri-Lim, who was advised by his palace prefect (*ARMT* VI 76: 20 ff.): 'You are the King of the Ḫaneans, but also King of the Akkadians are you . . .' (see above, pp. 2f.). Here, then, we see that both Zimri-Lim and Šamši-Adad regarded themselves as a blend of the civilized urban and the 'wild' tribal.

Birot was not able to make any sense out of the term *yaradu*, a *hapax*

[102] For the two king-lists, see Finkelstein 1966; and cf. the critical remarks of Lambert 1968; Röllig 1969; and see Grayson 1980–83; Charpin & Durand 1986, pp. 163 ff.

[103] See Malamat 1968.

[104] Despite this tribal descent, in a votive inscription for Ištar (A 4509), Šamši-Adad is designated 'king of Akkad'; see Charpin 1984, p. 44: 7.

legomenon in Akkadian.[105] The Bible, however, may shed light on the term in association with the *kispum* ritual text from Mari, for *yaradu* surely derives from the West Semitic root *yārōd*, 'to descend', so frequently applied in Biblical Hebrew and in the Ugaritic language, often in connection with Sheol—the netherworld.[106] This is well illustrated, for example, by Jacob's pathetic reaction to the 'false' report of Joseph's death (Genesis 37:35): 'I shall go down (*ērēd*) to Sheol, to my son, mourning.' In a royal context, a similar usage appears in Isaiah's warning to the king of Babylon (Isaiah 14:9ff.): 'Sheol beneath is stirred up to meet you when you come, it rouses the shades (*rᵉp̄āʾīm*) to greet you, all who were leaders of the earth, it raises from their thrones all who were kings of the nations. ... (11) Your pomp is brought down (*hurad*) to Sheol. ... (15) But you are brought down (*hurad*) to Sheol, to the depth of the pit. ... (19) with the slain, those pierced by the sword, who go down (*yōrᵉdē*) to the stones of the pit.' And on a larger scale it can be seen in Ezekiel 32:18–30, where Egypt, Assyrian, Elam, Meshech and Tubal, Edom and the princes of the North and every Sidonian are all condemned to be among 'those who have gone down (*yōrᵉdē*) to the pit ... amid those who are slain by the sword. ... And they do not lie with the fallen mighty men of old, who went down (*yārᵉdū*) to Sheol with their weapons of war....[107] Other parallel phrases in the Bible are 'who go down to the dust' (*yōrᵉdē ʿāp̄ār*; Psalms 22:30[29]); and 'any that go down into silence' (*yōrᵉdē dūmāh*; Psalms 115:17). Thus, the *yaradu* Ḫaneans and Numḫeans would also appear to be 'those who descended', that is, the deceased—the shades of Ḫanean and Numḫean ancestors summoned by the incumbent king to partake in the sacrificial meal.

At Ugarit, the Syrian coastal metropolis already noted here several times, an entire *kispum*-like liturgy in the Ugaritic language (closely akin to Canaanite) has come to light. This text has recently been the subject of intensive study,[108] and seems to reflect the accession rites of the kings of Ugarit, epitomizing the exclamation, 'The King is dead! Long live the King!' It was apparently to be recited in the royal palace in connection with sacrifices and invocations of the names of kings past—that is, it was a Ugaritic *kispum* ceremony. The most significant feature in this context is the fact that the Ugaritic royal line here is traced back to the 'Didanites' (or 'Ditanites')—

[105] Birot 1980, p. 144, on *l.* 19, does not explain the term, though he mentions the West Semitic root *yrd*, as well as *wardum*, 'servant', and the biblical PN Yered and Aramaic *yrt*, 'inherit'. Tsukimoto 1985, pp. 76–77, derives the word from the verb (*w*)*arādu*, 'to settle down', in his opinion referring to the settled Ḫaneans, etc., in contrast to nomadic tribal groups—a proposal rightly rejected by Charpin & Durand 1986, p. 166 and n. 121.

[106] For Hebrew *yrd* as applied to descent to the netherworld, see Mayer 1982, col. 899, s.v. *yrd*. And see also Tromp 1969, pp. 32–33 and 145; he cites Dahood's opinion that *'ereṣ yardēn* in Psalms 42:7, means the 'land of descent', i.e. the netherworld (pp. 91 and 145).

[107] On Ezekiel 32, see Zimmerli 1969, pp. 782 ff.; and Boadt 1980, pp. 150 ff.

[108] RS 34.126 (=KTU 1.161); from late in the 13th century BC, and properly collated only in 1982. See Bordreuil & Pardee 1982; and, based on their collation, Levine & Tarragon 1984, with earlier bibliography; and see Pitard 1978; Lewis 1986, pp. 1 ff.

identical with the Ditanu of AKL and GHD, noted above and appearing in the Ugaritic King List as well. In other words, Ditanu represents an early Amorite tribal group (late 3rd millennium BC) from which various entities derived, both in Mesopotamia and in the West. Indeed, the Ugaritic Keret Epic associates the protagonist Keret himself with the 'Rephaim of the netherworld and the assembly of the council (*qbṣ*)[109] of the Ditanites' (III Keret iii: 2–4). Regarding the last name, we may draw attention to the biblical name Dathan, who significantly was brother to Abiram and son of Eli-ab. All three of these eponyms are reminiscent of names in the Ugaritic sources, the last name reminiscent of an ancestor god, 'Il'ib', within the Ugaritic pantheon.[110] In the Bible, Dathan and Abiram rebelled against Moses in the Wilderness and, as punishment, 'the earth opened its mouth and swallowed them up. . . . So they and all that belonged to them went down (*wayyērᵉdū*) alive into Sheol; and the earth closed over them . . .' (Numbers 16: 30–33; and cf. Psalms 106: 17). The name Ditanu/Didanu occurs in several other early historical inscriptions, from which it can be concluded that it represents a major branch of the Amorites, or perhaps even a group comparable to the Amorites.[111] In any event, they seem to have been one more large West Semitic element in the Middle Euphrates region at an early period. And so here too, similarly to the Hebrews, the Ugaritic royal line traced its ancestry back into Old Babylonian times (and possibly earlier), and also to a region well within the Mesopotamian sphere.[112]

Of the seventy references to *kispum* in the Mari texts, several also make mention of special or variant features. One recently published example is unique in its use of the phrase *ana kispim ša abbē*, 'funerary offering (of oil) for the fathers',[113] that is, apparently, the deceased tribal chieftains, designated by *abū* in other Mari documents as well (see above, p. 42).

[109] For *qbṣ* (cf. Isaiah 57: 13) in a collective sense, meaning ancestors ('gathered ones'), i.e. of Ditānu, see Pope 1981; Heider 1985, n. 759. This would parallel Hebrew *'am* in such phrases as *neʾesap̱ 'el 'ammī*, lit. 'gathered unto my kin' (cf. *nl'esp̱ū 'el 'ᵃḇōtāw*, 'gathered unto his fathers'); and see now Lipiński 1987, cols. 185–186.

[110] I owe this observation of the biblical names to Jonas Greenfield. Might they represent ancient tribal entities which disappeared during their encounter with the Proto-Israelites, as may be inferred from the subsequent episode? For Il'ib at Ugarit, see Nougayrol 1968; and, e.g., de Moor 1976, p. 331; Margalit 1976, pp. 145–146. In this connection see the observation of Lambert 1981, that a deity Ilaba appears in Old Akkadian, as well as at Mari (in a PN) and Ugarit.

[111] For Ditānu/Didānu as a tribal organisation, see Buccellati 1966, pp. 236–237, 243–244 and 333. And see Levine & Tarragon 1984 and the literature cited there. And cf. Pardee 1983. This tribal name has also been compared to such biblical entities as (the tribal eponym) Dedan (Genesis 25: 3) or (the toponym) Dothan (Genesis 37: 17).

[112] On the basis of 28 to 30 kings registered in the Ugaritic royal line, Kitchen 1977 has reckoned that the eponym Didānu would hark back to the 22nd century BC. This, however, would seem too high since the entries prior to Yaqarum (immediate founder of the Ugaritic dynasty) should be regarded as 'putative' eponyms and thus lacking substantial timespan (further, they may not even have 'ruled' successively). And see Astour 1973.

[113] Charpin 1984, p. 89, No. 36.

This text, from the period of the Assyrian interregnum at Mari, thus provides and interesting variant from the common *kispum ša šarrāni*. Another unique feature is found in more than twenty Mari texts—all summaries of quantities of foodstuffs for the royal meals—which, in addition to *kispum*, mention *ana malikī* (in three cases this phrase appears alone), apparently a supplementary sacrifice of smaller proportions, normally occurring once a month, at the time of the New Moon. This obscure term may well be related to the West Semitic word *melek*, 'king' or 'counsellor' (*māliku*). At any rate, here it most likely refers to deceased rulers,[114] and if kings are intended—as we assume—*malikū* may perhaps refer to rulers of a more distant past than the *šarrāni* (sedentary, 'civilized' kings) invoked in the regular *kispum* ritual. Thus, *malikū* may refer to sheikhs still at the tribal-nomadic stage of society—living in a past so remote that their actual names could no longer be recalled.

A recently published Mari document (A 674) sheds more light on this particular term, *malikum*:[115] 'To Zimri-Lim, say: Thus says Išme-Dagan, your son. I am (used) to hold a *malikum* (rite). [Indeed, the *ma*] *likum* is come, but someone versed in the *malikum* ritual is not here. A servant (*ṣuḫārum*) of yours together with a servant of mine should get together and quickly seek out for me someone versed in the *malikum* ritual.' This is indicative of the specific and peculiar nature of this ritual (contacting the ancestral spirits of the kings?) which, as we have noted, is so far unique to the Mari documents. (In this latter text, however, it is significantly Išme-Dagan, king of Assyria and son of Šamši-Adad, who is appealing *to* the king of Mari.)

This assumed West Semitic concept—of a *malkum*/*malikum*, in contrast to the Akkadian *šarrum*/*šarrāni*—may find support in the following:

(a) At Mari and other sites during the 19th and 18th centuries BC—i.e. at the time of the Amorite expansion—there suddenly appear numerous personal names containing the element *mlk* (*malik*, *milki*, etc.), an element previously known only at such sites as Ebla.[116]

(b) At Ebla (c. 2500–2250 BC),[117] such words as *malikum*, 'ruler', 'king' (appearing at present only once as the ruler of a city: PN *ma-lik* GN) and frequently *maliktum*, 'queen', are found, and even the peculiar syllabic spelling *ma-li-gú-um*, 'kingship', appears in bilingual vocabularies, equated

[114] On the *malikū* at Mari, cf. Talon 1978; Tsukimoto 1985, pp. 65 ff.; Charpin & Durand 1986, pp. 168 ff.; Heider 1985, pp. 102 ff. The meaning of 'ancestral spirit', 'infernal demon', has been suggested for the word at Mari (cf. *CAD* M/1, pp. 168–169, s.v. *malku* B: 'netherworld god or demon'), and even the king's 'counsellor' (Wiseman 1965, p. 125).

[115] Finet 1985b, pp. 89–90.

[116] Cf. Huffmon 1965, p. 230.

[117] For the time being, there is too little documentary evidence from Middle Bronze Age Ebla (c. 2000–1600 BC) to be of use, but there are magnificent archaeological discoveries of princely tombs, indicative of a royal cult of the dead. See Matthiae 1979, 1981, 1984.

with Sumerian NAM.EN.[118] This surprising equation of Sumerian EN with *malikum*, rather than with the more usual Akkadian *šarrum*, would point to a western tradition.[119] It thus also lends to the *malikum* aspect of the *kispum* ritual at Mari (and possibly even to the entire ritual in its earlier manifestations) a distinctly western nuance.

(c) In the alphabetic Ugaritic texts, the common word for king is *mlk*, and in some lists we find the collective plural *mlkm*, presumably referring to deceased kings. In the lexical lists from Ugarit, Sumerian EN (as well as LUGAL) is equated with the syllabically spelled cuneiform *malku*, a West Semitic vocable.[120]

(d) In the biblical evidence, there may be a reference to Amorite *malikum* in Isaiah 57: 9, which should be translated: 'You have given offering to the *mlk* [the deceased king?] with oil, and you have provided many perfumes; and you have sent your envoys afar, you sent down to Sheol.' The Masoretic reading here is *melek̲*, 'king' (often emended to 'Moloch', which could merely be referring to a much earlier existence of the late Moloch cult).[121]

Such Western nuances of the cult of the dead may also be detected in two recently published documents from the 14th–13th centuries BC from the vicinity of Emar. There, a daughter is appointed by her father to serve as guardian of her junior brothers: 'She may call upon my gods and my dead (*meteia*).' The editor of these texts takes the phrase 'calling upon' here to mean that the daughter was allowed to *invoke* the household gods and family ancestors.[122] But rather than 'invoke', it might be better to read 'invite' (to partake in food), and thus a *kispum* offering would be intended. In an unpublished adoption text from Nuzi, we also read of

[118] See Müller 1980, pp. 11–14; Archi 1982, p. 37; Pettinato 1981, pp. 74 ff.; Krebernik 1982, p. 205; Muntingh 1984; Kienast 1984, p. 226.

[119] For the latest treatments available to me on *malikum* at Ebla, see Archi 1987; Artzi 1987.

[120] See the multilingual dictionary published by Nougayrol 1968, p. 234, *ll.* 13′ and 32′. In a recent study, (forthcoming), Pardee n. 49, equates the Rephaim, *rapa'uma*, at Ugarit, with the *malikū* at Mari; for a similar view, cf. Healey 1978, pp. 90–91 (*rp'um*, simply the deceased royalty). Cf. Dietrich & Loretz 1981. For additional recent studies on deceased kings at Ugarit, see del Olmo Lete 1986; 1987; for the connection between Ugaritic *mlkm* and dMalik, see Healey 1978; Healey 1984; 1986 and the literature cited in these.

[121] Müller 1980, p. 14, and 1984, col. 965, has already drawn attention to the possibility of this connection. For the emendation to *Molek̲*, see Heider 1985, p. 380. For an additional possible appearance of Amorite *malikum* in the Bible, see *malk̲ēhem* in Ezekiel 43: 7b, 9: 'But the house of Israel shall not defile my holy name again, neither they nor *malk̲ēhem* ('their kings' or 'the ancestral spirits of their kings') by their harlotry and by the *peḡārīm* of *malk̲ēhem bāmōtām* (in accord with numerous manuscripts and ancient versions, most likely to be emended to *bemōtām*, 'in their demise', i.e. the ancestral spirits of their deceased kings). . . . Now let them put away their idolatry and *pigrē malk̲ēhem* (for which see above, n. 91) far from me, and I will dwell in their midst forever.' The object of the prophet's wrath here was the burial of the dead kings and, presumably, the accompanying royal rites of the dead, adjacent to the Jerusalem Temple precincts; see already Schwally 1892, pp. 77–78; and, most recently, Lewis 1986, pp. 232 ff., and the literature cited there.

[122] Huehnergard 1983, esp. p. 28; and see Paradise 1987, pp. 203–204, 210–211.

a father bequeathing to his daughter his gods and his care of the spirits of the dead (*eṭemmū*).[123] Thus, it can be assumed that responsibility for the care of dead ancestors fell upon the shoulders of the guardian or heir (even if female).

Similar attitudes can also be felt among the Israelites in their *early* religious outlook toward the cult of the dead, which may not have been so very different from what we have just been reviewing. Saul's fear of having no one to invoke his name—and hence of oblivion in the hereafter—is seen in such passages as his plea before David, in 1 Samuel 24: 21: 'Swear to me therefore by the Lord that you will not cut off my descendants after me, and that you will not destroy my name out of my father's house.' In other words, Saul was begging David to leave his family line intact, so that there would be someone to commemorate his name. The childless Absalom also sought eventual invocation of his name: '"I have no son to keep my name in remembrance (*hazkēr šᵉmī*)"; he called the pillar after his own name (*yād wāšēm lᵉzikkārōn*), and it is called Absalom's monument to this day' (2 Samuel 18: 18). Eunuchs, too, could be assured by the Lord of a secure future after death: 'To the eunuchs who . . . hold fast my covenant, I will give . . . a monument and a name (*yād wāšēm*), better than sons and daughters; I will give them an everlasting name which shall not be cut off' (Isaiah 56: 4–5).

Certain fairly direct references to the cult of the dead do survive in the Bible, as does much related imagery, especially in the poetical sections,[124] despite the considerable efforts of Yahwistic and other (especially the Priestly) redactors to eradicate any and every heathen remnant from early Israelite worship.[125] Actual food-offerings are referred to at least twice, in Deuteronomy 26: 14, a negative confession (by Levites): 'I have not . . . offered any (of the tithe) to the dead'; and in Psalms 106: 28 (which relates to the Wanderings narrative; cf. Numbers 25), referring to the Israelites at Baal Peor in Moab, who sinfully 'ate sacrifices offered to the dead (*zib̲ḥē mētīm*).'[126] Two other passages imply such worship—in Isaiah 8: 19:

[123] Note the episode in Genesis 31, concerning Rachel's appropriation of Laban's family gods; and cf., e.g. Paradise 1987, pp. 212–213. For the ancestor worship in the Bible by means of the *tᵉrāp̲īm*, (again by women) see most recently Rouillard & Tropper 1987.

[124] See the treatments in Wächter 1967 and Tromp 1969, as well as the two basic studies in Saggs 1958 and Brichto 1973.

[125] Cf. Loretz 1978 and Spronk 1986. In an effort to counter long-standing custom, the priestly legislators acted to distance funerary activity from the Temple by declaring the dead to be impure in the extreme. Consequently, the dead were anathema to priests, and hence, apparently, the laws in Leviticus 21: 1–6, generally forbidding priests from participating in funerary rites. And see above, n. 121 on Ezekiel 43: 6–9 as an expression of opposition to the royal cult of the dead. (I wish to thank my colleague, Professor B. Levine, for this observation, based on his forthcoming commentary on Leviticus, to be published by the Jewish Publication Society, Philadelphia.)

[126] Perhaps corresponding to *zib̲ḥē ʾᵉlōhīm*, lit. 'sacrifices to the gods', but referring to the dead. For *ʾᵉlōhīm* as sometimes designating deceased persons, ancestral spirits, see, e.g., 1 Samuel 28: 13; Isaiah 8: 19.

'... Should not a people consult their God (or rather "their ancestral spirits"; *'el 'elōhāw yidrōš*)? Should they consult the dead on behalf of the living?'; and in Deuteronomy 18: 10–11: 'There shall not be found among you anyone who burns his son or his daughter as an offering, any one who practices divination, a soothsayer, or an augur, or a sorcerer, or a charmer, or a medium, or a wizard, or a necromancer (*dōrēš 'el hammētīm*)'.

There may even be at least one biblical reference to an actual *kispum*-like ritual of the Mari sort (albeit only of a king-to-be—David himself).[127] In 1 Samuel 20: 5–6 we read: 'David said to Jonathan, "Behold, tomorrow is the new moon, and I should not fail to sit at table with the king; but let me go that I may hide myself in the field. ... If your father misses me at all, then say, 'David earnestly asked leave of me to run to Bethlehem his city; for there is a *zebaḥ hayyāmīm* there for all the *mišpāḥāh* ("family")' "....' Saul held his feast upon the New Moon, seated on his throne, attended by his nobles; when he noticed that all were indeed present except David, Jonathan told him what David had asked him to tell. The two terms used for these sacrifices are *zebaḥ mišpāḥāh*, 'family sacrifice' (1 Samuel 20: 28–29) and *zebaḥ yāmīm*,[128] literally 'sacrifice of the days' and usually taken to mean 'yearly sacrifice' but possibly to be rendered 'sacrifice of yore', 'of (or 'for') generations long passed'.[129] Such a family gathering, held at the New Moon and at the ancestral home, might well have resembled the *kispum* ritual, as exemplified in the Old Babylonian period at Mari, and Babylon (and very likely Sippar) and possibly in Old Babylonian Ebla[130] as well as, later, Ugarit.

If indeed such a practice was current in early Israel, later Israelite belief sublimated it to the point where only the names of ancestors were invoked. There is a plethora of references to this effect in the Bible, the most forthright of which (though obscure) is in Psalms 49: 12 (MT). This verse has been misrendered by the traditional translations, and modern scholarship has till now offered no viable alternative.[131] We would now render it: 'The graves (of the dead) are their eternal homes, the dwelling place for all generations of those to be summoned by their names on earth.' This verse

[127] First hinted at in Malamat 1968, p. 173, n. 29, and since accepted by various scholars.

[128] The term also occurs in 1 Samuel 1: 21 and 2: 19.

[129] *Zbḥ ymm* also occurs in the Karatepe Inscription; see Donner & Röllig 1962, II, pp. 37, 42; and cf. *ANET*, p. 500; there, king Azitawwada records offering a sacrifice for all the molten images. For the usual meaning of *zebaḥ mišpāḥāh* and *zebaḥ yāmīm*, see, e.g., Haran 1978, index, s.v. Meal, sacrificial; Yearly sacrifice. Admittedly, our grasp here of *zebaḥ hayyāmīm* as 'sacrifice of yore' remains conjectural.

[130] For the cult for the dead royalty at Amorite Ebla, see Matthiae, above n. 117.

[131] On Psalm 49, see now Casetti 1982. The author reviews the previous interpretations of each verse; for v. 12 (MT), see pp. 63 ff. The *qirbām* is certainly a metathesis of *qibrām*; *qārᵉ'ū bᵉšēm* is a precise Hebrew rendering for calling *by* name, in contrast to *qārᵉ'ū šēm*, to call *a* name. And see Talmon 1987. For a critique of Casetti 1982, see Loretz 1985, pp. 189 ff. And cf. the above-cited Ugaritic liturgy invoking dead ancestors (see pp. 100f.), which employs the verb *qr'*, 'to call, to summon', throughout, in a similar context.

links in well with 2 Samuel 14: 7: 'and leave . . . neither name (*šēm*) nor remnant (*šᵉērīt*) upon the face of the earth.' Here, *šᵉērīt* should be taken in the legal sense of remnant—'heirs', 'descendants', actually deriving from the Hebrew root *šᵉēr*, 'flesh', 'kin'.[132] This parallels Isaiah 14: 22: '"I will rise up against them," says the Lord of hosts, "and will cut off from Babylon name (*šēm*) and remnant (*šᵉār*; perhaps the MT vowel pointing here should be modified to *šᵉēr*), offspring and posterity."'

The use of the word *šēm*, 'name', seems also to be reflected in the biblical concept of *anšē šēm*, 'men of renown', 'heroes'; note in Genesis 6: 4: 'They were the mighty men (*gibbōrīm*) that were of old, the men of renown (*anšē haššēm*).' Originally this term seems to have signified those worthy of being recorded by name in the ancestor cult. Indeed, the phrase also appears in Numbers 16: 2—in the story of Korah, Dathan and Abiram (see p. 101 and n. 110), in connection with the 'Ditanites' of the Ugaritic liturgy and the 'Ditanu' of AKL and GHD. The phrases are to be rendered: 'chosen from the assembly (*qᵉrīʾē mōʿēd*)', 'men of renown'.[133]

In short, the biblical attitude is that Sheol, the netherworld, was preferable to limbo (and cf. Psalms 88: 13), in which state the deceased had no one to invoke or remember his name (*hazkēr šēm*) and thus assure his continued welfare (cf., e.g., Jeremiah 11: 19 end; Job 18: 11; Ecclesiastes 9: 5).[134]

Among the Jews, the practice of commemorating famous ancestors has indeed survived to this very day. The outstanding instance is in the blessing of the New Moon (that is, on the first of every Hebrew, lunar month), where we find the exclamation: 'David, King of Israel, is alive and flourishes!' (referred to already in the Babylonian Talmud, Rosh Hashana 25a); there is even a vague reference in rabbinic literature to a memorial feast (*a̱bra'ah* in Aramaic), which was held on the New Moon,[135] a late survival of a *kispum*-like ceremony. Another such survival might be found in the so-called *Ushpizin* (an Aramaic word derived from the Latin *hospes*, 'guest'), first appearing in kabbalistic literature and referring to the seven mystical 'guests' visiting the *sukkāh* ('tabernacle') during the seven days of the Feast of Tabernacles.[136] The ancestral spirits, one each day, are invited to the festive meal, and they are named as: Abraham, Isaac, Jacob, Joseph, Moses, Aaron and David.

And during the Jewish memorial service for the principal holidays—Pesaḥ

[132] The expression *šᵉʾērīt*, *šᵉʾār*, in the sense of kin, like *šᵉʾēr*, has already been recognised by Ibn Ǵanah 1896, pp. 491–492, and Kimhi 1847, p. 364.

[133] Could *mōʿēd* here and elsewhere have assumed a specialised meaning of an assembly connected with a *kispum*-like ceremony?

[134] Cf. Brichto 1973, p. 53. For the importance of commemoration of the names of the deceased in Mesopotamia, see Bayliss 1973, pp. 116–117.

[135] Cf. Kutscher 1972, p. 88.

[136] Cf. *Encyclopaedia Judaica* 16, col. 19.

(Passover), Šāḇuōt (Pentecost) and Sukkōt (Tabernacles), and on Yom Kippur (Day of Atonement), in the *Yizkōr* ('Remembrance') prayer, the 'immortal' souls of Abraham, Isaac, Jacob, Sarah, Rebekah, Rachel and Leah are invoked, along with those of the deceased relatives of the congregants.

D. KINGLY DEEDS AND DIVINE EXPLOITS

It was a general aspiration of ancient Near Eastern kings to attain perpetual glory and fame, as we have seen in the previous section. In the world of the Old Babylonian period, this is well reflected in royal emulation of earlier, famous kings, and of epic heroes, with whom such kings as Yaḫdun-Lim and Šamši-Adad sought to identify. Nowhere is this better exemplified than in Yaḫdun-Lim's Foundation Inscription, two principal aspects of which are considered here: the king's deeds at the sacred sea—the Mediterranean; and those of the sacred forest—wooded mountains in the Levant. The mythological bases underlying these exploits appear to be the overcoming of the 'primordial waters' by a divine hero, and in the lumberjack heroics of Gilgameš in the 'Cedar Forest'.

The Sacred Sea

The divine nature of the Mediterranean Sea is another example of a western conceptualization which has not yet received the consideration worthy of it. Yaḫdun-Lim's Foundation Inscription was discovered in the temple of Šamaš at Mari, in nine identical copies.[137] This is the earliest known Western variation of an Old Babylonian royal inscription, a masterpiece of historiography. Here, Yaḫdun-Lim, Zimri-Lim's father, who reigned about 1800 BC, boldly describes a campaign to the West, and his reaching the Mediterranean coast, the crowning achievement of the entire effort. The relevant passage implies that the Mediterranean Sea was regarded as a divine–mythological entity at Mari—hundreds of years earlier than previously realized. The passage in question reads:

> Since days of old, when god built Mari, no king residing in Mari had reached the sea (*tâmtam*). To the Cedar Mountain and the Boxwood (Mountain), the great mountains, they had not reached; they had not felled their trees. (But) Yaḫdun-Lim, the son of Yaggid-Lim, the mighty king, a wild ox among kings, marched to the shore of the sea (*tâmtam*) in irresistible strength. To the Ocean

[137] Cf. Dossin 1955; for the passage discussed below, cf. pp. 13–14 and his notes on pp. 25–26; and see Malamat 1965; and Oppenheim's translations in *ANET*, pp. 556–557; and Borger 1984, p. 335.

(*ayaba*, 'Vast Sea')[138] he offered his great royal sacrifices,[139] and his troops cleansed themselves with water in the Ocean (*ayaba*). To the Cedar and Boxwood Mountain, the great mountains, he penetrated, and boxwood, cedar, cypress (or juniper?) and *elammakku* trees, these trees he felled. He stripped (the forest) bare (?),[140] established his name, and made known his might. He subjugated that land on the shore of the Ocean (*ayaba*). He made it obedient to his command; he caused it to follow him. He imposed a permanent tax upon them that they should bring their taxes to him regularly (i 34–iii 2).

The name of the god mentioned earlier in the inscription as the founder of Mari appears in the form of the cuneiform logogram AN, simply denoting divinity in both Sumerian and Akkadian. But in several of the copies of the inscription, the syllabically spelled variant *i-lu-um* appears, showing that the logogram is to be read as *ilum*. Now this term *ilum* can either signify the general Semitic concept for divinity or it can refer to a specific deity (despite its *-um* declension, which normally signifies a common noun)—El or Il. This latter well-known West Semitic god was chief of the pantheon at Ugarit which cultivated friendly ties with Mari, as we have previously seen. If we adopt the latter interpretation, as do several scholars,[141] we have here, in Yaḫdun-Lim's inscription, a clear West Semiticism in which the founder-god of the city of Mari was traditionally a West Semitic deity.

In dealing with this inscription many years ago, I touched upon this passage, and on the illuminating distinction between the two Akkadian words used here to designate the sea.[142] Twice we see the ordinary word for 'sea'—*tiamtum*/*tâmtum*, properly used in a secular, empirical aspect.[143] In contrast, the solemn term *ayaba* (spelled *a-a-ab-ba*/*a-ia-ba*), appearing three times, has a mythological colour to it, and is reminiscent of the Greek concept of *Oκεανος*, in both its mythological and its marine sense. In the

[138] Our translation, 'Vast Sea', is in accord with the apposition of [*t*]*a-ma-ti* DAGAL-*ti* to A.AB.BA in a Gilgameš fragment, and other sources; cf. Wiseman 1975, pp. 160–161, *l*. 38. In Hittite sources, too, the Mediterranean Sea is called 'Great Sea'.

[139] The text of col. ii: 10–11 is problematic, particularly the relationship of the adjective *rabiam*, which we have translated here as 'great', modifying 'sacrifice(s)' (similar to Dossin and *CAD* A/1, p. 221, s.v. *ajabba*). In Malamat 1965, we translated this phrase as 'multitude of royal sacrifices', which would call for an Akkadian adverbial form such as *rabiš*. In contrast, Oppenheim in *ANET*, p. 556a, translates the phrase as 'and offerred sacrifices to the Ocean as (befitting) his high royal rank', that is, he relates the adjective *rabiam* to the noun 'royal rank', rather than to 'sacrifice' (but he notes that 'the text is in disorder').

[140] Such a translation, in contrast to the more usual 'made a razzia (into the forest)' (cf. Dossin 1955 and *ANET*, p. 556a), was suggested to me by P. Artzi; and see below, n. 177.

[141] Dossin 1955, p. 25, favours the latter interpretation, as do de Vaux 1969, p. 508; and Lambert 1985, pp. 537–538, as well as others. On the other hand, Sollberger & Kupper 1971 regard the god here as Dagan, supreme deity of the Middle Euphrates region. Dalley 1979, p. 290, takes the god to be Itur-Mer, patron deity of Mari.

[142] See Malamat 1965. For the various terminological usages concerning the Mediterranean in later, neo-Assyrian sources, see Elayi 1984.

[143] The Hebrew cognate, *t*ᵉ*hōm*, however, occurs in the Bible only in mythological–poetical usage; cf., e.g., Job 28: 14; 38: 16, where it appears in parallel to *yām*.

El-Amarna Letters, too, *ayaba* appears several times to denote the Mediterranean Sea, particularly in the letters from the King of Byblos on the Syrian coast, and in a literary text (EA 340, which has escaped scholarly attention).[144]

The Akkadian phonetic spelling, *ayaba*, is most likely the equivalent of the Sumerogram A.AB.BA,[145] a somewhat obscure term often encountered in Sumero-Akkadian literature. It appears in the Akkadian lists of the 'Pantheon of Ugarit', and, significantly, in the parallel lists of the Ugaritic language its counterpart is Yamm, the West Semitic god of the sea.[146] In other words, several hundred years after Yaḫdun-Lim, the god bearing the West Semitic word for 'sea' as his name was identified at Ugarit with the Sumerogram A.AB.BA. Such an identity is also indicated, inter alia, by a personal name in an Akkadian text from Ugarit, written *Abdi*-A.AB.BA; this name was apparently pronounced Abdi-Yamm—and thus the element 'Yamm' appeared in names at Ugarit as well as at Mari.[147]

Now, one of the central themes in the comparative study of biblical literature and Ugaritic poetry relates to the motifs of the God of Israel and his conflict with the sea (and the daemonic creatures associated with it), on the one hand, and the myth of Yamm and his uprising against the other gods of Ugarit, on the other hand.[148] At Ugarit, Yamm plays a lofty role in the pantheon and is known by the epithets 'Prince' Yamm (*zbl ym*) and 'Judge Nahar' (*ṯpṭ nhr*; i.e. ruler of the river). He was the cosmic force of the raging waters, and this personification most probably originated in the character of the Mediterranean Sea, whose waters threaten the coast and occasionally inundate it.

Faint echoes of this concept, and numerous allusions to it, are found in poetic parts of the Bible, as well as more overtly in the talmudic literature. Thus, in Psalms 74: 13: 'Thou didst divide the sea (*yām*) by thy might; thou didst break the heads of the dragons on the waters'; or in Job 7: 12: 'Am I the sea (*yām*), or a sea monster, that thou settest a guard over

144 Noted by P. Artzi in a lecture at the Eighth World Congress of Jewish Studies, in Jerusalem, 1981; this literary text is very fragmentary (Knudtzon 1915, p. 954). Knudtzon gives the reading A.AB.BA in a note, but both he and Mercer 1939, p. 790, read *tâmtu* in EA 340: 6. Here, too, a royal (?), military campaign seems to be indicated.

145 Where it often refers to the Persian Gulf. For the term, see *CAD* A/1, p. 221, s.v. *ajabba*, where the difficulty of its being a loan from the Sumerian is noted. Cf. also Albright & Moran 1950, p. 167; Goetze 1955, p. 16, n. 58. Both Dossin 1955 and Oppenheim in *ANET*, p. 556, translate this word here as 'Ocean', in the mythical sense of the Greek epics.

146 See Nougayrol 1968, pp. 45 (*l.* 29) and 58; he reads the Sumerogram A.AB.BA as ^{d}*tâmtum*, but in his explanatory notes postulates the reading *yam(u)*; cf. Caquot *et al.* 1974, p. 110.

147 And compare the Ugaritic personal names *Ymy*, *Ymn*, *Ym-il*, etc.; cf. Gröndahl 1967, pp. 104, 144 and 316; for personal names with the element 'Yam' at Mari, cf. Huffmon 1965, p. 210. In this context, it is significant that personal names containing the Yamm element occur only from the Old Babylonian period onward; that is, beginning with the Amorites.

148 See Cassuto 1975, pp. 70 ff., and s.v. 'Prince of the Sea', p. 285. See also Day 1984; Kloos 1986.

me?'[149] The talmudic sages hinted at it in such words as 'When the Holy One, blessed be He, created the sea (*yām*), it went on expanding, until the Holy One, blessed be He, rebuked it and caused it to dry up.' (Babylonian Talmud, Hagigah 12, 1). And above all, this theme is to be seen in the talmudic appellation *śar šel yām*, 'prince of the sea', so reminiscent of 'Prince Yamm' at Ugarit.[150]

The extant material of the Ugaritic myth of Yamm,[151] which is too fragmentary to provide a full, continuous narrative, can be outlined briefly as follows: The god Yamm, called 'friend (*mdd*) of El' (El, as we have noted, was head of the Ugaritic pantheon), seeks majesty. El proclaims Yamm's majesty and promotes the building of his palace. Yamm's lofty aspirations are contested by Baal, Lord of Earth (and of fertility), who struggles with Yamm over hegemony. Eventually it is Baal who strikes the fateful, victorious blow. Two further stories, poorly preserved, are Yamm's contest with the goddess Anath, and his struggle against A<u>t</u>tr.[152] Also of special relevance to us is the inclusion of Yamm in two canonical lists of gods at Ugarit, recording recipients of sacrifices.[153] This demonstrates Yamm's integral position within the canonical pantheon at Ugarit.

Nor can we ignore two Egyptian legends from New Kingdom times, in which the sea deity bears the Canaanite appellation 'Yam'. This loan word appears in Late Egyptian, from the 18th dynasty (15th century BC) on as an alternative to the indigenous term *w3<u>d</u>-wr* (literally 'great green'), not only in mythological usage, but even in ordinary contexts.[154] One of these two legends is the 'Tale of Two Brothers',[155] in which Yam snatches a lock of hair from the head of the younger brother's wife. This part of the narrative takes place in the 'Valley of the Cedar (or Pine)', apparently in the Lebanon, more specifically in the Beqa' Valley.[156] Thus, we can assume that this Egyptian story was influenced by Canaanite mythology. In the second Egyptian story, the so-called Astarte Papyrus of the late 14th century BC, an actual Canaanite myth is to be found.[157] In this mere

[149] And see several notable instances in the prophetic literature, such as Isaiah 51: 9–10 and Jeremiah 5: 22; and in the Bible in general cf. Cross 1973, pp. 121 ff.

[150] See Cassuto 1975, p. 71.

[151] See Kaiser 1962; Loewenstamm 1980; and cf. Haussig 1965, pp. 98 ff., s.v. *Jamm*. For the reconstruction of the myth of Baal and Yamm, see Gibson 1978, pp. 37–45, and his glossary of Ugaritic, p. 148, s.v. *ym*.

[152] See Loewenstamm 1980, pp. 350, 354 ff.

[153] See Dietrich *et al.* 1976, I, 39: 13; 46: 6; and cf. Kaiser 1962, p. 58.

[154] Cf., besides Kaiser 1962, pp. 32 ff., and the references there; Erman & Grapow 1926, p. 78; Giveon 1980, pp. 242–243, s.v. *Jam* (Meer). Cf. also Faulkner 1962, s.v. *w3<u>d</u>-wr*, p. 56, where one form should probably be read *w3<u>d</u>-wr 'im* (!), that is, 'Great Green *Yam*'.

[155] Cf. Lichtheim 1976, pp. 203 ff.

[156] Cf. Gardiner 1933, p. 128.

[157] See Kaiser 1962, pp. 81 ff.; and especially Stadelmann 1967, pp. 125 ff.; and cf. Helck 1983.

fragment, Yam is ensnarled by Astarte's beauty, bringing him into conflict with her consort.[158]

It is in this light that we can return to the divine nature of the Mediterranean Sea in the Yaḫdun-Lim inscription from Mari, predating the Ugaritic and Egyptian evidence by about four centuries. The king (or rather, his scribes) heaps praise on his own 'unprecedented' campaign to the Mediterranean shore. The extraordinary encounter with the Mediterranean was accompanied by cultic ceremonies—the offering of sacrifices to the sea by the king, and the bathing of his troops in its waters in what was surely a cultic ritual—a sort of baptism. This latter nuance is presumably indicated also by the Akkadian verb employed, *ramākum*, meaning 'to cleanse' the entire body in water, especially in a ritual context.[159] The neo-Assyrian kings of the first millennium BC (such as Ashurnaṣirpal II and his son Shalmaneser III)[160] also recorded their arrivals on the Mediterranean coast: they too offered sacrifices at the seashore, though the deity so honoured was not the god of the sea, but 'the gods' in general, while their troops merely dipped their weapons into the water, symbolically purifying them, with no further ceremony.[161] Thus, Yaḫdun-Lim's description differs in certain essential details—in the deity involved and in the actual ritual use of the waters of the sea.

These descriptions are reminiscent of at least two episodes in classical or post-classical sources concerning seas—the Mediterranean and the Pontus. In the first episode, Herodotus (VII, 34 ff. and 54)[162] relates how, during the Persian actions against the Greeks in 480 BC, the bridges of ships crossing the Hellespont broke up and were scattered. Xerxes subsequently 'punished' the 'rebellious' sea, proclaiming that 'no man is to offer thee sacrifice, for thou art a turbid and briny river.' When the Persians were finally about to cross the straits, Xerxes brought incense and 'at sunrise poured a libation from a golden phial into the sea, praying to the sun that no accident should befall him' in his attempt to subdue Europe. This certainly echoes the belief that the Mediterranean Sea was a deity, or at least was conceived as having a divine nature. A seldom noted but intriguing passage from late antiquity reveals the tenacity of this cultic tradition. The Byzantine historian Procopius, in his *De bello persico* (II: xi, 1), describes

158 Kaiser 1962, pp. 38 and 90, even went so far as to postulate that the influence of the Canaanite myth of Yamm entered Egypt, apparently from Ugarit, already during the Middle Kingdom—that is, during the first quarter of the 2nd millennium BC (though he cites no actual proof in support).

159 Though the verb *ramākum* does mean 'wash', its ritualistic sense in certain contexts is indicated by the noun *rimkum*; cf. *AHw* II, p. 985: 'Bad[ekult], Ganzwaschung'. And note in particular the ritual series *bīt rimki*; Laessøe 1955.

160 Cf. their inscriptions, e.g., in *ANET*, pp. 276 ff.

161 It is not clear whether the ceremony took place prior to (as seems likely) or after the other events of the campaign, particularly the subjugation of the coastal population; that is, whether it was meant to assure success or was a sort of thanksgiving. See van Dijk 1973.

162 Herodotus 1922, pp. 349, 369–370.

how Chosroes, the Sassanian king, having taken Antioch from Justinian, went down to the Mediterranean shore and 'bathed himself alone in the sea water and after sacrificing to the sun and other such divinities, ... he went back.'[163]

Thus, we can conclude from Yaḫdun-Lim's inscription that already in the Mari period (and possibly earlier) the Mediterranean Sea was perceived as a divinity. This was undoubtedly based on early West Semitic–Canaanite concepts which find clear expression centuries later in the Ugaritic texts, on the one hand, and in the Egyptian stories, on the other hand, and are found still later in the biblical and talmudic traditions. The Canaanite concept of the divine nature of the Mediterranean Sea could well have taken hold at Mari (and, for that matter, at other Mesopotamian sites) at the time of its close ties with the West in general, and with such centres as Ugarit in particular.[164] Moreover, it has recently been suggested, rather boldly but reasonably, that the Babylonian Creation Epic, the *Enuma Eliš*, which describes the combat between the god Marduk and the primordial sea (in the person of Tiamat—*tᵉhōm* in Canaanite–Hebrew) is derived from the West—i.e. the Mediterranean coast, like the Ugaritic Yamm myth. The myth, it is held, spread from that region to Babylonia (and not vice versa!), apparently by means of the Amorites during the Old Babylonian period.[165]

The Sacred Forest

Many of the texts just discussed also reveal reverence for the extensive timber forests of the Lebanon, Anti-Lebanon and Amanus mountains in the west. It was especially the extraordinary properties of several species of wood to be obtained there—particularly cedar but also cypress or juniper, boxwood and *elammaku*—which drew the esteem of distant rulers in woodless lands, in both Mesopotamia and Egypt.[166] As usual with such exotic

[163] Procopius 1914, pp. 350–351.

[164] See above, pp. 57ff.; and the numerous references to Ugarit in *ARMT* XXIII, pp. 457 ff. and *ARMT* XXV, index, p. 247, s.v. Ugarit. Yarim-Lim, king of Yamḫad, apparently somehow also participated in Zimri-Lim's expedition to Ugarit (see above, p. 59); and he, too, may have brought sacrifices to the Mediterranean Sea (cf. *ARMT* XXIII, p. 473).

[165] See Jacobsen 1968, pp. 104–108. Charpin & Durand 1986, p. 174, refer to an unpublished Mari document indicating an early western tradition of the Yamm myth, according to which Adad (of Aleppo) had wielded a weapon against the (Mediterranean?) Sea. On the importance of Adad of Aleppo, and his widespread popularity, see Klengel 1965b.

[166] See Mikesell 1969; Klengel 1967. For Egypt, see also Giveon 1980. The challenge posed by the mountains of the west is well reflected in a cynical passage in the letter of king Hattušili III to Adadnirari I of Assyria, after the latter had annexed the land of Ḫanigalbat (the earlier Mittanni): '... verily, you have become a "Great King" ... but what are you talking about, of inspecting Mount Amanus?' Thus, a 'Great King' was presumed to have the prerogative of visiting the Cedar Mountains in the West. See Forrer 1928, pp. 262–263.

goods, their possession became symbolic of wealth and prestige.[167]

It is thus no wonder that Yaḫdun-Lim's Foundation Inscription should place such special emphasis on the mountains of the West and on the several specific species of wood which he obtained there. These woods are typical of the Amanus range in coastal northern Syria, no less than in the more southern Lebanon and Anti-Lebanon mountains.[168] Two principal kinds of wood in this inscription even lent their names to their mountains—'the Mountain of Cedar (*erēnum*) and Boxwood (*taskarinnum*)'.[169] While 'Cedar Mountain'[170] is often applied to the Amanus, Mount Lebanon and Mount Hermon (or Sirion), the Amanus is specifically denoted the 'Boxwood Mountain' in the Annals of Tiglath-pileser III (line 127). Thus, the Amanus (rather than Mount Lebanon) may have been intended in Yaḫdun-Lim's inscription.

Although there is no express association of boxwood with the Lebanon region in the sources, the other three woods are so attested. They can also be associated with the three kinds of timber ascribed to Mount Lebanon in the Bible: Hiram furnished Solomon with *'ᵃrāzīm*, 'cedars', and *bᵉrōšīm*, usually translated 'cypress' but actually juniper (see below, p. 114 and n. 176) for the Temple in Jerusalem (MT 1 Kings 5:22–24), as well as *'algummīm* (MT 2 Chronicles 2:7) or, preferably, *'almuggīm* (1 Kings 10:11–12), which corresponds to the Akkadian *elammakum*, noted above. This Akkadian and Hebrew evidence for *elammakum/'almuggīm* in the Mountains of Syria, together with the occurrence of *'almg* in the Ugaritic texts, precludes its earlier definition as sandalwood, a material imported from India.[171]

The biblical *bᵉrōš* is akin to the *šurmēnum* tree of Yaḫdun-Lim's inscription, which corresponds with *šurbīnā/šurbānā*, a tree found in Aramaic sources.[172] Thus, the Aramaic Targum of the Song of Solomon 1:17 and 3:15 renders one of the trees of Lebanon as *šurbīnā*, and the Peshitta specifically translates *bᵉrōš* in 1 Kings 5:22 as *šarvainā*. Further, in the ḪAR-*ra*=*ḫubullu* lexical text (XXII: 6′–7′), the list of mountains equates KUR *La-ab-na-nu* ('Mount Lebanon') with MIN (=ditto) *šur*-[*me-ni*] ('*Šur*-

167 King Solomon's fame and wealth are underscored in the Bible by the descriptions of his obtaining many of the same exotic woods as Yaḫdun-Lim; see 1 Kings 5:22–24 (MT); 10:11–12 ('. . . no such almug wood has come or been seen to this day'). For further prestige objects see Elat 1979, pp. 179 ff.

168 See Mikesel 1969; Rowton 1967; Mayer 1967.

169 Rowton 1967 has assumed that two different mountains are intended.

170 *CAD* E, s.v. *erēnu* A; in the Baal Epic from Ugarit (II, vi, 18 ff.), trees from Lebanon and cedars from Sirion were used in constructing Baal's mansion, even though Ugarit is much closer to the sources of cedar in the Amanus range.

171 Cf. both Akkadian dictionaries which, however, do not specify the wood intended: *CAD* E, p. 75; and *AHw*, p. 196, s.v. *elammaku*. Thompson 1949, p. 300, still took it as sandalwood. For further references, see Salonen 1963, pp. 215–216. The *almog* wood in 1 Kings 10:11–12, seemingly imported from Ophir, remains problematic and is probably intrusive there. Cf., e.g., Greenfield & Mayrhofer 1967, pp. 86–89.

172 Cf. Zimmern 1914, p. 53; Löw 1924, pp. 28–29. Cf. also Paul 1968, p. 183.

mēnu mountain'), immediately preceded by KUR *Ṣi-ra-a* (var. *Si-ra-a-ra*) = MIN [MIN (=*erinni*)], 'Mount Sirion (Anti-Lebanon) = Cedar Mountain'.[173]

The existence of cedar and *šurmēnu* trees on Mount Lebanon and in the Anti-Lebanon range is attested in the inscriptions of Ashurnaṣirpal II, Esarhaddon and Ashurbanipal, as well.[174] Ashurnaṣirpal II, in his Annals (iii: 89), states that he cut down cedar, *šurmēnum* and *burāšum* trees, among others, in the Amanus. In the Bible, Isaiah also testifies to the contiguity of cedar and *b^erōš* on Mount Lebanon: 'The *b^erōšīm* ("junipers") rejoice at you, the cedars of Lebanon: "Since you were laid low, no hewer comes against us"' (Isaiah 14: 8); 'I have gone up the heights of the mountains, to the far recesses of Lebanon; I felled its polished cedars, its choicest junipers' (37: 24; 2 Kings 19: 23). These passages, reminiscent of the phraseology of the neo-Assyrian royal inscriptions (and perhaps adapted from them) and the strong desire to exploit the choice woods, are indeed ascribed by Isaiah to Sargon II and Sennacherib, respectively.[175] Both Hebrew *b^erōš* and Akkadian *šurmēnum* (Aramaic *šurbīnā*) are generally identified with the cypress, but this was a rare tree in the Lebanon and altogether absent in the Anti-Lebanon. Therefore, they were more probably of the juniper family, which thrived alongside the cedar in the mountains of Lebanon, Hermon and Amanus.[176]

Yaḫdun-Lim's actions, after cutting down the trees, are not at all clear, but they were presumably connected with the commemoration of his campaign to the Mediterranean coast (see above, pp. 107ff.). He does not explain exactly how he perpetuated his heroic achievements; however, the records of the campaigns of Sargon the Great, Šamši-Adad I and other kings who reached the same coast strongly suggest the erection of a victory

[173] See Landsberger 1974, p. 23, *ll.* 9–10. Identical equations appear in the so-called *Lipšur* Litanies (Type I, *11.* 8–9); see Reiner 1956, pp. 132–133 and 146.

[174] See Luckenbill 1926, §538; Luckenbill 1927, §§697, 914 and 979, translating *šurmēnu* as Cypress. The Mari documents, too, indicate that *šurmēnum* wood was brought from Central Syria (i.e. the Qatna region); cf. *ARMT* I 7: 4–5.

[175] See Machinist 1983, pp. 723 ff.

[176] Löw 1924, pp. 15 and 33 ff., already discussed the identification of *b^erōš* with *Juniperus*; cf. also *HAL*, s.v. *b^erōš*. The botanist Zohary (1954) defined it more precisely as *Juniperus excelsa*. Finally, Landsberger suggested that its Akkadian counterpart, *burāšum*, is actually *Juniperus* (cf. *AHw*, p. 139). *CAD* B, p. 190, s.v. *burāšu*, identifies it as *Juniperus oxycedrus*. Thus, should we not also consider the *šurmēnu/šurbīnā* as a type of juniper rather than as a cypress, as generally accepted? This is also put forth as an alternative in Dalman 1922, s.v. *šurbīnā*, and in Brockelmann 1928, p. 205, s.v. *šarvainā* (Juniperus oxycedrus). The question, of course, remains as to which Akkadian term represents the cypress. Already in the pre-Sargonic palace at Mari (3rd millennium BC), the excavations revealed remains of wood which, after botanical examination, was defined as cedar from the Lebanon, indicating very early ties with the West; cf. Parrot 1965, p. 20.

stele at some prominent spot in the 'Great Mountains'.[177] But whether he left his inscription on a statue or on a bas-relief on some mountain cliff remains unknown. There are many references to commemorative stelae erected in connection with campaigns to the Mediterranean, and to the conquest of adjacent mountain regions. It is most illuminating, typologically, to compare Yaḫdun-Lim's inscription with other accounts of campaigns to the West: Ashurnaṣirpal II in his Annals; the throne-base inscription of Shalmaneser III from Nimrud; and the inscription of Adadnirari III's campaign to the Lebanon.[178] Only Yaḫdun-Lim, after relating his march to the Mediterranean Sea and the extraction of tribute, explicitly describes the feat of felling trees and also commemorates his royal prowess.

Ashurnasirpal recounts how he conquered Mount Lebanon and then went down to the Mediterranean shore, cleansed his weapons in the waters and offered sacrifices to the gods (as noted above, p. 111). After describing the tribute received from the Phoenician sea-ports, he relates how he went up into the Amanus range and hewed various kinds of wood, erecting there a stele in praise of his mighty deeds (Annals iii: 89). Shalmaneser III also went 'to the sea of the land of Amurru', purified his weapons, erected a stele and, after receiving tribute from the coastal kings, 'went up to Mount Amanus; I cut logs of cedar and juniper (*burāšum*); I set up on Mount Amanus a stele of myself as king.'[179]

In concluding the description of his campaign, Yaḫdun-Lim stresses his control of the coastal region and imposition of a tribute. Surprisingly, though Yaḫdun-Lim's description is much more detailed than the references to Sargon's campaigns, he makes no explicit mention of the name of the land or people conquered. Accordingly, the historicity of the campaign might be challenged, particularly since there is no corroborative evidence in the Mari archives, such as a date formula pertaining to his reign.[180]

Such arguments, however, hardly carry sufficient weight to discredit the specific testimony of the Foundation Inscription. Quite the contrary, the

[177] Thus we cannot accept the usual translation of the difficult phrase *ḫamūṣam iḫmuṣ* (Foundation Inscription, ii: 19) as 'il fit un grand carnage' (Dossin 1955, p. 14), nor von Soden's 'er plünderte gründlich' (*AHw*, p. 315)—which takes the unusual form *ḫamūṣam* as a Canaanite inf. abs. The ordinary meaning for *ḫamāṣum* in the G stem is 'to remove by force', 'to strip' (*CAD* Ḫ, p. 60). Thus, we take it to refer to the clearance or stripping of an area of trees in order to erect a stele (so that it could be seen from afar; cf. n. 140). Or perhaps the smoothing of the rock is intended, preparatory to carving an inscription there. For the Canaanite shift ā > ō in *ḫamūṣam* (<*ḫamāṣam*), see Moscati 1964, p. 48. However, this form is taken as an Assyrianism in the D stem by Hirsch 1967, p. 19, and thus would not be one of the earliest indications for the ā/ō shift; that is, for the appearance of the Canaanite language. But then these two twin verbal forms would belong to two different stems (D and G). See now Durand 1987b, p. 45, for a new interpretation of the above phrase, referring *per se* 'to erecting a stele'.

[178] For Adadnirari's campaign, see Tadmor 1973, pp. 142 ff.; Borger 1984, p. 368; for the other kings, cf. above, n. 160.

[179] See Hulin 1963, pp. 51–52, *ll.* 18–22.

[180] Cf. the list of Yaḫdun-Lim's year formulae, in Dossin 1950, p. 52.

erudition displayed concerning the nature of the Syrian forests would strongly support its authenticity. Yaḫdun-Lim could, of course, have acquired this knowledge through the special relations then prevailing between the Mari dynasty and the land and rulers of Yamḫad in northern Syria (see above, pp. 54ff.). Nevertheless, Yaḫdun-Lim's inscription includes several other authentic elements which recur in accounts of much later campaigns (see above, p. 115). It would thus be difficult to assume that such elements are mere figments of the imgination, or plagiarism, for there is no known earlier document even similarly resembling the contents of this inscription. Moreover, Yaḫdun-Lim's Foundation Inscription continues with an account of an organised uprising by three kinglets in the region of the bend of the Euphrates—'in the very same year' as his Mediterranean venture (iii: 3 ff.; and see above, pp. 107f.). This would suit the circumstances of a king and his army being off on an expedition to remote regions, a situation in which vassals, grasping an opportune moment, could have sought autonomy.[181]

We therefore conclude that Yaḫdun-Lim actually did carry out a military campaign to the Mediterranean coast, though it should be regarded as an ephemeral episode which left behind few permanent traces. Mariote economic activity with the coast—flourishing under successive reigns at Mari—was apparently well established by Yaḫdun-Lim's time.[182]

The Lebanon, Gilgameš and a Hebrew Psalm

Despite Yaḫdun-Lim's boast, he was not the first Mesopotamian ruler to reach the Mediterranean shore. Sargon, king of Akkad (mid-24th century BC) already reached A.AB.BA, the Mediterranean Sea, and had even sailed ships on it; but unlike our information on Yaḫdun-Lim, our data on Sargon the Great is based on later and indirect sources.[183] Naram-Sin (c. 2291–2255 BC), Sargon's grandson, also led a campaign to Northern Syria as far as the coast, as is described in (an Old Babylonian copy of) his inscription.[184] Boasting of his 'unprecedented' feat, he specifically names the Cedar Moun-

[181] They may well have received their punishment when Yaḫdun-Lim and his army returned to Mari. The only two published *letters* in the Mari archives from the reign of Yaḫdun-Lim witness his political influence in and suzerainty over western areas adjacent to Carchemish and Yamḫad (*ARMT* I, 1–2). Further, according to one of his year formula (Dossin 1950, p. 52, No. 4), Yaḫdun-Lim defeated Emar, the important town on the great bend of the Euphrates, on the main road from Mari to the Levant coast (see above, p. 64 and map, p. 65.).

[182] For trade between Mari and the Levant coast, see Dossin 1939a, p. 111 (with reference particularly to Byblos); and Limet 1985 (Byblos, Ugarit, Crete and inland cities); for a general study of foreign trade at Mari, see Cornelius 1985.

[183] See Malamat 1965, pp. 365–367, and the apparatus there; and see Gadd 1971, pp. 417–434. In the continuation of this inscription, Sargon claims that Dagan at Tuttul promised him dominion over the 'Upper Country': 'Mari, Yarmuti and Ebla, as far as the Cedar Forest (i.e. the Amanus) and the Silver Mountain (i.e. the Taurus)'.

[184] Hirsch 1963, pp. 73 ff. (b5, col. I: 22–27; col. II: 25–27); and Foster 1982, pp. 29 ff.

tain in the West as the Amanus (again in contrast to Yaḫdun-Lim).[185] No less significant is one of Naram-Sin's year formulae (appearing in a recent published economic text):[186] 'The year when Naram-Sin conquered [unintelligible GN] and personally (?) felled cedars in Mount Lebanon ([KUR *La-a*]*b-na-an*)'. This is the earliest clear historical mention of the name 'Lebanon'.[187]

Only a few years after Yaḫdun-Lim's expedition, perhaps even under its influence, his footsteps were followed by Šamši-Adad I, king of Assyria. This campaign took place after Mari and its territories on the Middle Euphrates had already fallen under Assyrian control. Unlike Yaḫdun-Lim's relatively detailed account, notable for its excellent historiographical presentation, the description of Šamši-Adad's expedition is confined to a laconic notice appended to a building inscription of a temple dedicated to Enlil at Ashur.[188] After noting tribute received from the land of Tukriš and the king of the 'Upper Country',[189] Šamši-Adad states: 'I established my great name and my (victory) steles in the land of Lebanon (*ma-a-at La-ab-a-an*[ki]) on the shore of the "Great Ocean"' (rev. iv: 12–18).[190] Here, then, we read of an explicit name for the land to which the king had marched and where he erected his stele.[191] Although the spelling of the toponym is somewhat unusual, it certainly refers to the land of the Lebanon on the Mediterranean coast. This reference, then, is more or less contemporaneous with the mention of Mount Lebanon and Sirion in literary texts extant from or composed in the Old Babylonian period.[192] Here, in Šamši-

185 The suggestion to read *Na-ab*-NUM before Amnanum, and to identify it with the Lebanon, as proposed in *CAD* G, p. 25b, is unacceptable; see, e.g., the reading in Foster 1982, p. 29, II: 23–25 (the proposal was derived from Landsberger).

186 I am indebted to Joan and Aage Westenholz for drawing my attention to this source from the Ekur archive at Nippur; see Westenholz 1987, p. 41 (text 1b iv: 6–7).

187 Since the reference to Lebanon at Ebla remains doubtful. See Pettinato 1980, p. 238, *ll.* 8–9: KUR *La-ba-na-an*, in a campaign of king Enna-Dagan (of Ebla or Mari).

188 Cf. Ebeling *et al.* 1926, pp. 24–25. For the inscription, see Borger 1961, pp. 14–15; *ANET*, p. 274; Grayson 1972, pp. 20–21.

189 One of the rulers in the 'Upper Country', surely one of those who presented the tribute, was Abi-Samar who, as a vassal of Yaḫdun-Lim (see above, n. 180), sought his protection against the intrigues of Šamši-Adad I (*ARMT* I 1). When the kingdom of Mari fell to Šamši-Adad, its dependents also passed under Assyrian domination.

190 For the inscription, see above, n. 188. 'Lebanon' there appears in a shortened form and is designated a land (*mātum*), and not a mountain (with the ambiguous determinative KUR).

191 Grayson 1972, p. 21, n. 65, negates the historicity of this campaign: 'In view of the presence of important Amorite states in Syria at this time, a military conquest of this region by Shamshi-Adad is out of the question'—a rather enigmatic and difficult assumption.

192 See below. The ḪAR-*ra* = *ḫubullu* lexical text and the *Lipšur* Litanies (see above, n. 173) are preserved only in later copies though they probably originated in the Old Babylonian period; see Reiner 1956, p. 131. In an Assyrian 'Dream-Book' having Old Babylonian forerunners, the Lebanon is also mentioned, again in the shortened form found in the Šamši-Adad I inscription; see Oppenheim 1956, p. 312 (Sm 29 + 79-7-8, 94): *La-ba-an*[ki]. Oppenheim prefers locating this GN in Babylonia (p. 268, n. 36), but, as we have already pointed out (Malamat 1960, p. 16, n. 19), its identification with the Lebanon is surely more appropriate.

Adad's inscription, the Mediterranean is referred to specifically as the 'Great Ocean' (A.AB.BA *rabītum*)—a term later used widely in the Assyrian inscriptions. A parallel term also appears frequently in the Bible, nearly always in precise geographical contexts (cf. Numbers 34: 6–7; Joshua 1: 4; Ezekiel 47: 15). Particularly illuminating is Joshua 9: 1: 'All along the coast of the Great Sea (*hayyām haggādōl*) toward Lebanon'. This Canaanite–Hebrew expression is even borrowed into Late Egyptian. In the tale of Wen-Amon (i: 8, 49), we find the Mediterranean Sea denoted 'the great sea (*p3 ym '3*) of the land of Kharu (i.e. Canaan)'.

From the formulation of his text, it is not clear whether Šamši-Adad erected a statue (or stele) or cut an inscription on a rock-face; neither is it clear whether it was situated by the sea or at some dominant spot in the mountains. The remains of such reliefs and inscriptions of various rulers (later Egyptian, neo-Assyrian and neo-Babylonian) can still be seen near the mouth of the Dog River (Nahr el-Kalb), south of Byblos, as well as at Wadi Brissa (Nebuchadnezzar II) in Mount Lebanon, which descends eastward toward the Beqa' valley. Shalmaneser III tells of erecting stelae both on the sea-coast and in Mount Lebanon.[193]

In the light of these royal campaigns to the mountain forests of the West, we can hardly ignore the tradition reflected in the Gilgameš Epic concerning the adventures of the protagonist, accompanied by his boon companion Enkidu, in the forests of the Cedar Mountain. Typologically and geographically, this epic is most interesting. The heroic pair penetrated the depths of the cedar forest and cut down the sacred cedar, which was guarded by Huwawa the ogre.[194] After slaying Ḫuwawa, they set out to hew the trees of the forest. A recurrent phrase in this part of the epic is 'My hand I will poise and will fell the cedars, a name that endures I will make for me.'[195] This is clearly paralleled by the self-lauditory commemorations by Yaḫdun-Lim and Šamši-Adad (and others) and the recording of their exploits in the cedar mountains. But whereas the perpetuation of Gilgameš's deeds is epic in nature, in the royal inscriptions it rests on an historical plane. In both cases, of course, bold expeditions to obtain exotic woods are narrated.

The most interesting point in the Gilgameš Epic, as far as we are concerned here, is found in an Old Babylonian fragment hinting at the location

193 This last fact remained unknown until the discovery of a new recension of Šalmanesser III's annals; cf. Safar 1951, pp. 3 ff.; Michel 1954–59, pp. 38–39. The word *ṣalmum*, used in the inscriptions discussed above, can mean either a statue or a rock relief (with inscription); cf. *CAD* Ṣ, pp. 78 ff., s.v. *ṣalmu*. For the above noted stelae and inscriptions, see Malamat 1965, pp. 371–372.

194 See the Gilgameš Epic, Tablets III–V (E. A. Speiser, in *ANET*, pp. 79–83). The distinction between the sacred cedar which Gilgameš first chopped down and the other trees of the forest, which he felled only after slaying Ḫuwawa, appears in a single tablet from Old Babylonian times (for which see below, n. 196). For the relationship between Gilgameš and Ḫuwawa, cf. Shaffer 1983.

195 See, e.g., Thompson 1930, pp. 27–28, Tablet III, v: 6–7: *qātī luškunma luksuma ^{giš}erēnam šuma ša dārû anāku luštaknam.*

of the cedar forest.[196] There, we read of 'Saria (=Sirion, Anti-Lebanon) and Lebanon[197] which trembled at Ḫuwawa's "word"'. Thus, according to the Old Babylonian recension of the epic, the two heroes went forth from Uruk to the cedar forests in the Lebanon mountains and to the Valley of the Lebanon.[198]

As we have already noted, Sirion and Lebanon are mentioned together in various sources: the Gilgameš Epic; the lexical series ḪAR-*ra* = *ḫubullu*; the *Lipšur* Litanies; and later, the Ugaritic texts,[199] as well as a Mari text of the Šamši-Adad period.[200] The pair also appears in biblical poetry, most significantly in Psalm 29, which is of a distinctly Canaanite tenor, if not Canaanite derivation.[201] In the Israelite rendition of the theme, it is Yahwe who holds sway over the cedar mountains, and in vss. 5–6, a motif similar to that in the Old Babylonian Gilgameš fragment is seen:[202] 'The voice of the Lord breaks cedars; the Lord shatters the cedars of Lebanon, He makes Lebanon skip like a calf; Sirion like a young wild ox.'[203] Here, as in Gilgameš, the cedar forest is perceived as sacred, as it is in Psalms 104: 16: 'The trees of the Lord . . . the cedars of Lebanon which he planted.'

A common motif is to be found in the stripping of the forest bare of trees—linking Psalm 29 not only with the Gilgameš Epic but notably with

[196] Discovered at Ishchali and published in Bauer 1957. Cf. *ANET*, pp. 504–505; and see Tigay 1982, p. 78 and nn. 12, 19.

[197] The reading here is *Sa-ri-a* and *La-ab-na-an*. The former is mentioned at about the same period in the Egyptian Execration Texts (E 30—*s3ynw*—Posener 1940, p. 80). Note also the listing of various names for the Anti-Lebanon in Deuteronomy 3: 9 (ascribing use of the toponym Sirion to the Sidonians).

[198] The same can be said of the Hittite version, in which the heroes pass the Euphrates on their route, offering a sacrifice on the river bank. See Kammenhuber 1967, p. 50. Gilgameš's westward journey can also be inferred from the reference to a table used by him, made of *elammakum* (i.e. a Syrian) wood; see Greenfield & Mayrhofer 1967, p. 87, n. 7; and possibly even from the very name of Huwawa, which might be related to Kubaba (or Cybele), the deity worshipped in later times in the Amanus region, Cilicia and Lydia; cf. Hawkins & Bittel 1980–83.

[199] See above, n. 170; Loretz 1984, pp. 111–126; and Fisher 1972, p. 248; Fisher 1975, pp. 333–334.

[200] See the abstract of D. Charpin's lecture at the AOS Meeting at Los Angeles, March 1987; according to a still unpublished Mari document from the time of Šamši-Adad, troops from Mari went to Qatna, reached the Mediterranean coast and then proceeded from Mount Lebanon (*Labnan*) to Mount Sirion (*Sariah*).

[201] The strong Canaanite influence in this psalm, in the light of the Ugaritic, was first pointed out by Ginsberg 1935; and see Dahood 1966, pp. 175 ff. For the recent voluminous literature on Psalm 29, consult Cunchillos 1976; Seybold 1980; Loretz 1984; and Kloos 1986.

[202] For the connection between the Gilgameš fragment and Psalm 29 (which I noted soon after the initial publication of the fragment), see Lipiński 1971, pp. 18 ff.; Stolz 1972, where the sacred character of the cedar forest is noted. Cf. also Cunchillos 1976, pp. 86 ff.

[203] NJPS and various modern commentators; older translations, such as the RSV, and numerous commentaries, conform with the MT division of the text: 'He makes them skip like a calf, Lebanon and Sirion. . . .' The new translation is based on the seminal discovery of Ginsberg 1935, p. 474, of the enclitic *m* in Ugaritic, which also penetrated into Biblical Hebrew. Thus, the *-ēm* in *wayyarqīdēm* (v. 6) would not designate the accusative suffix, but the emphatic verbal form.

Yaḫdun-Lim's Foundation Inscription. Psalms 29:9 reads: 'The voice of the Lord makes the *'ylwt* whirl and strips the forest bare.' The crux here is, of course, the word *'ylwt*, vowel pointed in the MT as *'ayyālōt*, 'hinds'. Such a reading, however, seems awkward and ignores the internal parallelism of the verse. Thus, we would accept emendations of the pointing, read *'ēlōt*, 'oaks', 'mighty trees'.[204]

During Yaḫdun-Lim's campaign to the Mediterranean coast, 'he entered into the Cedar- and Boxwood-Mountains, the great mountains . . . he felled the trees and stripped (the forest) bare,[205] (thus) established his fame and proclaimed his power' (ii, 15–21). If our reading here is accepted, this inscription represents another significant parallel to Psalm 29, where it is God (rather than a mortal king) who achieves the deed.

Another theme common to Psalm 29 and Yaḫdun-Lim's inscription is the 'mighty waters', apparently originally referring to the stormy Mediterranean Sea. In the psalm, this theme is expressed in two verses encompassing the cedar forest pericope: verse 3 reads: 'The voice of the Lord is over the waters (*mayīm*) . . . over the mighty waters (*mayīm rabbīm*)', while according to verse 10: 'the Lord sat enthroned at the Flood (*mabbūl*);[206] the Lord sits enthroned, king for ever.' Here, too, the mythical, primordial waters are associated with the stripping of the (sacred) forests.

A final element emphasised in all three sources—the Gilgameš Epic, Yaḫdun-Lim's Foundation Inscription and Psalm 29—is the perpetuation of the protagonist's name.[207] Actually, it is this latter feature which is the *raison d'être* of all such texts. Psalm 29 is indeed replete with motifs of great antiquity and, regardless of the date of composition of the Hebrew psalm as such, it derives from traditions harking back beyond Late Bronze Age Ugarit, to Old Babylonian (or rather Amorite) times.

It was suggested some time ago that the Sumerian prototype of the epic concerning the expedition of Gilgameš and Enkidu against Ḫuwawa (known as 'Gilgameš and the Land of the Living') was inspired by the extensive campaigns of Sargon the Great to the West.[208] Even if this were accepted,

[204] The latter translation is from Kloos 1986, pp. 38, 41. The emendation was suggested as early as the mid-18th century, in Lowth 1753, p. xxvii.

[205] For the phrase *ḫamūṣam iḫmuṣ*, see above, n. 117; and cf. Malamat 1965, p. 369a on the commemoration of Yaḫdun-Lim's fame.

[206] *Mabbūl* here is the only occurrence in the Bible outside the Flood Story and remains problematic. It has been interpreted by J. N. Epstein (1941, p. 82) as 'throne', while, e.g., B. Margulis (1970) emends it to read *lmlk* (verb) or *lmšl*. But the lexeme most likely refers to the flood or Ocean; see Kloos 1986, pp. 62 ff., where the *mabbūl* is believed to be the source of the fructifying rains sent down by Yahwe (p. 93). The word may also occur at Ebla, where the bilingual equation A-KUL (Sumerian, 'heavy [or, preferably, 'mighty'] water') = *ma-ba-lum*. See Gordon 1987, p. 28.

[207] In Psalms 29:2, it is termed *k^{e}ḇōd š^{e}mō*, for which see Kloos: 1986, pp. 23 ff., 256 ff.; and cf. Weinfeld 1984, pp. 23 ff. For further details on the Amorite background of this psalm, see Malamat 1988b.

[208] See Matouš 1960, p. 92; as well as Afanasjeva 1964. See also Matouš 1964, where various views are noted, holding that this epic echoes the campaigns of kings of the Third Dynasty at Ur. And see Tigay 1982, pp. 34–35.

there is nothing in the extant traditions relating to Sargon which could have served as the source of the specific reference to the Lebanon region as it appears in the Old Babylonian version of the epic. Thus, we may suggest that this part of the Gilgameš Epic crystallized under the stimulus of the western campaigns of such kings as Yaḫdun-Lim and Šamši-Adad in the Old Babylonian period, expeditions which doubtless were a source of inspiration to poets and narrators alike.

ABBREVIATIONS

AAAS	*Annales archéologiques arabes syriennes*
AbB	*Altbabylonische Briefe*, Leiden
AfO	*Archiv für Orientforschung*
AHw	W. von Soden, *Akkadisches Handwörterbuch*, I–III Wiesbaden, 1965–81
AIPHOS	*Annuaire de l'Institut de Philologie et d'Histoire Orientales et Slaves*
ANEP	J. B. Pritchard, *The Ancient Near East in Pictures*^{2}, Princeton, 1955
ANET	J. B. Pritchard, *Ancient Near Eastern Tests Relating to the Old Testament*^{3}, Princeton, 1969
AnOr	*Analecta Orientalia*
ArOr	*Archiv Orientálni*
AOAT	*Alter Orient und Altes Testament*
ARET	*Archivi Reali di Ebla Testi*
ARMT	*Archives royales de Mari: Transcrite et Traduite* (see *ARMT* list p. 124)
AS	*Assyriological Studies*
BA	*Biblical Archaeologist*
BaM	*Baghdader Mitteilungen*
BAR	*Biblical Archaeologist Review*
BASOR	*Bulletin of the American Schools of Oriental Research*
BDB	F. Brown, S. R. Driver, C. A. Briggs, *A Hebrew and English Lexicon of the Old Testament*, Oxford, repr. 1959
BiOr	*Bibliotheca Orientalis*
BZ	*Biblische Zeitschrift*
BZAW	*Beihefte zur Zeitschrift für die alttestamentliche Wissenschaft*
CAD	*Chicago Assyrian Dictionary*
CAH	*Cambridge Ancient History*^{3}, I–II, Cambridge, 1970–75
CRAIBL	*Comptes-rendus de l'Académie des Inscriptions et Belles Lettres*
DBS	*Dictionnaire biblique Supplément*
EAEHL	M. Avi-Yonah, E. Stern (eds.), *Encyclopaedia of Archaeological Excavations in the Holy Land*, Jerusalem, 1975–78
EI	*Eretz-Israel*
EJ	*Encyclopaedia Judaica*, Jerusalem, 1971
ETL	*Ephemerides Theologicae Lovanienses*
GGA	*Göttingische gelehrte Anzeigen*
HAL	L. Köhler, W. Baumgartner, J. J. Stamm, *Hebräisches und aramäisches Lexikon zum Alten Testament*^{3}, Leiden, 1967–00
HAT	W. Gesenius, F. Buhl, *Handwörterbuch über das Alte Testament*^{17}, Leipzig, 1921
HTR	*Harvard Theological Review*

HUCA	*Hebrew Union College Annual*
IEJ	*Israel Exploration Journal*
IOS	*Israel Oriental Studies*
JANES	*Journal of the Ancient Near Eastern Society (Columbia University)*
JAOS	*Journal of the American Oriental Society*
JBL	*Journal of Biblical Literature*
JCS	*Journal of Cuneiform Studies*
JEA	*Journal of Egyptian Archaeology*
JESHO	*Journal of the Economic and Social History of the Orient*
JJS	*Journal of Jewish Studies*
JNES	*Journal of Near Eastern Studies*
JNSL	*Journal of Northwest Semitic Languages*
JSS	*Journal of Semitic Studies*
JTS	*Journal of Theological Studies*
KAI	H. Donner, W. Röllig (eds.), *Kanaanäische und aramäische Inschriften,* I–III, Wiesbaden, 1962–64
LÄ	W. Helck, E. Otto (eds.), *Lexikon der Ägyptologie*, Wiesbaden, 1975–1986
MARI	*Mari Annales Recherches Interdisciplinairés*
MSL	B. Landsberger, *Materialien zum Sumerischen Lexikon*, Roma
N.A.B.U.	*Nouvelles Assyriologiques Brèves et Utilitaires*
NJPS	*A New Translation of the Holy Scriptures*, The Jewish Publication Society (one volume edition), Philadelphia, 1985
OA	*Oriens Antiquus*
OLA	*Orientalia Lovaniensia Analecta*
OLP	*Orientalia Lovaniensia Periodica*
OLZ	*Orientalistische Literaturzeitung*
RA	*Revue d'Assyriologie*
RAI	*Rencontre Assyriologique Internationale*
RB	*Revue biblique*
RÉS	*Revue des Études sémitiques*
RHPR	*Revue d'Histoire et de Philosophie Religieuses*
RLA	E. Ebeling, B. Meissner ... D. O. Edzard (eds.), *Reallexikon der Assyriologie*, Berlin—New York, 1928–00
RSO	*Rivista degli Studi Orientali*
RSV	*Revised Standard Version*
SEL	*Studi Epigrafici e Linguistici*
SVT	*Supplements Vetus Testamentum*
THAT	E. Jenni, C. Westermann (eds.), *Theologisches Handwörterbuch zum Alten Testament*, München—Zürich, 1971–76
TUAT	O. Kaiser (ed.), *Texte aus der Umwelt des Alten Testament*, Gütersloh, 1981–00
TWAT	G. J. Botterweck, H. Ringgren, H.-J. Fabry (eds.), *Theologisches Wörterbuch zum Alten Testament*, Stuttgart, 1973–00
TZ	*Theologische Zeitschrift*
UF	*Ugarit-Forschungen*
VDI	*Vestnik Drevnei Istorii*
VT	*Vetus Testamentum*
WO	*Welt des Orients*
WZKM	*Wiener Zeitschrift für die Kunde des Morgenlandes*
ZA	*Zeitschrift für Assyriologie*
ZAW	*Zeitschrift für die alttestamentliche Wissenschaft*

ZDMG	*Zeitschrift der Deutschen Morgenländischen Gesellschaft*
ZDPV	*Zeitschrift des Deutschen Palästina-Vereins*
ZTK	*Zeitschrift für Theologie und Kirche*

ARMT

ARMT I	G. Dossin, *Correspondance de Šamši-Addu et de ses fils*, Paris, 1950
ARMT II	C.-F. Jean, *Lettres diverses*, Paris, 1950
ARMT III	J.-R. Kupper, *Correspondance de Kibri-Dagan, gouverneur de Terqa*, Paris, 1950
ARMT IV	G. Dossin, *Correspondance de Šamši-Addu et de ses fils* (*suite*), Paris, 1951
ARMT V	G. Dossin, *Correspondance de Iasmaḫ-Addu*, Paris, 1952
ARMT VI	J.-R. Kupper, *Correspondance de Baḫdi-Lim*, Paris, 1954
ARMT VII	J. Bottéro, *Textes économiques et administratifs*, Paris, 1957
ARMT VIII	G. Boyer, *Textes juridiques*, Paris, 1958
ARMT IX	M. Birot, *Textes administratifs de la salle 5 du Palais*, Paris, 1960
ARMT X	G. Dossin & A. Finet, *Correspondance féminine*, Paris, 1978
ARMT XI	M. Burke, *Textes administratifs de la salle 111 du Palais*, Paris, 1963
ARMT XII	M. Birot, *Textes administratifs de la salle* 5, 2e partie, Paris, 1964
ARMT XIII	G. Dossin *et al.*, *Textes divers*, Paris, 1964
ARMT XIV	M. Birot, *Lettres de Yaqqim-Addu, gouverneur de Sagaratum*, Paris, 1974
ARMT XV	J. Bottéro & A. Finet, *Répertoire analytique des tomes I à V*, Paris, 1954
ARMT XVII/1	M. Birot *et al.*, *Répertoire analytique (tomes I–XIV, XVIII et textes divers hors-collection)*, 1: *Noms Propres*, Paris, 1979
ARMT XVII/1	J.-G. Heintz, *Index documentaire des textes de Mari, Fascicule 1, Liste/Codage des textes, Index des ouvrages de référence*, Paris, 1975
ARMT XVIII	O. Rouault, *Mukannišum: L'administration et l'économie palatiales à Mari*, Paris, 1977
ARMT XIX	H. Limet, *Textes administratifs de l'époque des šakkanakku*, Paris, 1976
ARMT XXI	J.-M. Durand, *Textes administratifs des salles 134 et 160 du Palais de Mari*, Paris, 1983
ARMT XXII	J.-R. Kupper, *Documents administratifs de la salle 135 du Palais de Mari*, I–II, Paris, 1983
ARMT XXIII	G. Bardet, F. Joannes, B. Lafont, D. Soubeyran, P. Villard, *Archives administratives de Mari I*, Paris, 1984
ARMT XXIV	P. Talon, *Textes administratifs des salles 'Y et Z' du Palais de Mari*, Paris, 1985
ARMT XXV	H. Limet, *Textes administratifs relatifs aux métaux*, Paris, 1986

BIBLIOGRAPHY

Abdallah, F. 1987. 'La femme dans le royaume d'Alep au XVIIIe siècle av. J.-C.', in J. M. Durand (ed.), *La femme dans le Proche Orient antique*, Paris, pp. 13–15.

Adams, R. McC. 1975. 'The Mesopotamian Social Landscape . . .' in C. B. Moore (ed.), *Reconstructing Complex Societies* (*Suppl. BASOR* 20), pp. 1–22.

Afanasjeva, V. K. 1964. *VDI* 87/1, pp. 84 ff (Russian).

Albright, W. F. 1937. 'Western Asia in the Twentieth Century B.C.: The Archives of Mari', *BASOR* 67, pp. 26–30.

—— 1941. 'The Land of Damascus between 1850 and 1750 B.C.', *BASOR* 83, pp. 30–36.

—— 1953. 'Dedan', in *Geschichte und Altes Testament* (*A. Alt Festschrift*), Tübingen, pp. 1–12.

—— 1954. 'Northwest Semitic Names in a List of Egyptian Slaves from the 18th Century B.C.', *JAOS* 74, pp. 222–233.

—— 1957. 'The High Place in Ancient Palestine', *SVT* 4, pp. 242–258.

—— 1961. 'Abram the Hebrew', *BASOR* 163, pp. 36–54.

—— 1965 'Some Remarks on the Archaeological Chronology of Palestine before about 1500 B.C.', in R. W. Ehrich (ed.) *Chronologies in Old World Archaeology*[2], Chicago, pp. 47–60.

—— 1968. *Yahweh and the Gods of Canaan*, London.

Albright, W. F. & Moran, W. L. 1950. 'Rib-Adda of Byblos and the Affairs of Tyre (EA 89)', *JCS* 4, pp. 163–168.

Alt, A. 1953. 'Die Landnahme der Israeliten in Palästina', *Kleine Schriften* I, München, pp. 89–125 (original in 1925).

—— 1954. 'Beziehungen zu Ägypten in den Briefen von Mari?' *ZDPV* 70, pp. 130–134.

Anbar, M. 1975. 'Aspect moral dans un discours 'prophètique' de Mari', *UF* 7, pp. 517–518.

—— 1979. 'La durée du règne de Zimri-Lim, roi de Mari', *IOS* 9, pp. 1–8.

—— 1981. in 'Notes brèves', *RA* 75, p. 91.

—— 1985. *The Amorite Tribes in Mari,* Tel Aviv (Hebrew).

—— & Na'aman, N. 1986/87. 'An Account Tablet of Sheep from Ancient Hebron', *Tel Aviv* 13/14, pp. 3–12.

Arbeli, S. 1981. in M. Heltzer, *The Suteans*, Naples, pp. 101–104.

Archi, A. 1985. 'Le synchronisme entre les rois de Mari et les rois d'Ebla au IIIe mill.'; 'Les noms de personne mariotes à Ebla (IIIe mill.)'; 'Les rapports politiques et économiques entre Ebla et Mari', *MARI* 4, pp. 47–51; 53–58; 63–83.

—— 1986. 'Die ersten zehn Könige von Ebla', *ZA* 76, pp. 213–217.

—— 1987. 'Les titres de EN et LUGAL à Ebla et des cadeaux pour le roi de Kish', *MARI* 5, pp. 37–52.

—— & Biga, M. G. 1982. *Testi Administrativi di Vario Contenuto, ARET* 3, Rome.

Artzi, P. 1968. S.v. '*nāweh*', *Encyclopaedia Biblica* V, cols. 791–792, (Hebrew).

—— 1984. In M. Haran *et al.* (eds.), *Ezekiel* (*Encylopedia of the World of the*

Bible 12), pp. 176–177 (Hebrew).
—— 1987. 'Ten Years of Ebla Research . . .', in L. Cagni (ed.), *Ebla in Retrospect*, Naples, pp. 409–417.
Artzi, P. & Malamat, A. 1960. apud Y. Yadin *et al., HAZOR* II, Jerusalem, pp. 115–116.
—— 1971. 'The Correspondance of Shibtu Queen of Mari', *Orientalia* 40, pp. 75–87.
Astour, M. 1973. 'A North Mesopotamian Locale of the Keret Epic?', *UF* 5, pp. 29–39.
Bahat, D. 1978. 'Did the Patriarchs Live at Giv'at Sharet?', *BAR* 4/3, pp. 8–11.
Barrelet, M. T. 1950. 'Une peinture de la cour 106 du palais de Mari', in A. Parrot (ed.), *Studia Mariana*, Paris, pp. 9–35.
Bartlett, J. B. 1969. 'The Use of the Word [*rō'š*] (*ro'š*) as a Title in the Old Testament', *VT* 19, pp. 1–10.
Batto, B F. 1974. *Studies on Women at Mari*, Baltimore.
—— 1980. 'Land Tenure and Women at Mari', *JESHO* 23, pp. 209–239.
Bauer, J. 1969. 'Zum Totenkult im altsumerischen Lagasch', *ZDMG* Suppl. 1, pp. 107–114.
Bauer, T. 1926. *Die Ostkanaanäer*, Leipzig.
—— 1957. 'Ein viertes altbabylonisches Fragment des Gilgameš-Epos', *JNES* 16, pp. 254–262.
Bayliss, M. 1973. 'The Cult of the Dead Kin in Assyria and Babylonia', *Iraq* 35, pp. 115–125.
Beitzel, B. L. 1976. *The Placenames in the Mari Texts: An Onomastic and Topographic Study* (Unpublished Doctoral Dissertation. The Dropsie University).
Ben Barak, Z. 1980. 'Inheritance by Daughters in the Ancient Near East', *JSS* 25, pp. 22–33.
Bendor, S. 1986. *The Bet-Ab in Israel from the Settlement to the End of the Monarchy*, Haifa (Hebrew).
Benjamin, W. 1974. *Gesammelte Schriften* 1/2, Frankfurt a.M.
Beyer, D. 1985. 'Scellements de portes du palais de Mari', *MARI* 4, pp. 375–384.
Biran, A. 1975. 'Tel Dan', in M. Avi-Yonah (ed.), *EAEHL* 1, pp. 313–321.
—— 1980. 'Tel Dan: Five Years Later', *BA* 43, pp. 168–182.
—— 1984. 'The Triple Arched Gate of Laish at Tel-Dan', *IEJ* 34, pp. 1–19.
Birot, M. 1953/55. 'Trois textes économiques de Mari', *RA* 47, pp. 121–130, 161–174; 49, pp. 15–31.
—— 1973. 'Nouvelles découvertes épigraphiques au palais de Mari (salle 115)', *Syria* 50, pp. 1–12.
—— 1978. 'Données nouvelles sur la chronologie du règne de Zimri-Lim', *Syria* 55, pp. 333–343.
—— 1980. 'Fragment de rituel de Mari relatif au *kispum*', in B. Alster, (ed.), *Death in Mesopotamia*, (26e RAI), Copenhagen, pp. 139–150.
Blenkinsopp, J. 1983. *A History of Prophecy in Israel*, Philadelphia.
Boadt, L. 1980. *Ezekiel's Oracles against Egypt*, Rome.
Bohlen, R. 1980. *Der Fall Nabot*, Trier.
Bonneterre, D. 1985. *Banquets, rations et offrandes alimentaires à Mari sur l'Euphrate* (Unpublished doctoral dissertation, University of Montreal.)
Boochs, W. 1982. *Siegel und Siegeln im alten Ägypten*, St. Augustin.
Bordreuil, P. & Pardee, D. 1982. 'Le rituel funéraire Ougaritique, *RS* 34.126', *Syria* 59, pp. 121–128.
Borger, R. 1961. *Einleitung in die assyrischen Königsinschriften* I, Leiden.
—— 1984. 'Jaḫdun-Lim von Mari am Mittelmeer', *TUAT* 1/4, p. 355.

Bottéro, J. 1974. In J. P. Vernant *et al., Divination et Rationalité*, Paris, pp. 70–197.
—— 1981. 'L'ordalie en Mésopotamie ancienne', *Annali della Scuola Normale Superiore di Pisa*, Vol. XI, 4, pp. 1005–1067.
—— 1987. 'La mythologie de la mort', in *Mésopotamie*, Paris, pp. 232–346.
Botterweck, G. J. & Clements, B. 1973. S.v. '*gōy*', *TWAT* 1, cols. 695–973.
Brekelmans, C. H. W. 1959a. *De Herem in het Oude Testament*, Nijmegen.
—— 1959b. 'Le *ḥerem* chez les prophètes du Royaume du Nord et dans le Deutéronome', *Bibliotheca Ephemeridum Theologicarum Lovaniensium*, 377–383.
Brichto, H. C. 1973. 'Kin, Cult, Land and Afterlife—A Biblical Complex', *HUCA* 44, pp. 1–55.
Brockelmann, C. 1928. *Lexicon Syriacum²,* Halle.
Buber, M. 1950. *Der Glaube der Propheten*, Zurich.
Buccellati, G. 1966. *The Amorites of the Ur III Period*, Naples.
Burke, M. L. 1964. 'Lettres de Numušda-Nahrari et de trois autres correspondants à Idiniatum', *Syria* 41, pp. 67–103.
Caquot, A. *et al.* 1974. *Textes ougaritiques* I, Paris.
Caquot, A. & Lemaire, A. 1977. 'Les textes araméens de Deir 'Alla', *Syria* 54, pp. 189–208.
Casetti, P. 1982. *Gibt es ein Leben vor dem Tod?*, Friebourg/Göttingen.
Cassin, E. 1969. 'Cycles du temps et cadres de l'espace en Mésopotamie ancienne', *Revue de Synthèse* 55/56, pp. 241–257.
Cassuto, U. 1975. *Biblical and Oriental Studies* II, Jerusalem.
Cazelles, H. 1966. 'Patriarches', in *DBS* VII, cols. 136–141.
—— 1967. 'Mari et l'ancien Testament', 15e *RAI*, pp. 73–90.
—— 1977. S.v. '*ḥabar*', in *TWAT* 2, cols. 721–726.
Chaney, M. L. 1983. 'Ancient Palestinian Peasant Movements and the Formation of Premonarchic Israel', in D. N. Freedman & D. F. Graf (eds.), *Palestine in Transition*, Sheffield, pp. 39–90.
Charpin, D. 1983. 'Une inventoire générale des trésors du palais de Mari', *MARI* 2, pp. 211–214.
—— 1984. 'Inscriptions votives d'époque assyrienne', *MARI* 3, pp. 41–81.
—— 1985. 'Les archives du devin Asqudum dans la résidence du chantier A', *MARI* 4, pp. 453–462.
—— 1987a 'Les Elamites à Šubat-Enlil' in L. de Meyer, H. Gasche et F. Vallat (eds.), *Fragmenta Historiae Elamicae, Mélanges offerts à M.-J. Steve*, Paris, pp. 129–137.
—— 1987b. 'Mari and the "Western Coast" during the Reign of Šamši-Addu', *American Oriental Society Meeting, Abstracts*, No. 7, Los Angeles, p. 3.
Charpin, D. & Durand, J.-M. 1985. 'La prise du pouvoir par Zimri-Lim', *MARI* 4, pp. 293–343.
—— 1986. '"Fils de Sim'al": Les origines tribales des rois de Mari', *RA* 80, pp. 141–183.
—— 1987. 'Le nom antique de Tell Rimāh', *RA* 81, pp. 125–148.
Cleuziou, S. & Berthoud, T., 1982. 'Early Tin in the Near East—A Reassessment in the Light of New Evidence from Western Afganistan', *Expedition* 25/1, pp. 14–19.
Cody, A. 1979. 'The Phoenician Ecstatic in Wenamun', *JEA* 65, pp. 99–106.
Cornelius, I. 1985. *Aspects of the Economy of Mari in the Middle Bronze Age: Foreign Trade in the Old Babylonian Period (c. 1830–1758 B.C.E.)*, (Unpublished doctoral dissertation, Stellenbosch, R.S.A.).
Cowley, A. 1923. *Aramaic Papyri of the Fifth Century B.C.,* Oxford.

Craghan, J. F. 1974. 'The *ARM* X "Prophetic" Texts: Their Media, Style and Structure', *JANES* 6, pp. 39–57.

Cross, F. M. 1973. *Canaanite Myth and Hebrew Epic*, Cambridge, Mass.

Crüsemann, F. 1978. *Der Widerstand gegen das Königtum. Die antiköniglichen Texte des Alten Testamentes und der Kampf um den frühen israelitischen Staat*, Neukirchen-Vluyn.

Cunchillos, J. L. 1976. *Estudio del Salmo 29*, Valencia (concluded 1970).

Dahood, M. 1966. *Psalms I* (Anchor Bible), Garden City, N.Y.

Daiches, S. 1909. 'Balaam—A Babylonian *barû*', in *Assyrian and Archaeological Studies (H.V. Hilprecht Anniversary Volume)*, Leipzig, pp. 60–70.

Dalley, S. 1979. 'ARMT X Reviewed (with a discussion of ^{d}šar mātim and sitrum)', *BiOr* 36, pp. 289–292.

—— 1984. Mari and Karana—Two Old Babylonian Cities, London and New York.

—— *et al.* 1976. *The Old Babylonian Tablets from Tell al Rimah*, Hertford.

Dalman, G., 1922. *Aramäisch-neuhebräisches Handwörterbuch*^{2}, Frankfurt a.M.

Day, J. 1984. *God's Conflict with the Dragon and the Sea in the Old Testament*, Cambridge.

Delcor, M. 1962. 'Le trésor de la maison de Yahweh', *VT* 12, pp. 353–377.

Deller, K. 1985. 'SAG.DU UR.MAḪ, Löwenkopf-situla, Löwenkopf-becher', *BaM* 16, pp. 327–346, esp. pp. 337–340 (on Mari).

Dent, J. 1981. *The Quest for Nonsuch*, Sutton (Surrey).

Dever, W. G., 1987. 'Palestine in the Middle Bronze Age . . .', *BA* 50, pp. 149–177.

Dietrich, W., 1979. *Israel und Kanaan. Vom Ringen zweier Gesellschaftssysteme*, Stuttgart.

—— 1986. 'Prophetenbriefe aus Mari', *TUAT* II/I, Gütersloh, pp. 83–93.

—— *et al.* 1976. (with Loretz, O. & Sanmartin, J.), *Die Keilalphabetischen Texte aus Ugarit*, Neukirchen-Vluyn.

—— & Loretz, O., 1981. 'Neue Studien zu den Ritualtexten aus Ugarit (I)', *UF* 13, pp. 63–100.

Van Dijk, J. 1973. 'Un rituel de purification des armes et de l'armée . . .', *Symbolae F.M. Th. de Liagre Böhl*, Leiden, pp. 107–117.

Donner, A. & Röllig, W. 1962. *Kanaanäische und aramäische Inschriften* I, Wiesbaden.

Dossin, G., 1937. 'La correspondance de Zimrilim, dernier roi de Mari (vers. 2000 avant J.-C.)', *CRAIBL*, pp. 12–20.

—— 1938. 'Les archives épistolaires du palais de Mari', *Syria* 19, pp. 105–126.

—— 1939a. 'Les archives économiques du palais de Mari', *Syria* 20, pp. 97–113.

—— 1939b. 'Benjaminites dans les textes de Mari', in *Mélanges syriens offerts à M.R. Dussaud*, II, Paris, pp. 981–996.

—— 1948. 'Une revelation du dieu Dagan de Terqa', *RA* 42, pp. 125–134.

—— 1950. 'Les noms d'années et d'éponymes dans les Archives de Mari', in A. Parrot (ed.) *Studia Mariana*, Leiden, pp. 51–61.

—— 1955. 'L'inscription de fondation de Iahdun-Lim, roi de Mari', *Syria* 32, pp. 1–28.

—— 1957. 'Kengen, pays de Canaan', *RSO* 32, pp. 35–39.

—— 1958. 'À propos du nom des Benjaminites dans les "Archives de Mari"' *RA* 52, pp. 60–62.

—— 1966. 'Sur le prophètism à Mari', in *La divination en Mésopotamie ancienne*, Paris, pp. 77–86.

—— 1970. 'La route de l'étain en Mésopotamie au temps de Zimri-Lim', *RA* 64, pp. 97–106.
—— 1971. 'Documents de Mari. 1', *Syria* 48, pp. 1–6.
—— 1973. 'Une mention de Canaanéens dans une lettre de Mari', *Syria* 50, pp. 277–282.
—— 1975. 'Le songe d'Ayala', *RA* 69, pp. 28–30.
Driver, G. R. & Miles, J. C. 1955. *The Babylonian Laws* II, Oxford.
Durand, J. M. 1982. 'In vino veritas', *RA* 76, pp. 43–50.
—— 1984a. 'Trois études sur Mari', *MARI* 3, pp. 127–180.
—— 1984b. 'Sur un emploi du verbe *bulluṭum*', *MARI* 3, pp. 260–263.
—— 1985a. 'Les dames du palais de Mari', *MARI* 4, pp. 385–436.
—— 1985b. 'La situation historique des Šakkanakku: Nouvelle approche', *MARI* 4, pp. 147–172.
—— 1987a. 'Villes fantômes de Syrie et autres lieux', *MARI* 5, pp. 199–234.
—— 1987b. '**hamāṣum*', in *N.A.B.U.* No. 3, p. 45 (para. 85).
—— & Margueron, J. 1980. 'La question du harem royal dans le palais de Mari', *Journal des Savants,* Oct.–Dec., pp. 253–280.
Ebach, J., 1982. 'Der Blick des Engels', in N.W. Bolz & R. Faber (eds.), *Walter Benjamin*, Würzburg, pp. 57–102.
Ebeling, E. *et al.* 1926. (with Meissner, B. & Weidner, E. F.), *Die Inschriften der altassyrischen Könige* I, Leipzig.
Edelstein, G. & Eisenberg, I. 1985. 'Emeq Repha'im' in *Excavations and Surveys in Israel* 4, pp. 54–56.
Eichrodt, W., 1957. *Theologie des Alten Testaments* I^7, Göttingen.
Eigner, D. 1985. 'Der ägyptische Palast eines asiatischen Königs', *Jahresheft, Österreichisch Archäologisches Institut* 56, pp. 19–25.
Eissfeldt, O., 1975. 'The Hebrew Kingdom', in *CAH* II/2, pp. 537 ff.
Elat, M. 1979. 'Trade and Commerce' in A. Malamat (ed.), *The Age of the Monarchies* 4/2 (*World History of the Jewish People*), Jerusalem, pp. 173–186.
Elayi, J. 1984. 'Terminologie de la Mer Méditerranee dans les annales assyriennes', *OA* 23, pp. 75–92.
Ellermeier, F., 1968. *Prophetie in Mari und Israel*, Herzberg.
Ellis, M. De Jong, 1987. 'The Goddess Kititum Speaks to King Ibalpiel: Oracle Texts from Ishchali', *MARI* 5, pp. 235–257.
Eph'al, I. 1976. S.v. '*qedem*', *Encyclopaedia Biblica* VII, col. 26 (Hebrew).
Epstein, J. N. 1941. 'Mabbul (Psalms 29:10)', *Tarbiz* 12, p. 82 (Hebrew).
Erman, A. & Grapow, H. (eds.), 1926. *Wörterbuch der Ägyptischen Sprache* I, Berlin.
Faulkner, R. O. 1962. *A Concise Dictionary of Middle Egyptian*, Oxford.
Fiandra, E., 1981. 'The Connection between Clay Sealings and Tablets in Administration', in H. Härtel (ed.), *South Asian Archaeology 1979*, Berlin, pp. 29–43.
—— 1982. 'Porte e chiusure de Sicurezza nell'antico Oriente', *Bolletino d'Arte* 13, pp. 1–18.
Finet, A. 1969. 'L'Euphrate, route commerciale de la Mésopotamie', *AAAS* 19, pp. 37–48.
—— 1982. 'Un cas de clédonomancie à Mari', in G. van Driel *et al.* (eds.), *Zikir Šumim* (F. R. Kraus Festschrift), Leiden, pp. 48–55.
—— 1985a. 'Le port d'Emar sur l'Euphrate, entre le royaume de Mari et le pays de Canaan', in E. Lipiński (ed.), *The Land of Israel: Cross-Roads of Civilization* (*OLA* 19), pp. 27–38.

—— 1985b. 'Une requête de'Išme-Dagan', in J. M. Durand & J. R. Kupper (eds.), *Miscellanea Babylonica, Mélanges M. Birot*, Paris, pp. 87–90.

Finkelstein, J. J. 1966. 'The Genealogy of the Hammurapi Dynasty', *JCS* 20, pp. 96f.

—— 1968. 'An Old Babylonian Herding Contract and Genesis 31: 38f.', *JAOS* 88 (*Essays in Memory of E. A. Speiser*), pp. 30–36.

Finkelstein, I. 1988. *The Archaeology of the Israelite Settlement*, Jerusalem.

Fisher, L. R. (ed.) 1972, 75. *Ras Shamra Parallels* I–II, Rome.

Forrer, E. 1928. *Assyrien*, in *RLA* I, pp. 228–297.

Forshey, H. D., 1975. 'The Construct Chain *naḥ^{a}lat YHWH/'^{e}lohim*', *BASOR* 220, pp. 51–53.

Foster, B. 1982. 'The Siege of Armanum', *JANES* 14, pp. 27–36.

Frankena, R. 1966. *Briefe aus dem British Museum* (= *AbB* 2), Leiden.

Freedman, D. N., 1963. 'The Original Name of Jacob in Deut. 33: 28', *IEJ* 13, pp. 125–126.

—— 1987 '"Who is Like Thee Among the Gods?", The Religion of Early Israel', in P. D. Miller *et al., Ancient Israelite Religion* (*Essays in Honor of F. M. Cross*), Philadelphia, pp. 315–335.

Frick, F. S., 1977. *The City in Ancient Israel*, Missoula.

Gadd, C. J. 1971. 'The Dynasty of Agade and the Gutian Invasion', Chapter 19, *CAH* 1/2, pp. 414–463.

Von Gall, A. 1900. *Zuzammensetzung und Herkunft der Bileam Perikope*, Giessen.

Gardiner, A. H. 1933. 'Tanis and Pi-Ra'Messe: A Retractation', *JEA* 19, pp. 122–128.

Gelb, I. J., 1961. 'The Early History of the West Semitic Peoples', *JCS* 15, pp. 27–47.

—— 1968. 'The Word for Dragoman in the Ancient Near East', *Glossa* 2, pp. 93–104.

—— 1980. 'Comparative Method in the Study of the Society and Economy of the Ancient Near East', *Rocznik Orientalistyczny* 41, pp. 29–36.

De Geus, G. H. 1976. *The Tribes of Israel*, Assen.

Gesenius, W., 1909. *Hebräische Grammatik*^{28} *(E. Kautzsch, ed.), Leipzig.*

Gibson, J. L., 1975. Textbook of Syrian Semitic Inscriptions II: Aramaic Inscriptions, Oxford.

—— 1978. *Canaanite Myths and Legends*, Edinburgh.

Gibson, McG. & Biggs, R. D. (eds.), 1977. *Seals and Sealing in the Ancient Near East*, Malibu, Calif.

Ginsberg, H. L. 1935. 'A Phoenician Hymn in the Psalter', *Atti del 19 Congresso Internazionale degli Orientalisti, Roma 1938*, pp. 472–476.

—— 1946. 'The Legend of King Keret', *BASOR Suppl* 2–3.

Giveon, R. 1980. 'Jam, Libanon', in *LÄ* III, Wiesbaden, cols. 242–243, 1013–1014.

Glaeseman, R. R., 1978. *The Practice of the King's Meal at Mari . . .* (Unpublished Doctoral Dissertation, University of Calif. at Los Angeles).

Glock, A. 1968. *Warfare in Mari and Ancient Israel*, (Unpublished Doctoral Dissertation, Ann Arbor, Mich.)

Glueck, N. 1959. *Rivers in the Desert*, New York.

Gnuse, R. K. 1984. *The Dream Theophany of Samuel*, Lanham, N.Y.

Goetze, A., 1953. 'An Old Babylonian Itinerary', *JCS* 7, pp. 51–72.

—— 1955. 'An Incantation against Diseases', *JCS* 9, pp. 8–18.

Gordon, C. H. 1963. 'Hebrew Orgins in the Light of Recent Discovery', in A. Altmann (ed.), *Biblical and Other Studies*, Cambridge, Mass., pp. 3–14.

—— 1987. in C. H. Gordon, G. A. Rensdburg and N. H. Winter (eds.), *Eblaitica* I, Winona Lake, Indiana.

Gottwald, N. K. 1979. *The Tribes of Yahweh*, Maryknoll, N.Y.

Gray, G. B. 1912. *Numbers* (*International Critical Commentary*), Edinburgh.

Grayson, A. K. 1972. *Assyrian Royal Inscriptions* I, Wiesbaden.

—— 1980/83. 'Königslisten und Chroniken', *RLA* 6, pp. 101 ff.

—— 1987. *Assyrian Rulers of the Third and Second Millennia B.C.*, Toronto.

Greenberg, M. 1971. S.v. '*ḥerem*' in *EJ*, Vol. 8, cols. 344–350.

Greenfield, J. C. & Mayrhofer, M. 1967. 'The *'algummim/'almuggim* Problem Reexamined', *Hebräische Wortforschung* (*SVT* 16 = *W. Baumgartner Festschrift*), Leiden, pp. 86–89.

—— & Shaffer, A. 1985. 'Notes on the Curse Formulae of the Tell Fekherye Inscription', *RB* 92, pp. 47–59.

Gröndahl, F. 1967. *Die Personennamen der Texte aus Ugarit*, Rome.

Grosz, K. 1987. 'Daughters Adopted as Sons at Nuzi and Emar', in J. M. Durand (ed.), *La femme dans le Proche-Orient antique*, Paris, pp. 81–86.

Guy, P. L. O. & Engberg, R. M. 1938. *Megiddo Tombs*, Chicago.

Hackett, J. A. 1984. *The Balaam Text from Deir 'Alla*, (Harvard Semitic Monographs 31), Chico, Calif.

Haldar, A. 1952. 'On the Wall Painting from Court 106 of the Palace of Mari', *Orientalia Suecana* 1, pp. 51–65.

Hallo, W. W. 1964. 'The Road to Emar', *JCS* 18, pp. 57–88.

—— 1980. 'Biblical History in its Near Eastern Setting: The Contextual Approach', in C. D. Evans *et al.* (eds.), *Scripture in Context—Essays on the Comparative Method*, Pittsburgh, pp. 1–26.

—— & Tadmor, H. 1977. 'A Lawsuit from Hazor', *IEJ* 27, pp. 1–11.

Halpern, B. 1983. *The Emergence of Israel in Canaan*, Chico, Calif.

Hamlin, 1977. 'Agricultural Seasonality at Mari ...', in L. D. Levine & J. C. Young (eds.), *Mountains and Lowlands: Essays in the Archaeology of Greater Mesopotamia*, Malibu, Calif., pp. 35–74.

Hammel, E. A. M. 1980. 'The Comparative Method in Anthropological Perspective', *Society for Comparative Study of Society and History* 22, pp. 145–155.

Hanson, J. S. 1978. 'Dreams and Visions in the Graeco-Roman World and Early Christianity', in H. Temporini & W. Haase (eds.) *Aufstieg und Niedergang der Römischen Welt* II, 23/2, Berlin.

Haran, M. 1962. S.v. '*mekes*' in *Encyclopaedia Biblica* IV, Jerusalem (Hebrew).

—— 1977. 'From Early to Classical Prophecy: Continuity and Change', *VT* 27, pp. 385–397.

—— 1978. *Temples and Temple Service in Ancient Israel*, Oxford.

Harel, M. 1983/84. 'The Geographical Orientation and the Use of the Map in the Bible Lands', *Yearbook, Museum Ha'aretz* 1, pp. 157–168 (Hebrew).

Haussig, H. W.(ed.) 1965. *Wörterbuch der Mythologie* I, Stuttgart.

Hawkins, J. D. & Bittel, B. K. 1980–83. S.v. '*Kubaba*' A, '*Kubaba*' B, *RLA* 6, pp. 257–264.

Healey, J. F., 1978. 'MLKM/RP'M and the *kispum*', *UF* 10, pp. 89–91.

—— 1984. 'The Immortality of the King: Ugarit and the Psalms', *Orientalia* 53, pp. 245–254.

—— 1986. 'The Ugaritic Dead: Some Live Issues', *UF* 18, pp. 27–32.

Hecker, K., 1986. Assyrische Prophetien, in *TUAT* II/I, pp. 56 ff.

Heider, G. C., 1985. *The Cult of Molek*, Sheffield.

Heinrich, E. 1984. *Die Paläste im Alten Mesopotamien*, (= DAA XV), Berlin.

Heintz, J. G. 1969. 'Oracles prophètiques et 'guerre sainte' selon les archives royales de Mari et l'Ancien Testament', *SVT* 17, pp. 112–138.

Helck, W. 1971. *Die Beziehungen Ägyptens zu Vorderasien im 3. und 2. Jahrtausend v. Chr.*², Wiesbaden.

—— 1983. 'Zur Herkunft der Erzählung des sog. Astarte Papyrus', in M. Görg (ed.), *Fontes Atque Pontes* (*H. Brunner Festschrift*), Wiesbaden, pp. 215–223.

Held, M. 1970. 'Philological Notes on the Covenant Rituals', *BASOR* 200, pp. 32–37.

Heltzer, M. 1981. *The Suteans*, Naples.

Herodotus, 1922. A. D. Godley (ed.) *Herodotus* (Loeb Ed.), London—Cambridge, Mass.

Herrmann, S. 1965. *Die prophetischen Heilserwartungen im Alten Testament*, Stuttgart.

—— 1980. 'Zwischen Stamm und Staat', *XX. Deutscher Orientalistentag (1977), ZDMG*, Suppl. 4, pp. 21–40.

——1988. *Israels Frühgeschichte im Spannungsfeld neuer Hypothesen*, Rheinisch-Westfälische Akademie der Wissenschaften, Abh. 78.

Hirsch, H., 1963. 'Die Inschriften der Könige von Agade', *AfO* 20, pp. 73 ff.

—— 1967. Einige Bemerkungen zu einer vergl. Betrachtung der Semit. Sprachen., *WZKM* 61, pp. 19 f.

Hoftijzer, J. & Van der Kooij, G. 1976. *Aramaic Texts from Deir 'Alla*, Leiden.

Holma, H. 1914. *Die assyrisch-babylonischen Personennamen der Form quṭṭulu*, Helsingfors.

Hölscher, G. 1914. *Die Profeten*, Leipzig.

Horst, F. 1969. *Hiob* 1² (*BK*), Neukirchen-Vluyn.

Hossfeld, F. L. & Meyer, I. L. 1973. *Prophet gegen Prophet*, Fribourg/Göttingen.

Hour, J. L. 1962. 'L'alliance de Sichem', *RB* 69, pp. 5–36, 101–184, 350–368.

Hrouda, B. 1971. *Vorderasien* I, München.

Huber, P. J. *et al.* 1982. *Astronomical Dating of Babylon I and Ur III* (*Occasional Papers on the Near East* 1/4), Malibu, Calif.

—— 1987. 'Astronomical Evidence for the Long and against the Middle and Short Chronologies', in P. Åström (ed.), *High, Middle or Low?* (*Acts of an International Colloquium*), Gothenburg, pp. 5–17.

Huehnergard, J., 1983. 'Five Tablets from the Vicinity of Emar', *RA* 77, pp. 11–43.

Huffmon, H. B. 1965. *Amorite Personal Names in the Mari Texts*, Baltimore,

—— 1970. 'Prophecy in the Mari Letters', *BA·Reader* III, Garden City, N.Y., pp. 199–224.

Hulin, P. 1963. 'The Inscriptions on the Carved Throne-base of Shalmanesser III', *Iraq* 25, pp. 48–69.

Hutter, M. 1982. *Hiskija König von Juda*, Graz.

Ibn Ğanah, A. M. 1896. W. Bacher (ed), *Sepher Hashorashim*, Berlin, (repr. 1966, Jerusalem), (Hebrew).

Jacobsen, T., 1968. 'The Battle between Marduk and Tiamat', *JAOS* 88, pp. 104–108.

Jean, C. F. 1939. 'Excerpta de la correspondance de Mari', *RÉS* 6, pp. 62–69.

Jeremias, J. 1971. 'Lade und Zion', in H. W. Wolff (ed.), *Probleme biblischer Theologie. G. von Rad zum 70. Geburtstag*, München, pp. 183–198.

Joüon, P. 1947. *Grammaire de l'hebreu biblique*, Rome.

Kaiser, O., 1962. *Die mythische Bedeutung des Meeres in Ägypten, Ugarit und Israel*², (*BZAW* 78), Berlin.

Kammenhuber, A. 1967. 'Die hethitische und hurrische Überlieferung zum "Gilgameš Epos"', *Münchener Studien zur Sprachwissenschaft* 21, pp. 45–58.

—— 1976. *Orakelpraxis, Träume und Vorzeichenschau bei den Hethitern*, Heidelberg.

Kantor, H. J. 1986. in *The Oriental Institute 1985–1986 Annual Report*, Chicago, pp. 23–26.

Kaufmann, Y. 1942. *The History of the Israelite Faith*, II/1, Tel Aviv (Hebrew).

—— 1963. *The Book of Joshua*², Jerusalem (Hebrew).

Kempinski, A. 1985. 'The Hyksos Dynasty', in S. Groll (ed.), *Pharaonic Egypt*, Jerusalem, pp. 132–134.

Kerestes, T. M. 1982. *Indices to Economic Texts from the Palace of Zimri-Lim*, (Unpublished Doctoral Thesis, University of Michigan).

Al-Khalesi, Y. M. 1978. *The Court of Palms: A Functional Interpretation of the Mari Palace*, Malibu, Calif.

Kienast, B. 1984. 'Nomina mit T-Präfix ... in der Sprache von Ebla ...', in L. Cagni (ed.), *Il Bilinguismo a Ebla*, Naples.

Kimchi, D. 1847. J. H. R. Biesenthal & F. Lebrecht (eds.), *Sefer Hashorashim*, Berlin (repr. N.Y. 1947/48).

Kitchen, K. A. 1977. 'The King List of Ugarit', *UF* 9, pp. 131–142.

Klengel, H. 1958/59. 'Benjaminiten und Hanäer', *Wissenschaftliche Zeitschrift der Humboldt-Universität, Berlin, Gesellsch.-und Sprachwissenschaftl. Reihe* 8, pp. 211 ff.

—— 1965a. *Geschichte Syriens im 2. Jahrtausend v.u.Z.* 1: *Nordsyrien*, Berlin.

—— 1965b. 'Der Wettergott von Halab', *JCS* 19, pp. 87–93.

—— 1967. 'Der Libanon und seine Zedern in der Geschichte des alten Vorderen Orients', *Das Altertum* 13, pp. 67–76.

—— 1972. *Zwischen Zelt und Palast*, Leipzig.

—— 1980. 'Mord und Bussleistung im spätbronzezeitlichen Syrien', in B. Alster (ed.), *Death in Mesopotamia*, Copenhagen, pp. 189–197.

Kloos, C. 1986. *Yhwh's Combat with the Sea*, Leiden.

Knudtzon, J. A. 1915. *Die El-Amarna Tafeln* I–II, Leipzig.

Kraus, F. R. 1958. *Ein Edikt des Königs Ammi-Ṣaduqa von Babylon*, Leiden.

—— 1964. '*Briefe aus dem British Museum*' (*AbB* 1), Leiden.

—— 1976. 'Akkadische Wörter und Ausdrücke X–XI', *RA* 70, pp. 165–179.

—— 1984. *Königliche Verfügungen in altbabylonischer Zeit*, Leiden.

Krebernik, M. 1982. 'Zu Syllabar und Orthographie der lexikalischen Texte aus Ebla. Teil 1', *ZA* 72, pp. 178–236.

Kupper, J. R. 1957. *Les nomades en Mésopotamie au temps des rois de Mari*, Bruxelles.

—— 1973. 'Le caléndrier de Mari', *Symbolae de M.T. de Liagre Böhl*, Leiden, pp. 266–270.

—— 1976. 'L'inscription du "disque" de Yaḫdun-Lim', *Kramer Anniversary Volume, AOAT* 25, Neukirchen-Vluyn.

—— 1982. 'Mari entre la Mésopotamie et la Syrie du Nord à l'époque paléo-babylonienne', in H. Kühne, H. J. Nissen & J. Renger (eds.), *Mesopotamien und seine Nachbarn*, 1, Berlin, pp. 173–185.

Kutscher, E. K. (ed.), 1972. *Archive of the New Dictionary of Rabbinic Literature* I, Ramat Gan (Hebrew).

Kutscher, R. & Wilcke, C. 1978. 'Eine Ziegel-Inschrift des Königs Takil-ilišśu von Malgium ...', *ZA* 68, pp. 95–128.

Laessoe, J. 1955. *Studies on the Assyrian Ritual and Series bīt rimki*, Copenhagen.

Lafont, B. 1984. 'Le roi de Mari et les prophètes du dieu Adad', *RA* 78, pp. 7–18.

—— 1987. 'Les filles du roi de Mari', *La femme dans le Proche Orient antique* (33e RAI), Paris, pp. 113–123.

Lambert, W. G. 1960. *Babylonian Wisdom Literature*, Oxford.

—— 1967. 'The Language of Mari', in J. Kupper (ed.), *La Civilisation de Mari* (15e RAI), Liège, pp. 29–38.

—— 1968. 'Another Look at Hammurabi's Ancestors', *JCS* 22, pp. 1–2.

—— 1981. 'Old Akkadian Ilaba = Ugaritic Ilib?', *UF* 13, pp. 299–301.

—— 1985. 'The Pantheon of Mari', *MARI* 4, pp. 525–539.

—— 1987. 'A Vocabulary of an Unknown Language', *MARI* 5, pp. 409–413.

Landsberger, B. 1915. Review H. Holma, 'Die assyrisch-babylonischen Personennamen der Form *quṭṭulu*', *GGA* 117, pp. 363–366.

—— 1933. 'Assaku II = "Tabu"', *ZA* 41 (NF 7), pp. 218–219.

—— 1954. 'Assyrische Königsliste und "Dunkles Zeitalter"', *JCS* 8, pp. 31–73, 106–133.

—— 1955. 'Remarks on the Archive of the Soldier Ubarum', *JCS* 9, pp. 121–131.

—— 1957. 'The Series ḪAR-*ra*=*ḫubullu*, Tablets I–IV', *MSL* V, Rome.

—— 1967. '*The Date Palm*', (*AfO* Beiheft 17) Graz.

—— 1974. 'The Series ḪAR-*ra*=*ḫubullu*, Tablets XX–XXIV', *MSL* XI, Rome.

—— & Tadmor, H. 1964. 'Fragments of Clay Liver Models from Hazor', *IEJ* 14, pp. 201–218.

Laroche, E. 1957. 'Fragment hourrite provenant de Mari', *RA* 51, pp. 104–106.

Larsen, M. T. 1967. *Old Assyrian Caravan Procedures*, Istanbul.

Leemans, W. F. 1960. *Foreign Trade in the Old Babylonian Period*, Leiden.

—— 1968. 'Old Babylonian Letters and Economic History', *JESHO* 11, pp. 171–226.

—— 1982. 'La fonction des sceaux apposés à contrats vieux—babyloniens', in G. van Driel *et al.* (eds.), *Zikir Šumim* (*Assyriological Studies Presented to F. R. Kraus*), Leiden, pp. 219–244.

Lemaire, A. L. 1981. 'Une inscription paléo-hebraique sur grenade en ivoire', *RB* 88, pp. 236–239.

—— 1984. 'La haute Mésopotamie et l'origine des Benê Jacob', *VT* 34, pp. 95–101.

—— 1985. 'Mari, la Bible et le monde nord-ouest sémitique', *MARI* 4, pp. 549–558.

Lemche, N. P. L. 1985. *Early Israel*, Leiden.

Levine, B. A. 1983. 'Late Language in the Priestly Source: Some Literary and Historical Observations', *8th World Congress of Jewish Studies, Panel Sessions, Bible Studies and Hebrew Language*, Jerusalem, pp. 69–82.

—— & Tarragon, J. M. 1984. 'Dead Kings and Rephaim: The Patrons of the Ugaritic Dynasty', *JAOS* 104, pp. 649–659.

Lewis, T. J. 1986. *Cults of the Dead in Ancient Israel and Ugarit*, (Unpublished Dissertation, Harvard University, Cambridge, Mass.)

Lewy, J. 1952. 'Studies in the Historical Geography of the Ancient Near East', *Orientalia* 21, pp. 393–425.

Lichtheim, M. 1976. *Ancient Egyptian Literature* II, Berkeley, Calif.

—— 1980. *Ancient Egyptian Literature* III, Berkeley, Calif.

Limet, H. L. 1960. *Le travail du métal au pays de Sumer au temps de la IIIe dynastie d'Ur*, Liège.

—— 1985. 'Les relations entre Mari et la côte Méditerranéenne sous le règne de

Zimri-Lim', *Studia Phoenicia III: Phoenicia and Its Neighbours*, Leuven, pp. 13–20.

Lindblom, J. 1962. *Prophecy in Ancient Israel*, Oxford.

Lipiński, E. 1971. 'El's Abode—Mythological Traditions Related to Mount Hermon . . .', *OLP* 2, pp. 504 ff.

—— 1986. S.v. '*naḥ^{a}lah*', *TWAT* 5, cols. 341–360.

—— 1987. S.v. '*'amm*', *TWAT* 6/1–2, cols. 177–194.

Liverani, M. 1973. 'The Amorites', in D. J. Wiseman (ed.), *Peoples of Old Testament Times*, Oxford, pp. 100–133.

—— 1977. 'Segni Arcaici di Individuazione Personale', *Rivista di Filologia* 105, pp. 106–118.

Loewenstamm, S. 1958. S.v. '*ḥāṣēr*' '*ḥ^{a}ṣērīm*', *Encyclopaedia Biblica* III, cols. 273–274 (Hebrew).

—— 1980. *Comparative Studies in Biblical and Ancient Oriental Literatures* (*AOAT* 204), Neukirchen-Vluyn.

—— 1986, S.v. '[*nah^{a}lat Yahure*] in S. Japhet (ed.), *Studies in the Bible* (*Scripta Hierosolymitana* 31), Jerusalem, pp. 155–192.

Lohfink, N. 1982. S.v. '*ḥērem*' in *TWAT* 3, cols. 192–213.

Loretz, O. 1978. 'Vom kanaanäischen Totenkult zur jüdischen Patriarchen- und Elternverehrung', *Jahrbuch für Anthropologie und Religionsgeschichte* 3, pp. 149–204.

—— 1984. *Psalm 29*, Altenberg.

—— 1985. 'Ugaritisches und Jüdisches—Weisheit und Tod in Psalm 49', *UF* 17, pp. 189–212.

Loud, G. 1948. *Megiddo* II, Chicago.

Löw, I. 1924. *Die Flora der Juden* III, Wien & Leipzig.

Lowth, R., 1753. *De sacra poesi Hebraeorum*, Oxford.

Luckenbill, D. D. 1926–27. *Ancient Records of Assyria and Babylonia* I, II, Chicago.

Luke, J. T. 1965. *Pastoralism and Politics in the Mari Period*, (unpublished Doctoral Dissertation, University of Michigan).

Macalister. R. A. S. 1911/12. *The Excavation of Gezer* I–III, London.

Machinist, P. 1983. 'Assyria and its Image in First Isaiah', *JAOS* 103, pp. 719–737.

Mafico, T. L. 1987. 'The Term *Šāpiṭum* in Akkadian Documents' *JNSL* 13, pp. 69–87.

Maisler (Mazar), B. 1930. *Untersuchungen zur alten Geschichte und Ethnographie Syriens und Palästinas*, Giessen.

—— 1946. 'The Genealogy of the Sons of Nahor and the Historical Background of the Book of Job', *Zion* 11, pp. 1–16 (Hebrew). See Mazar B. below.

Malamat, A. 1952. *The Aramaeans in Aram Naharaim and the Rise of their States*, Jerusalem (Hebrew).

—— 1954. Jeremiah Chapter One—The Call and the Visions, *Iyyunim* 21, Jerusalem (Hebrew).

—— 1956. 'Prophecy in the Mari Documents', *EI* 4, pp. 74–84 (Hebrew; English summary, pp. vi–v).

—— 1958. 'History and Prophetic Vision in a Mari Letter', *EI* 5, pp. 67–73 (Hebrew; English summary, pp. 86*–87*).

—— 1960. 'Hazor, Head of All those Kingdoms', *JBL* 79, pp. 12–19.

—— 1962. 'Mari and the Bible: Some Patterns of Tribal Organization and Institutions', *JAOS* 82, pp. 143–150.

—— 1965. 'Campaigns to the Mediterranean by Iahdunlim and Other Early

Mesopotamian Rulers', in H. Güterbock & T. Jacobsen (eds.), *Studies in Honor of B. Landsberger* (*AS* 16), Chicago, pp. 367 ff.

—— 1966a. 'Prophetic Revelations in New Documents from Mari and the Bible', *SVT* 15, pp. 207–227.

—— 1966b. 'The Ban in Mari and the Bible', in *Biblical Essays—Proceedings of the 9th Meeting of Die Ou-Testamentiese Werkgemeenskap in Suid-Africa*, pp. 40–49.

—— 1967. 'Aspects of Tribal Society in Mari and Israel', *15th RAI*, Liège, pp. 129–138.

—— 1968. 'King Lists of the Old Babylonian Period and Biblical Genealogies', *JAOS* 88 (*E. A. Speiser Memorial Volume*), W. W. Hallo (ed.), pp. 163–173.

—— 1970. 'Northern Canaan and the Mari Texts', in J. A. Sanders (ed.), *Near Eastern Archaeology in the Twentieth Century* (*Essays in Honor of N. Glueck*), Garden City, N.Y., pp. 164–197.

—— 1971a. 'Mari', *BA* 34, pp. 1–22.

—— 1971b. 'Syro-Palestinian Destinations in a Mari Tin Inventory', *IEJ* 21, pp. 31–38.

—— 1973a. 'The Arameans', in D. J. Wiseman (ed.), *Peoples of Old Testament Times,* Oxford, pp. 134–155.

—— 1973b. 'Review of R. de Vaux, *Histoire ancienne d'Israel*', *RB* 80, pp. 82–92.

—— 1979a. 'Conquest of Canaan: Israelite Conduct of War According to Biblical Tradition', *Revue internationale d'Histoire Militaire* 42, pp. 25–52.

—— 1979b. '*Ummatum* in Old Babylonian Texts and Its Ugaritic and Biblical Counterparts', *UF* 11, pp. 527–536.

—— 1980. 'A Mari Prophecy and Nathan's Dynastic Oracle', in J. Emerton (ed.), *Prophecy—Essays G. Fohrer*, Berlin–New York, pp. 68–82.

—— 1982. 'Silver, Gold and Precious Stones from Hazor—Trade and Trouble in a New Mari Document', *JJS* 33 (*Essays in Honor of Y. Yadin*), pp. 71–79.

—— 1983. 'The Proto-History of Israel: A Study in Method', in C. L. Meyers & M. O'Connor (eds.), *The Word of the Lord Shall Go Forth* (*Essays in Honor of D. N. Freedman*), Philadelphia, pp. 303–313.

—— 1985. 'Mari and Early Israel', in *Biblical Archaeology Today*, Jerusalem, pp. 235–243.

—— 1986. '"Doorbells" at Mari—A Textual-Archaeological Correlation', in K. R. Veenhof (ed.), *Cuneiform Archives and Libraries* (*30e RAI*), Istanbul, pp. 160–167.

—— 1987. 'A Forerunner of Biblical Prophecy: The Mari Documents' in P. D. Miller, P. D. Hanson, S. Dean McBride (eds.), *Ancient Israelite Religion, Essays in Honor of F. M. Cross*, Philadelphia, pp. 33–52.

—— 1988a. 'Pre-monarchical Social Institutions in Israel in the Light of Mari', *SVT* 40, pp. 165–176.

—— 1988b. 'The Amorite Background of Psalm 29', *ZAW* 100, pp. 156–160.

—— 1989. 'Hazor Once Again in New Mari Documents', in P. Talon & M. Lebeau (eds.), *Reflets des Deux Fleuves, Acta assyriologica in honorem André Finet*, pp. 95–96.

Malul, M. 1986. '"Sissiktu" and "sikku"—Their Meaning and Function', *BiOr* 43, pp. 20–36.

Mandelbaum, M. 1979/80. 'Some Forms and Uses of Comparative History', *American Studies International* 18, pp. 19–34.

Mann, Thomas. 1934. *Joseph und seine Brüder*, I: *Geschichten Jakobs*, (Vorspiel: Höllenfahrt), Berlin.

[Margalit] Margulis, B. 1970. 'The Canaanite Origin of Psalm 29 Reconsidered', *Biblica* 51, pp. 332–348.

—— 1976. 'Studia Ugaritica II: Studies in KRT and AQHT', *UF* 8, 137–192.
Margueron, J. C. 1982a. *Recherches sur les palais mésopotamiens de l'âge du bronze* I–II, Paris.
—— 1982b. 'Rapport préliminaire sur la campagne de 1979', *MARI* 1, pp. 9–30.
—— 1983. 'Rapport préliminaire sur la campagne de 1980', *MARI* 2, pp. 9–35.
—— 1984a. 'Rapport préliminaire sur la campagne de 1982', *MARI* 3, pp. 7–39.
—— 1984b. 'Les derniers moments du palais de Mari', *Art et Fact* 3, pp. 41–44.
—— 1985. 'L'architecture de la fin du IIIe millénaire à Mari ...', in M. Durand & J. R. Kupper (eds.), *Miscellanea Babylonica* (*Mélanges Maurice Birot*), Paris, pp. 211–222.
—— 1987a. 'Du nouveau sur la Cour du Palmier', *MARI* 5, pp. 413–482.
—— 1987b. 'Mari: Principaux résultats des fouilles conduites depuis 1979', *CRAIBL*, pp. 163–185.
Marx, E. 1977. 'The Tribe as Unit of Substinence: Nomadic Pastoralism in the Middle East', *American Anthropologist* 79, pp. 343–363.
Marzal, A. 1969. *The Organization of the Mari State* (Unpublished Doctoral Dissertation, University of Chicago).
—— 1971. 'The Provincial Governor of Mari', *JNES* 30, pp. 186–217.
Materne, J. P. 1985. 'Remarques sur l'écriture des "repas royaux" sous Zimri-Lim', in J. M. Durand & J. R. Kupper (eds.), *Miscellanea Babylonica* (*Mélanges M. Birot*), Paris, pp. 223–231.
Matthews, V. H. 1978. *Pastoral Nomadism in the Mari Kingdom*, Cambridge, Mass.
Matthiae, P. 1979. 'Princely Cemetery and Ancestors Cult at Ebla during the Middle Bronze Age II', *UF* 11, pp. 563–569.
—— 1980. *Ebla*, London (original Italian edition, 1978).
—— 1981. 'A Hypothesis on the Princely Burial Area of Middle Bronze II at Ebla', *ArOr* 49, pp. 55–65.
—— 1984. 'New Discoveries at Ebla: The Excavation of the Western Palace and the Royal Necropolis of the Amorite Period', *BA* 47, pp. 18–32.
Matouš, L, 1960. 'Les rapports entre la version sumérienne et la version akkadienne de l'épopee de Gilgameš', in P. Garelli (ed.), *Gilgameš et sa legende*, pp. 83–94.
—— 1964. 'Zur neueren Literatur über das Gilgameš-Epos', *BiOr* 21, pp. 3–10.
Mayer, H. 1967. 'Das Bauholz des Tempel Salomos', *BZ* (NF) 11, pp. 53–66.
Mayer, W. 1982. S.v. '*yrd*', *TWAT* 3, cols. 894–901.
Mazar, B. 1965. 'The Sanctuary of Arad and the Family of Hobab the Kenite', *JNES* 24, pp. 297–303.
—— 1968. 'The Middle Bronze Age in Palestine', *IEJ* 18, pp. 65–97.
—— 1969. 'The Historical Background of the Book of Genesis', *JNES* 28, pp. 73–83.
—— 1986. 'The Early Israelite Settlement in the Hill Country', in S. Ahituv & B. Levine (eds.), *The Early Biblical Period*, Jerusalem, pp. 35–48.
McCarter, P. K. 1980a. *I Samuel*, Garden City, N.Y.
—— 1980b. The Balaam Texts from Deir 'Alla: The First Combination', *BASOR* 239, pp. 49–60.
McEwan, J. P., 1980. 'A Seleucid Augural Request', *ZA* 70, pp. 58–69.
Meissner, B. 1926. in E. Ebeling *et al.*, *Die Inschriften der altassyrischen Könige*, Leipzig.
Mendenhall, G. 1962. 'The Hebrew Conquest of Palestine', *BA* 25, pp. 66–87.
Mercer, S. A. B. 1939. *The Tell el-Amarna Tablets* I–II, Toronto.
Michalowski, P. 1985. 'Third Millennium Contacts: Observations on the Relationships between Mari and Ebla', *JAOS* 105, pp. 293–302.

Michel, E. 1954/59. 'Die Assur-Texte Salmanessars III . . .', *WO* 2, pp. 27–45.

Mikesell, M. W. 1969. 'The Deforestation of Mount Lebanon', *The Geographical Review* 59, pp. 1–28.

Milgrom, J. 1976. 'The Concept of *MA'AL* in the Bible and the Ancient Near East', *JAOS* 95, pp. 236–247.

Millard, A. R. 1980. 'Methods of Studying the Patriarchal Narratives as Ancient Texts', in A. R. Millard & D. J. Wiseman (eds.), *Essays on the Patriarchal Narratives*, Leicester, pp. 43–92.

De Moor, J. C. 1976. '*Rapi'uma*—Rephaim', *ZAW* 88, pp. 323–345.

Moortgat, A. 1964. 'Die Wandgemälde im Palaste zu Mari und ihre historische Einordnung', *BaM* 3, pp. 63–74.

Moortgat-Correns, U. 1952/53. 'Westsemitisches in der Bildkunst Mesopotamiens', *AfO* 16/2, pp. 287–294.

Moran, W. L. 1969a. 'New Evidence from Mari on the History of Prophecy', *Biblica* 50, pp. 15–56.

—— 1969b. 'Akkadian Letters', *ANET*, pp. 623–632.

—— 1987. *Les Lettres d'El-Amarna*, Paris.

Moscati, S. (ed.) 1964. *An Introduction to the Comparative Grammar of the Semitic Languages*, Wiesbaden.

Mosis, R. 1987. S.v. ''*kr*', *TWAT* 6/1, cols. 74–79.

Muffs, Y. 1969. *Studies in Aramaic Legal Papyri from Elephantine*, Leiden.

Muhly, D. 1973. *Copper and Tin. The Distribution of Mineral Sources and the Nature of the Metals Trade in the Bronze Age*, Hamden, Conn.; and *Supplement* to *ibid*, pp. 77–136.

Müller, H. P. 1976. S.v.'*qdš*', *THAT* 2, cols. 590–609.

—— 1980. 'Religionsgeschichtliche Beobachtungen zu den Texten von Ebla', *ZDPV* 96, pp. 1–19.

—— 1984. S.v. '*molaek̲*', *TWAT* 4, cols. 957–968.

Munn-Rankin, J. M. 1956. 'Diplomacy in Western Asia in the Early Second Millennium B.C.', *Iraq* 18, pp. 68–110.

Muntingh, L. M. 1984. 'The Conception of Ancient Syro-Palestinian Kingship in the Light of Contemporary Royal Archives with Special Reference to the Recent Discoveries at Tell Mardikh (Ebla) in Syria', in Prince T. Mikasa (ed.), *Bulletin of the Middle Eastern Culture Center in Japan* 1, Wiesbaden, pp. 1–10.

Muntz, P. 1956. 'History and Myth', *Philosophical Quarterly* 6, pp. 1–16.

Na'aman, N. 1981. 'East-west Diplomatic Relations in the Days of Zimrilim', *RA* 75, pp. 171/2.

Nakata, I. 1982a. 'Two Remarks on the So-called Prophetic Texts from Mari', *Acta Sumerologica* 4, pp. 143–148.

—— 1982b. 'Rezension zu: Noort, Edward, Untersuchungen zum Gottesbescheid in Mari, *AOAT* 202, 1977', *JAOS* 102, pp. 166–168.

Neiman, D. 1948. 'PGR: A Canaanite Cult Object in the Old Testament', *JBL* 67, pp. 55–60.

Niehr, H. 1986a. *Herrschen und Richten—Die Wurzel špṭ im Alten Orient und im Alten Testament*, Würzburg.

—— 1986b '*nāśī*'', *TWAT* 5, cols. 647–665.

Noort, E. 1977. *Untersuchungen zum Gottesbescheid in Mari* (*AOAT* 202), Neukirchen-Vluyn.

Noth, M. 1956. *Geschichte Israels*³, Göttingen.

—— 1958. 'Amt und Berufung im Alten Testament', *Bonner Akad. Reden* 19, Bonn.
—— 1961. *Die Ursprünge des alten Israel im Lichte neuer Quellen*, Köln-Opladen.
Nougayrol, J. 1955/56. *Le palais royal d'Ugarit*, III, IV, Paris.
—— 1968. *Ugaritica* V, Paris.
Oded, B. 1985. 'The Story of the Babylonian Delegation to Hezekiah . . .', *Shnaton, Annual for Biblical and Ancient Near Eastern Studies* 9, pp. 115–126 (Hebrew).
Del Olmo Lete, G. 1986. 'Liturgia Funeraria de los reyes de Ugarit (KTU 1.106)', *SEL* 3, pp. 55–71.
—— 1987. 'Los nombres "divinos" de los reyes de Ugarit', *Aula Orientalia* 5, pp. 39–69.
Oppenheim, A. L. 1952. 'The Archives of the Palace of Mari: A Review Article', *JNES* 11, pp. 129–134.
—— 1956. *The Interpretation of Dreams in the Ancient Near East* (*Transactions of the American Philosophical Society* 46), Philadelphia.
—— 1964. *Ancient Mesopotamia*, Chicago.
Orlinsky, H. M. 1939. '*Ḥaṣer* in the Old Testament', *JAOS* 59. pp. 22–37.
Otto, E. 1984. 'Historisches Geschehen—Überlieferung—Erklärungsmodell-Sozialhistorische Grundsatz—und Einzelprobleme in der Geschichtsschreibung des frühen Israel . . .', *BN* 23, pp. 63–80.
Pack, M. D. 1981. *The Administrative Structure of the Palace at Mari* (*ca. 1800–1750 B.C.*) I–II, (Unpublished Dissertation, University of Pennsylvania.)
Paradise, J. 1987. 'Daughters as "Sons" at Nuzi', in M. A. Morrison & D. I. Owen (eds.), *Studies on the Civilization and Culture of Nuzi and the Hurrians* II, Winona Lake, Ind., pp. 202–213.
Pardee, D. 1983. 'Visiting Ditanu' *UF* 15, pp. 127–140.
—— (forthcoming). 'La fête des mânes', Chapter 5 in *Les textes para-mythologiques de la 24e campagne (Ras Shamra-Ougarit)*, Paris.
Parpola, S. 1983. *Letters from Assyrian Scholars to the Kings Esarhaddon and Assurbanipal* II (*AOAT* 5/2), Neukirchen-Vluyn. pp. 486–491.
Parrot, A. 1950a. 'Les tablettes de Mari et l'Ancien Testament', *RHPR* 30, pp. 1–11.
—— 1950b. '"Cérémonie de la main" et réinvestiture', *Studia Mariana*, Paris, pp. 37–40.
—— 1958a. *Le Palais* 1: *Architecture* (Mission Archéologique de Mari II/1), Paris.
—— 1958b. *Le Palais* 2: *Peintures murales* (Mission Archéologique de Mari II/2), Paris.
—— 1959. *Le Palais* 3: *Documents et monuments* (Mission Archéologique de Mari II/3), Paris.
—— 1962. *Abraham et son temps*, Neuchâtel.
—— 1965. 'Les fouilles de Mari. Quatorzième campagne (printemps 1964)', *Syria* 42, pp. 1–24, pl. 1–2.
—— 1966. 'La vie d'un chef d'état du IIe millénaire', *Institut Francaise, Cinq Académies* 26, Paris, pp. 5–11.
—— 1967. 'Mari', in D. Winton Thomas (ed.), *Archaeology and Old Testament Study*, Oxford, pp. 136–144.
—— 1974. *Mari, capitale fabuleuse*, Paris.
Paul, S. M. 1968. 'Deutero-Isaiah and Cuneiform Royal Inscriptions', *JAOS* 88 (*E. A. Speiser Memorial Vol.*, W. W. Hallo, ed.), pp. 180–186.

Petersen, D. L. 1981. *The Roles of Israel's Prophets*, Sheffield.

Pettinato, G., 1980. 'Bolletino Militare della campagne di Ebla contra la atta di Mari', *OA* 19, pp. 231–245.

—— 1981. *The Archives of Ebla*, Garden City, N.Y. (Italian edition, 1979.)

Pitard, W. T. 1978. 'The Ugaritic Funerary Text RS 34.126', *BASOR* 232, pp. 65–75.

—— 1986. 'Is the Area of Apum-Damascus mentioned in the Mari Archives?', *BASOR* 264, pp. 73–77.

Pitt-Rivers, J. 1977. *The Fate of Shechem or the Politics of Sex,* Cambridge.

Pope, M. H. 1973. *Job*, Garden City, N.Y.

—— 1981. 'The Cult of the Dead', in G. D. Young (ed.), *Ugarit in Retrospect*, Winona Lake, Ind.

Porten, B. 1979. 'Aramaic Papyri & Parchments', *BA* 42, pp. 74–103.

Porter, J. R. 1981. '[*bᵉ nē nᵉb̲ī'īm*]', *JTS* 32, pp. 423–429.

Posener, G. 1940. *Princes et pays d'Asie et de Nubie*, Brussels.

Postgate, J. N. 1980. 'Excavations at Abu Salabikh 1978–79', *Iraq* 42, pp. 87–104, pl. 10–11.

Procopius, 1914. H. B. Dewing, *Procopius* (Loeb Ed.), London.

Von Rad, G. 1951. *Der heilige Krieg im alten Israel*, Zürich.

Radcliffe-Brown, A. R. 1969 (1952). *Structure and Function in Primitive Society*, London.

Rainey, A. F. 1979. 'Toponymic Problems', *TA* 6, pp. 158–161.

Reiner, E. 1956. 'Lipšur Litanies', *JNES* 15, pp. 129–149.

Rendtorff, R. 1962. 'Erwägungen zur Frühgeschichte des Prophetentum in Israel', *ZTK* 59, pp. 145–167 ff.

Renger, J. 1969. 'Untersuchungen zum Priestertum in der altbabylonischen Zeit', *ZA* 59 (NF 25), pp. 104–230.

Reviv, H. (forthcoming). *The Elders in Ancient Israel—A Study of a Biblical Institution*, Jerusalem.

Ringgren, H. 1986. '*nāweh*', *TWAT* 5, cols. 293–297.

Roberts, J. J. M. 1972. *The Earliest Semitic Pantheon*, Baltimore.

Rofé, A. 1979. *The Book of Balaam*, Jerusalem, (Hebrew).

Röllig, W. 1969. 'Zur Typologie und Entstehung der babylonischen und assyrischen Königslisten', *AOAT* 1, pp. 265–277.

Ross, J. 1970. 'Prophecy in Hamath, Israel and Mari', *HTR* 63, pp. 1–28.

Rouault, D. 1984. *L'archiv de Puzurum* (Terqa Final Reports 1), Malibu, Calif.

Rouillard, D. H. & Tropper, J. 1987. '*TRPYM*, rituels de guérison et culte des ancêtres . . .', *VT* 37, pp. 340–361.

Rowton, M. B. 1967. 'The Woodlands of Ancient Western Asia', *JNES* 26, pp. 261–277.

—— 1970. Ancient Western Asia, *CAH* I/1, Part II, pp. 193–239.

—— 1974. 'Enclosed Nomadism', *JESHO* 17, pp. 1–30.

—— 1976a. 'Dimorphic Structure and the Tribal Elite', *Studia Instituti Anthropos* 28, pp. 219–257.

—— 1976b. 'Dimorphic Structure and the Problem of the *'apiru—'ibrim'*', *JNES* 35, pp. 13–20.

—— 1977. 'Dimorphic Structure and the Parasocial Element', *JNES* 36, pp. 181–198.

Rudolph, W. 1966. *Hosea* (*KAT*), Gütersloh.

—— 1968. *Jeremia*³ (*HAT*), Tübingen.

Rutten, M. 1938. 'Trente-deux modeles de foies en argile inscrits provenant de Tell-Hariri (Mari)', *RA* 35, pp. 36–52.

Safar, F. 1951. 'A Further Text of Shalmanesar III from Assur', *Sumer* 7, pp. 3 ff.

Safren, J. 1979. 'New Evidence for the Title of the Provincial Governor', *HUCA* 50, pp. 1–15.

Saggs, H. W. F. 1958. 'Some Ancient Semitic Conceptions of the Afterlife', *Faith and Thought* 90, pp. 152–182.

—— 1960. 'Review *ARMT* VII, VIII', *JSS* 5, pp. 411–417.

—— 1978. *The Encounter with the Divine in Mesopotamia and Israel*, London.

Salonen, A. 1963. *Die Möbel des alten Mesopotamien*, Helsinki.

—— 1966. *Die Hausgeräte der alten Mesopotamier* II, Helsinki.

—— 1973. *Vögel und Vogelfang im alten Mesopotamien,* Helsinski.

Salonen, E. 1968. 'Zum altbabylonischen Kriegswesen', *BiOr* 25, pp. 160–162.

Salzman, P. C. 1980. 'Introduction: Processes of Sedentarization as Adaption and Response', in P. C. Salzman (ed.), *When Nomads Settle*, New York, pp. 1–19.

Sasson, J. M. 1971. 'Mari Notes', *RA* 65, p. 172.

—— 1972a. 'Zimri-Lim's March to Victory', *RA* 66, pp. 177–178.

—— 1972b. 'Some Comments on Archive Keeping at Mari', *Iraq* 34, pp. 55–67.

—— 1979. 'The Calendar and Festivals of Mari during the Reign of Zimri-Lim', in M. A. Powell & R. H. Sack (eds.), *Studies in Honor of Tom B. Jones* (*AOAT* 203), Neukirchen-Vluyn, pp. 119–141.

—— 1980. 'Two Recent Works on Mari', *AfO* 27, pp. 127–135.

—— 1983. 'Mari Dreams', *JAOS* 103, pp. 283–293.

—— 1984. 'Zimri-Lim Takes the Grand Tour', *BA* 47, pp. 246–251.

Schaeffer, C. F. A. 1939, 49. *Ugaritica* I, II, Paris.

Schäfer-Lichtenberger, C. 1983. *Stadt und Eidgenossenschaft im Alten Testament* (*BZAW* 156), Berlin.

Scharbert, J. 1982. *Beyt 'ab* als soziologische Grösse im Alten Testament, in *Von Kanaan bis Kerala (FS J. P. M. van der Ploeg)*, Neukirchen-Vluyn, pp. 213–237.

Schmitt, A. 1982. *Prophetischer Gottesbescheid in Mari und Israel*, Stuttgart.

Schmitt, G. 1970. *Du sollst keinen Frieden schliessen mit den Bewohnern des Landes*, Stuttgart.

Scholem, G. 1983. *Walter Benjamin und sein Engel*, Frankfurt a.M.

Schwally, F. 1892. *Das Leben nach dem Tode*, Giessen.

—— 1901. *Semitische Kriegsaltertümer* I, Leipzig.

Seebass, H. 1973. '*'aḥ^{a}rīt*', *TWAT* 1, cols. 224–228.

—— 1978. *Geschichtliche Zeit und theonome Tradition in der Josephserzählung*, Gütersloh.

Van Seters, J. 1975. *Abraham in History and Tradition*, New Haven.

Seybold, K. 1980. 'Die Geschichte des 29. Psalms und ihre theologische Bedeutung', *TZ* 36, pp. 208–219.

Shaffer, A. 1983. 'Gilgamesh, the Cedar Forest and Mesopotamian History', *JAOS* 103, pp. 307–313.

Sibawayhi. 1889. *Le livre de Sîbawaihi, Traité de grammaire Arabe . . .*, par H. Derenbourg, II, Paris.

Sigrist, M. (forthcoming). 'Le Deuil de Šu-Sin', FS *Å. Sjöberg*, Philadelphia.

Smith, W. R. 1894. *The Religion of the Semites*, New York, (repr. 1956.)

Smith, S. 1940. *Alalakh and Chronology*, London.

Von Soden, W. 1949. 'Zum akkadischen Wörterbuch', *Orientalia* 18, pp. 385–403.

—— 1953. 'Neue Bände der Archives Royales de Mari', *Orientalia* 22, pp. 193–204.

Soggin, J. A. 1985. *A History of Israel*, London.

Sollberger, E. & Kupper, J.-R. 1971. *Inscriptions royales sumériennes et akkadiennes*, Paris.

Speiser, E. A. 1958. 'Census and Ritual Expiation in Mari and Israel', *BASOR* 149, pp. 17–25.

—— 1963. 'Background and Function of the Biblical Nasi', *CBQ* 25, pp. 111–117.

—— 1964. *Genesis* (Achor Bible), Garden City, N.Y.

Sperling, D. 1972. 'Akkadian *egirru* and Hebrew *bt qwl*', *JANES* 4, pp. 63–74.

Spronk, K. 1986. *Beatific Afterlife in Ancient Israel* (*AOAT* 219), Neukirchen-Vluyn.

Spycket, A. & Strommenger, E. 1981. in B. Hrouda, *Isin-Išān Baḫriyāt* II, München, pp. 55–58 and Pl. 20: 2–3.

Stadelmann, R. 1967. *Syrisch-Palästinensische Gottheiten in Ägypten*, Leiden.

Stager, L. E. 1985. 'The Archaeology of the Family in Ancient Israel', *BASOR* 260, pp. 1–35.

Stamm, J. J. 1939. *Die akkadische Namengebung*, Leipzig.

Starr, I. 1983. *The Ritual of the Diviner*, (Bibliotheca Mesopotamica 12), Malibu, Calif.

Steiner, F. 1956. *Taboo*, Harmondsworth.

Stoebe, H. J. 1973. *Das erste Buch Samuels* (*KAT*), Gütersloh.

Stol, M. 1972. 'Akkadisches *šāpiṭum*, *šapāṭum* und westsemitisches *špṭ*', *BiOr* 29, pp. 276–277.

Stolz, F. 1972. 'Die Bäume des Gottesgarten auf dem Libanon', *ZAW* 84, pp. 141–156.

Störk, L. 1977. 'Gold', *LÄ* II, cols. 725–731.

Strommenger, E. *et al.* 1987. 'Tell Bi'a', *MDOG* 119, pp. 10–16.

Tadmor, H. 1958. 'The Correct Rendering of Akkadian *dâku*', *JNES* 17, pp. 129–141.

—— 1970. 'The Chronology of the Ancient Near East in the Second Millennium B.C.', in B. Mazar (ed.), *Patriarchs* (*World History of the Jewish People* II), Jerusalem, pp. 63–101.

—— 1973. 'The Historical Inscriptions of Adad-Nirari III', *Iraq* 35, pp. 141–150.

—— 1977. 'A Lexicographical Text from Hazor', *IEJ* 27, pp. 98–102.

Tallqvist, K. 1926. 'Himmelsgegende und Winde', *Studia Orientalia* 2, pp. 106–185.

Talmon, S. 1984. S.v. '*midbār*', *TWAT* 4, cols. 660–695.

—— 1987. '*Yad vašem*', in H. Beinart & S. Loewenstamm (eds.), *Studies in Bible* (*U. Cassuto Memorial Volume*), Jerusalem, pp. 137–147, (Hebrew).

Talon, P. 1978. 'Les offrandes funéraires à Mari', *AIPHOS* 22, pp. 53–75.

—— 1985. 'Quelques réflexions sur les clans hanéens', in J.-M. Durand & J.-R. Kupper (eds.), *Miscellanea Babylonica* (*Mélanges M. Birot*), Paris, pp. 277–284.

—— 1986. 'Les nomades et le royaume de Mari', *Akkadica* 48, pp. 1–9.

Thiel, W. 1985. *Die soziale Entwicklung Israels in vorstaatlicher Zeit*[2], Neukirchen.

Thompson, L. T. 1974. *The Historicity of the Patriarchal Narratives*, *BZAW* 133, Berlin.

Thompson, L. & Lamar, H. 1981. *The Frontier in History*, New Haven.

Thompson, R. C. 1930. *The Epic of Gilgamesh*, Oxford.

—— 1949. *A Dictionary of Assyrian Botany*, London.

Thureau-Dangin, F. 1936. 'Iaḫdunlim, Roi de Hana', *RA* 33, pp. 49–54.

—— 1939. 'Sur des étiquettes de paniers à tablettes provenant de Mari', in J. Friedrich *et al.* (eds.), *Symbolae Paulo Koschaker Dedicatae*, Leiden, pp. 119–120.

—— 1941. 'Asakku', *RA* 38, pp. 41–43.

—— 1943. 'La terme šipṭum dans les lettres de Mari', *Orientalia* 12 (NS), pp. 110–112.
Tigay, J. H. 1982. *The Evolution of the Gilgamesh Epic*, Philadelphia.
Van der Toorn, K. 1985. *Sin and Sanction in Israel and Mesopotamia*, Assen.
—— 1987. 'L'oracle de victoire comme expression prophètique au Proche Orient ancien', *RB* 94, pp. 63–97.
Tromp, N. J. 1969. *Primitive Conceptions on Death and the Netherworld in the Old Testament*, Rome.
Tsukimoto, A. 1985. *Untersuchungen zur Totenpflege (kispum) im Alten Mesopotamien*, Neukirchen-Vluyn.
Ucko, P. J. *et al.* 1972. *Man, Settlement and Urbanism*, London.
Uffenheimer , B. 1973. *Early Israelite Prophecy*, Jerusalem, (Hebrew).
Ullendorff, E. 1977. *Is Biblical Hebrew a Language?*, Wiesbaden.
De Vaux, R. 1961. *Die hebräischen Patriarchen und die modernen Entdeckungen*, Düsseldorf.
—— 1969. 'El et Baal', *Ugaritica* VI, Paris, pp. 501–517.
—— 1978. *The Early History of Israel* I–II, London.
Veenhof, K. R. 1972. *Aspects of Old Assyrian Trade and its Terminology*, Leiden.
—— 1985. 'Eponyms and Mari Chronology', *MARI* 4, pp. 191–218.
Villard, P. 1986. 'Un roi de Mari à Ugarit', *UF* 18, pp. 387–412.
De Vries, S. 1978. *Prophet against Prophet*, Grand Rapids, Mich.
Wächter, L. 1967. *Der Tod im Alten Testament*, Stuttgart.
Weinfeld, M. 1977. 'Ancient Near Eastern Patterns in Prophetic Literature', *VT* 27, pp. 178–195.
—— 1983. in M. Bar Asher *et al.* (eds.), *Meḥqᵉrē Lāshōn* (Z. Ben-Hayyim Festschrift), Jerusalem, (Hebrew), pp. 195–200.
—— 1984. S.v. '*kābōd*', *TWAT* 4, cols. 23–34.
Weippert, M. 1967. *Die Landnahme der israelitischen Stämme in der neueren wissenschaftlichen Diskussion*, Göttingen.
—— 1981. 'Assyrische Prophetien der Zeit Asarhaddons und Assurbanipals', in F. M. Fales (ed.), *Assyrian Royal Inscriptions: New Horizons* (*OAC* 17), Rome, pp. 71–17.
—— 1985. 'Die Bildsprache der neuassyrischen Prophetie', in H. Weippert *et al.* (eds.), *Beiträge zur prophetischen Bildsprache in Israel und Assyrien*, Fribourg & Göttingen, pp. 55–93.
—— & Weippert, H. 1982. 'Die "Bileam" Inschrift von Tell Der 'Alla', *ZDPV* 98, pp. 77–103.
Westenholz, A. 1987. *Old Sumerian and Akkadian Texts in Philadelphia* II (*OSP*), Copenhagen (Carsten Niehbur Institute).
Westermann, C. 1981. *Genesis II, 12–36*, Neukirchen-Vluyn.
Wilcke, C. 1983a. 'Nachlese zu A. Poebels: Babylonian Legal and Business Documents from the Time of the First Dynasty of Babylon chiefly from Nippur (*BE* 6/2)', *ZA* 73, pp. 48–66.
—— 1983b. '*ittātim ašqi aštāl*: Medien in Mari?', *RA* 77, pp. 93 f.
Willmes, B. 1984. *Die sogennante Hirtenallegorie Ez. 34*, Frankfurt a.M.
Wilson, R. R. 1980. *Prophecy and Society in Ancient Israel*, Philadelphia.
Wiseman, D. J. 1965. 'Review: M. L. Burke', *ARMT* XI, 1963, *JSS* 10, pp. 124–126.
—— 1975. 'A Gilgamesh Epic Fragment from Nimrud', *Iraq* 37, pp. 157–163.
Wolff, H. W. 1974. *Anthropology of the Old Testament*, London.
Worschech, V. 1983. *Abraham*, Frankfurt a.M.
Yadin, Y. 1972. *Hazor* (The Schweich Lectures, 1970), London.

—— 1976. 'Hazor', in M. Avi-Yonah (ed.), *EAEHL* II, Jerusalem, pp. 474–495.
Yaron, R. 1969. 'Foreign Merchants at Ugarit', *Israel Law Review* 4, pp. 70–79.
Yeivin, S. 1963. 'The Age of the Patriarchs', *RSO* 38, pp. 277–302.
Yenner, K. A. & Özbal, H. 1987. 'Tin in the Turkish Taurus Mountains: The Bolkardag Mining District', *Antiquity* 61, pp. 220–226.
Yonick, S. 1970. *Rejection of Saul as King of Israel*, Jerusalem.
Yorkoff, H. 1972. 'A Mold from Mari and its Relations', *JANES* 4, pp. 21–32.
Al-Zeebari, A. 1964. *Altbabylonische Briefe des Iraq-Museums*, Münster.
Zettler, R. L. 1987. 'Sealings as Artifacts of Institutional Administration in Ancient Mesopotamia', *JCS* 39, pp. 197–240.
Zimmerli, W. 1969. *Ezechiel* II, Neukirchen-Vluyn.
Zimmern, H. 1901. *Beiträge zur Kenntnis der babylonischen Religion*, Leipzig.
—— 1914. *Akkadische Fremdwörter*, Lipsiae.
Zohary, M. 1954. S.v. '*b^{e}roš*', *Encyclopaedia Biblica* II, Jerusalem, cols. 340–344, (Hebrew).
Van Zyl, A. H. 1960. *The Moabites*, Leiden.

INDEX I
GENERAL

Aaron 106
Abdi-Yamm 109
Abel-Beth-Maacah 43, 50
Abi-Ram 31, 32
Abiram (and Dathan) 101, 106
Abi-Samar 117
Abraham 29, 30, 31, 45, 52, 54, 106, 107
Abram 31
Absalom 104
Achan 74, 75, 79
Adad 50, 55, 72, 75, 86
Adad of Aleppo 83, 86, 87, 112
Adad of Maḫanum 58
Adadnirari I 112
Adadnirari III 115
Adar 98
Addi-Addu 57
Addu-Dūri 12, 84
administration 6, 12, 55, 72, 86, 97
administrative documents 8, 56, 60
Aegean 58, 59
afterlife 96
Afghanistan 57
Agag 78
Ahab 21, 78, 86, 89, 91
Aḫatum 90
Aḫi-Laban 31
Aḫum 90
Akkad, Akkadian 2, 4, 23, 25, 55, 58, 62, 63, 67, 68, 70–4, 76, 79, 80, 85, 86, 87, 93, 96, 97, 98, 99, 100–3, 108, 109, 111, 113, 114, 116
Alaḫtum 50
Alalaḫ 55
Aleppo 2, 11, 12, 50, 57, 58, 59, 61–4, 72, 86
alliance 5
Amalek(ite) 54, 78
Amanus mountains 112, 113, 115–17, 119
Amarna see el-Amarna
Amaz 53
Amaziah 90
Amenhotep II 55
Amenhotep IV (Ikhnaton) 66
Ammi-ṣaduqa 99
Ammonite 88
Amnanum 117
Amorite 2, 6, 10, 24, 25, 27, 30, 32, 35, 39, 57, 84, 97, 99, 101, 102, 103, 109, 112, 117, 120
Amos 82, 90
Amud-pi-El of Qatna 4, 57, 58
Amurru(m) 6, 8, 38, 39, 53, 56, 62, 76, 115
anathema 70, 78, 104
ancestors 98, 99, 104, 105, 106; ancestor cult 96, 106; ancestor god 101; ancestor worship 25
ancestral home 105
ancestral spirits 98, 102, 104, 105, 106
ancestral clan/tribe 54, 99
answerer/respondent 86–8
Anath 110
Anatolia (Kaniš) 2, 52, 57, 84
Anatot 82
Annunītum 86, 87, 90, 94
Anti-Lebanon 112, 113, 114, 119
Antioch 112
anthropological (terms) 40
Annu-tabni 86
Appān 40
Arabian-Syrian desert 53, 84
Arad 73
Aram Naharaim 40, 52, 53, 54
Aramaic 20, 33, 52, 84, 88, 100, 106, 113, 114
Aramaic Targum 113
Aramean 78, 91
archives 11, 15, 16, 19, 20, 53, 62, 115
army 39, 42, 59, 77, 91, 116
Arrapḫum, Arrapḫa 61, 62
Asher 41
Ashera 86
Ashtar-Chemosh 79
Ashur 10 (city), 57, 90, 117
Asqudum 8, 16, 80
Assyria(n) 4, 10, 13, 52, 65, 87, 98, 100, 102, 117, 118
Assyrian interregnum 56, 102
Assyrian King List 99
Astarte 111
Astarte Papyrus 110
Ashurbanipal 62, 81, 114
Ashurnasirpal II 111, 114, 115
Atar-Aya 59
Aṯtr 110
auditory 'experience' 93
Avvites 47
Awīn, bīt Awīn (clan) 40, 41, 48, 71
Ayala 94

Baal 86, 110, 113
Baal myth, Ugarit 51
Baal Peor, Moab 104
Baalšamayn 88
Babylon 2, 13, 14, 56, 60, 61, 62, 66, 86, 88, 89, 99, 100, 106, 112
Babylonian Wisdom Literature 14
Babylonian-Akkadian civilization 2
Baḫdi-Lim 8, 60, 61, 62, 64, 80, 90
Baḫlu-gāyim 38
Balaam 5, 87, 88
Balaam Inscription 88; oracles of Balaam 29, 87
Balak of Moab 87, 88
Baliḫ 24, 52, 53, 87
ban (= taboo) 70–4, 76, 78, 79
Baruch son of Neriah 84
bathroom 22, 24
Beer sheba 37, 44, 73
Ben-Hadad 78
Benjamin 31, 35, 74; *Bi-ni-ya-mi-na* 31, 35
Benjamin, Walter 69
Beor 87
Beqa Valley 110, 118
Bethel 37, 90
Bethlehem 105
biblical historiographer 30, 56
Blessing of Jacob 29, 31
Blessing of Moses 29
Book of Job 45, 46
Book of Judges 34
bronze 13
Bronze Age: Early 1; Middle 1, 56, 65, 102; Middle I 29; Middle II 29, 45, 63; II A 55; II B 37, 55, 56, 58; Late 1, 29
bureaucracy 6, 7
butler (royal) 20, 21
Burnaburiaš II 66
Byblos 54, 62, 84, 109, 116, 118, and see Gubla
Byzantine 111

cakes (cultic) 22
campaign 59, 62, 89, 91, 107, 109, 111, 114, 115, 116, 117, 118, 120, 121; campaign of Sennacherib 89
Canaan(ite) 6, 30, 35–7, 40, 41, 45, 49–57, 60, 61, 63, 66, 78, 79, 82, 100, 110, 111, 115, 118, 119
Caphtor(ite) (= Crete) 8, 57, 58, 59
Cappadocian Texts 52, 57, 58
caravans, caravan trade 52, 53, 63, 64, 65, 66
Carchemish (Karkamiš) 45, 57, 62, 116
cardinal directions, points 66, 67
Carthaginians 34
cedar 112–14, 118–20
cedar forest 107, 116, 119
cedar mountain 107, 108, 112, 114, 116, 118
cella 24, 25
census-taking 70
centre and periphery 82
ceremonial hall 19, 23, 24, 25
Chemosh 79
Chosroes 112
Chronicles (Book) 83
chronology 1 (Middle, Low) 29, 30, 56, 58
Cicero 93
Cilicia 119
clan 34, 37–9, 43, 51–4, 71
Classical, classic 84, 93, 94, 111
Codex Hammurabi 65, 66
commemoration, commemorative stelae 106, 115
commerce 2 (banking), 4, 6, 58 (colony), 59, 60, 61, 63, 64
comparative anthropology 34
comparative study 27, 28, 37, 109
comparison (Mari-Bible) 11, 13, 27, 28, 30–32, 67, 68, 73, 81
concubine 54
conquest (Israelite) of Canaan 30, 56, 79
consecrated 70, 72, 73, 76, 77, 79, 86
contract 71, 72, 74
contrast (Mari-Bible) 28, 34, 52, 81, 83, 96; antithesis 5
contrasting approach 28
court of the palm in the Mari Palace 8, 9, 13, 22
court prophet 86
covenant-making 70
credibility (prophetic) 94, 95
Crete 2, 16, 57, 58 (Cretans), 116
cult of the dead 96, 104
cult prophet 85
cultic ritual 111
cylinder seal, impressions 8, 14
Cybele 119

Dagan 71, 72, 76, 83, 88, 89, 96, 97, 108
Dagan at Tuttul 116
Dagan of Terqa 87
Dan/Laish 58
Daniel 20
Dariš-libūr 60
Darius 20
Dathan 101, 106
David 21, 29, 45, 50 (army), 77, 86, 95, 104, 105, 106
Deborah 40, 92
Dedan 101
Deir ʿAlla (Inscription) 88
desert 54
diachronic (view of the Bible) 35, 44
Didanites/Ditanites 100, 106
Didanu/Ditanu 99, 101

dimorphic society 36, 37, 45
Dinah 36
diplomacy, diplomatic 2, 4, 61, 62, 63, 83
disc inscription of Yaḫdun-Lim 14
divination, divine 79, 81–4, 89, 91–6, 107, 108, 111, 112
divine word 80
diviner prophet 79–87, 96
Diyala 87
'doorbell' (door sealing) 16, 19, 20
Dothan 44, 45, 101
drainage system 24
dream book 62, 117
dream, dreamer 62, 81, 83, 87, 90–4, 96
dreamer prophet 95
dynastic 21 (forefathers), 98 (genealogy)

Ea-Maṣi 86
Ea-mudammiq 86
Ebla 1, 2, 10, 27, 52, 55, 65, 102, 105, 116, 117, 120
economy 36, 55, 57, 60, 116; economic centre 52; economic list, texts 38, 56; economic unit 34
ecstatic 81, 84, 85
Edom(ites) 79, 100
Egypt(ian) 2, 15, 24, 31, 52, 55, 61–3, 66, 84, 100, 110–12, 118
Ekallatum 61
Ekur archive 117
El 110, El/Il 108
-El (theophoric element) 31
el-Amarna 52, 56, 62, 66; archive 1, 9, 11, 109; Amarna Age, Period 2, 29
El-Laban 31
Elam 67, 87, 100
Elephantine 49; Elephantine Papyrus 20
Eli-ab 101
Elide clan 93
Emar 57, 62–5, 103, 116
Emori 8
En-Gedi (*midbār*) 44, 95
Enkidu 118, 120
Enlil 117
Enna-Dagan 117
Enuma Eliš 112
eponym 40, 41, 101
Erišti-Aya 86
Esarhaddon 81, 114
Eski-Haran 52
Ešnunna 4, 10, 56, 61, 87
Euphrates 10, 24, 46, 53, 54, 59, 62, 65, 67, 87, 99, 101, 108, 116, 117, 119
Europe 111
Ewri-Talma 57
Execration Texts 119
Exodus 30
extispicy 80
Ezekiel 51, 85

family 37, 40, 41, 43, 98, 104; ancestors 103; life 6; sacrifice 105; extended family 34, 40
Flood 120
food offerings 104
foodstuffs 20
forests 112, 118
forms of settlement 38
fresco 22, 23
Full Moon 97
funeral, funerary offering 97, 101; rites 104; sacrifice 82, 97; stele/statue 97

Gad 86
Galilee 43, 48, 50
Garden of Eden 23
garment (hem) 93
Gašera 12
Gaza 2, 62
Gebal (= Byblos) 8
genealogical list 41, 54, 99
Genealogy of Hammurabi Dynasty (GHD) 99
Genesis 31, 40, 45, 53; narratives 30
genetic, genetic connection 28, 29, 37, 40
gentilic, gentilic unit 38, 51
geographical setting 52, 53, 54, 62, 67, 118
geopolitical setting 5
Gezer 63
ghosts 98
Gibeon 82, 89
Gilgameš 107, 108, 116, 118–21
Giv'at Sharett 37
Great Green 110
Great King 112
Greece, Greek 16, 108, 109, 111
Gubla/Gebal (Byblos) 8, 62

Habiru 40, 53, 55
Ḫabur 53, 54, 99
Hagarites 54
hair, see lock of hair
Ḫaman 42
Hamath 84, 88
Ḫammurabi of Babylon 1, 4, 6, 10, 11, 13, 29, 58, 83, 89, 96, 99
Ḫammurabi of Aleppo 25, 58
Ḫammurabi period 32
Ḫana 44, 71, 96, 99 (Ḫeana); Ḫaneans 2, 25, 34, 35, 38–40, 42, 44, 46, 80, 98–100
Ḫanat (godess) 71
Hananiah 82, 89
Ḫanigalbat 112
(Ḫ)aqba-aḫum 31
(Ḫ)aqba/u-Ḫammû 31
Ḫaqbu-El 31
haruspex, haruspicy 79, 80, 84, 95, 96
Haran 52, 53, 54

harem 10, 11, 12
Ḥaṣar-addar 48
Ḥaṣar-asam ('sm) 48
Ḥaṣar-gaddah 48
Ḥaṣar-shual 48
Ḥaṣar-susah 48
Hattušili III 66, 112
Hazazar 57
Hazor, Hazorite 2, 4, 5, 48, 55–66, 73
Ḫeana 99 (= Ḫana)
Heber 40, 41
Heber the Kenite 39, 40
Hebrew lexicography 28
Hebrews 52; Hebrew tribes 30
Hebron 37, 41, 45, 60
Hellespont 111
hem of the garment 94, 95
Ḫēn 44
hepatoscopy 13
Hermon 113, 114
Herodotus 111
heroes 106, 107, 118, 119
Hezekiah 13, 90
high priest/priestess 90, 94
Hilkiahu 90
Hiram 113
historicity 29, 115, 117
historiographic books 83, 107, 117
Hittite 66, 84, 92, 94, 108, 119
Hobab 40, 41
holiness 70, 71, 73, 74
Holy One 110
holy people 79
holy war 78, 89
Hormah 78
hospes 106
Huldah 90, 92
Hurrian 14
Ḫuwawa 118–20
Hyksos 31, 32

Ibal-pī-El 4, 87
Ibn Ǧanah (Janaḥ) 106
Ibni-Adad 57, 58, 60
Idamaraṣ 4, 10, 53, 59
Idrimi Inscription 55
Igmilum 15
Il'ib 101
Ilā-Kabkabû 10, 98
Ilaba 101
Ili-Ummati 42
inheritance 37, 40, 48, 49, 50, 51
Inib-šina 15
international age 2
international trade 66
intuitive prophecy 1, 11, 79, 81, 83, 84, 95, 96
investiture of Zimri-Lim 23
invocations 100–7
Iran 2, 16, 57
Irra-gamil 86
Isaac 29, 30, 52, 54, 106, 107
Isaiah 90, 91, 100, 114
Išar-Lim 8
Ishchali 87, 119
Išḫi-Adad 56
Ishmael(ites) 31, 47, 54; Ishmaelite genealogy 42
Isin 16
Išme-Adad 55
Išme-Dagan 87, 90, 91, 102
Israel 5, 21, 27, 31, 32, 36; and Judah 82; ancestors 32; proto-history 30
Israelite-Gileadite 88
Israelite cradle 28
Ištar 4, 25, 99
Ištar = Astarte 21
Ištup-ilum 24, 25
itinerary 52, 62
Itūr-Asdu 4, 5, 53
Itūr-Mer 71, 72, 74, 76, 86, 108

Jabesh-Gilead 74
Jabin 56, 58
Jacob 29, 30, 32, 36, 52, 100, 106, 107; Jacob's sons 45
Jacob-El 31
Jehoiachin 21
Jehoiakim 90
Jeremiah 22, 43, 82, 83, 84, 87, 89, 90, 92, 93, 94, 96
Jericho 72, 74, 75, 78
Jeroboam 90
Jeruel 44
Jerusalem 37, 89, 90, 103, 113
Jesus 20
jewellery 13
Jews 106
Jezebel 86
Jezirah 52
Job 45, 51, 82
Jonathan 105
Jordan 54
Joseph 45, 100, 106
Joshua 30, 49, 59, 78
Josiah 90
Jubilee year 51
Judah(ites) 21, 40, 44, 48, 73, 82, 89, 90; and Israel 82
judge 34, 58
'Judge Nahar' 109
juniperus 113–15
Justinian 112

Kabbalistic literature 106
Kadašman-Enlil II 66
Kadesh 44
Kallassu 50

Kaptara 8, 58, 59
Karana 38, 60, 61
Kassite 62
Kedar 47, 48
Kenite 40, 41
Keret 101
Kharu 118
Kibri-Dagan 88, 89, 93
Kimḫi 106
Kings (book) 83
king's table 20; meals 97
kings, dead, deceased 97, 98, 103
kinglet 4
kinship system 39
kispum ritual 24, 25
kitchen 21
Kititum 87
kledon 91
Kubaba (Cybele) 119

Laban 31, 52; Laban's family gods 104
Lagaš 97
Laish (= Dan) 58, 62
Landnahme 36
Lapidoth 92
Larsa 4, 45
lay-persons 90
Layaš/Layašim/Layiš 57, 58
Leah 41, 51, 107
Lebanon, Mount Lebanon 54, 110–21
legal practices 37
letters 15, 25, 26
Letter to God 10
Levant, Levant Coast 2, 107, 116
Levites 104
lexicographical text 55
Lim dynasty 9, 10, 35, 96
lineage 54
linguistic factor 32
Lipšur Litanies 114, 117, 119
liturgy 100
liver, clay model livers 13, 14, 16, 55, 56
lock of hair (of prophet) 93–6, 110
Lydia 119

Maḫ(ḫ)an 2
Malgium 97
Malik 103
Manahat 37
mantic 79, 81, 95, 96
Maon 44
Marduk 87, 112
Mari archive 1, 6, 12, 14, 27
Mari dialect, Mari idiom 32, 48
matrilineal 41
Mediterranean 2, 59, 68, 107, 108, 109, 111–20
Megiddo 62, 63
memorial feast/service 106
merchants 52, 58, 64, 66; merchant caravans 53
Merodach-baladan 13
Meṣad Ḥashavyahu 48
Mesha Inscription 79
Meshech 100
Meskene 65
Mesopotamia 2, 27, 52, 56, 61, 62, 84, 96, 101, 112, 116
Mesopotamian archaeology 6
Mesopotamian commerce 2
Mesopotamia-Syria-Palestine 4, 46
message dreams 92
messenger 56, 60–6
metals, precious 6
Micah 82
Micaiah son of Imlah 91
midbār, midbār Gibeon etc. 44, 54
Middle Euphrates 2, 34, 42
Middle Kingdom 111
Midian(ites) 42, 77
Midrash 5
migration, migratory group 44
Milcah 54
missions 53
Mittani 112
Moab 79, 87, 104
Molek, Moloch 103
Moreshet 82
Moses 30, 96, 101, 106
mother city 43
moulds (kitchen) 21, 22
Mount Lebanon, see Lebanon
Mount Zaphon 51
Mukannišum 8, 9, 10, 14, 15
multi-polar system 4
Muršili 92
Muzunnim 57
mythical 120; mythological 108, 110, 112

Naboth 51, 52
Naharin(a), Nahrima, Nārima 52
Nahor(ites) 4, 40, 52, 53, 54
Nahr el-Kalb 118
Namḫu 99
Naram-Sin 25, 98, 99, 116, 117
Nathan 86
Nebo 79
Nebuchadnezzar II 89, 118
Negeb 48
Nehemiah 21
neo-Assyrian 80, 81, 108, 111, 114, 118
neo-Babylonian 118
Nergal (of Hubšalum) 86, 87
netherworld 100, 102, 106
New Kingdom 110
New Moon 25, 97, 102, 105, 106
Nimrud 115

Ninḫursag 86
Nippur 117
nomadism 34–6, 40–2, 44, 47, 48, 52, 53, 71, 76, 84, 100, 102; enclosed nomadism 36, 37, 45
Nonsuch Palace 26
Nuabu 99
Numḫā, Numḫû, Numḫeans 25, 98, 99, 100
Nuzi 103

oath 72; oath-formula 72
ocean 107, 108, 109, 118, 120
offerings 97, 98, 99, 105, 111
omens 80, 96
onomasticon 31, 32
Ophir 113
oracles 29, 79, 86–8, 91
orientation 67

P source 50
palace 1, 5, 6, 8, 11, 14, 15, 19, 20, 21, 23, 25, 26, 56, 59, 60, 73, 80, 83 84, 86, 87, 90, 98–100
Palestine 1, 2, 37, 40, 45, 55, 58, 60–3, 84
palm 8; see court of the palm
Paradise 23
Pashḥur (son of Immer) 85, 90
Passover see Pesaḥ
Passover Papyrus 20
pastoral semi nomads 36, 44
pasturage 44–7
Patriarchs 22, 28, 29, 32, 37, 45, 50, 52–4, 61; Age 29, 30; family 31; names 32; narratives 28–30, 44
patriarchal-tribal 51
patrilineal regimes 34
patrimony 38, 48, 49, 50, 51, 52
Pentecost 107
Persian 111
Persian Gulf 109
Pesaḥ (Passover) 106, 107
Peshitta 113
phenomenological method 28, 92
Philistine 89
Phoenician 115
Piankhy, Piye (king) 15
plain of Jezreel 40
politics, political relationship 2, 4, 11, 53, 62, 89; political system 36
Pontius Pilate 20
pre-Sargonic (period) 2; palace 114
premonarchic (period) 37; institutions 37
priesthood 85, 90, 94, 104; diviner priest 8; priestess 88
Prince Yamm 109, 110
Procopius 111
prophecy 79–96; false prophets 89, 92; lay prophet 91, 92; cf. intuitive prophecy
proto-history of Israel 30, 31, 101
Psalms 47, 120

Qabra 61
Qatna (Qaṭna) 2, 4, 5, 46, 53–8, 60, 61, 62, 114, 119
Qišatum 87
Queen of Heaven 22
Queen of Sheba 21

Rabbean (tribe) 40, 41, 48; *Rabbû* 71
Rabbinic, rabbinic literature 93, 106
Rachel 41, 51, 104, 107
Ramah of Benjamin 45
Ras al-ʿAin 53
Razama 47
realia 6
Rebekah 107
redactors 104
reflection 30
religion 6
Rephaim 101; Rephaim valley 37
respondent 88
Reumah 54
Ribbatum 86
Rīm-Sin 4
ritual 70, 76, 79, 97, 99, 102, 103, 105, 111; ritual meal (*kispum*) 21
royal administration 38; royal ancestors 24, 25; royal apartments 11; royal ceremonial complex 22; royal cult 96, 97, 102; royal kitchens 21; royal meals 20, 102

Šāb̲uot (Pentecost) 107
sacred 70, 73, 107, 118, 119, 120
sacred chapels 26
Sacred Sea 107
sacrifice(s) 73, 78, 79, 88, 96, 97, 98, 100, 102, 104, 105, 108, 110, 111, 112, 115, 119
sacrifice(s) of the 'days' 105
sacrificial animals 25
sacrificial meal 98, 100, 106
safe (coffer) 8
Saggarātum 74
šakkanakku 16, 24
Samānum 42
Samaria 67
Šamaš 25, 71, 72, 74, 75, 107
Šamaš of Sippar 72, 84, 86
Šamši-Adad 10, 14, 23–5, 35, 56, 59, 71, 72, 74–6, 78, 98, 99, 102, 107, 114, 117–18, 119, 121
Samuel 78, 83, 89, 93
Sarah 107
Sargon the Great 25, 98, 114–16, 120, 121
Sargon II 114

Saria (= Sirion, Anti Lebanon) 119
Šarmaneḫ (Tarmanni) 4, 5
Sassanian 112
sattelite village 37
Saul 77, 78, 87, 89, 92, 95, 104, 105
scribe of Amurru 76
scribes 6, 12, 32, 56, 60, 76, 83–5, 111
sea 107–12, 118
seal 8, 14, 15, 16, 19, 21, 64; sealing 20, 35
sealed baskets 15; sealed chambers 14, 20; sealed document 63; sealed doors 15, 19; sealed room 15; sealed store-room 13, 22
sedentarisation, sedentary 34–6, 38, 39, 44
Šeḫrum 94
Semitic peoples 41, 67, 68, 70, 108
Sennacherib 13, 89, 114
Septuagint 34
settlements 48; open settlement 47
Shallum 92
Shalmaneser III 111, 115, 118
Shechem 36, 37, 45
sheikhs 4, 102
Sheol 100, 101, 103, 106
Shiloh 93
Shunā 60
Sibawayhi 49
Šibtu 12, 15, 19, 84, 90, 91
Sidonian 100, 119
Silver Mountain 116
Sim'alites (Northerners) 10, 35, 39, 44, 86
Simeon 48
Sin 52, 97
Sin-Naṣir 97
Sippar 5, 45, 86
Sirion (Anti-Lebanon) 113, 114, 117, 119
social system 34, 36–8, 81, 84
societies 34, 37, 82
socio-ethical/moral 79, 83
sociology 34, 36, 37, 82
Sodom 67
Solomon 21, 86, 113
Song of Deborah 29, 41
Song of the Sea 29, 50, 51
sons of the prophets 82; cf. *b^e^ne n^e^bi'im* (Index III)
space (Mari-Bible) 29, 66, 67, 68
spatial-temporal 68
spirits 98, 104
spoils of war 75–9
Standard Akkadian 32, 34, 43, 67, 68
Standard Babylonian 98
statues, steles 23, 24, 25, 98, 115, 117, 118
statue of Ištar 23
store-rooms 13, 14, 15, 20
suffetes 34
Šu-Sin 97
Ṣubatum 72
Sukkot (Tabernacles) 107
Sumerian 103, 108, 109, 120; Sumerian cult 97
Sumero-Akkadian 109
Sumu-Erah 57
Sumu-Yamam 10, 35
Ṣuprum 10
Suteans 40, 44, 46
synchronic (picture of Mari) 35
Syria 2, 24, 27, 52, 54, 57, 60, 61, 64, 66, 86, 100, 109, 113, 114, 116, 117
Syro-Arabian Desert 27; Syro-Mesopotamia 14; Syro-Palestine 30

Tabernacles 107; feast of- 106
taboo 70, 75, 77, 78
Tadmer/Tadmor (= Palmyra) 8
Takil-iliššu 97
Talmud 91, 109, 112
Tarmanni 4
Taurus 57, 116
Tekoa 44, 82
telescoping 30
Tell Biʿya 10, 24 (= Tuttul 24)
Tell al-Rimaḥ 38, 41, 95 (= Karana? Qaṭṭara?)
Tell el-Dabʿa 24
temporal 68; time (Mari-Bible) 29, 66
Terah 52
Terqa 10, 71, 72, 80, 82, 88, 96
Thailand 57
throne 23, 25; throne room 6, 23, 25, 98
Thutmose III 63
Tiamat 112
Tiglath-pileser III 113
Tigris 61, 62
tin 4, 57, 58; inventory 5; trade 57
trade 57, 64, 116
Transjordan 88
treasury 13, 68 (treasure)
tribes 34, 36–8, 40–2, 44, 45, 48, 49, 52–4, 74, 75, 80, 84, 86, 99–101; confederation 42, 54; eponyms 99, 101; institutions 37; leadership 34, 37; regimes 34; settlement 37; tribal structure 38, 39
tribe and city (relationship) 37
troops 37
Tubal 100
Turukkeans 53
Tuttul 10, 82, 87, 88, 116
typological method 28

Ugarit 2, 25, 42, 47, 51, 54, 57–60, 66, 97, 100, 101, 103, 105, 106, 108–13, 116, 120; Ugaritic line of kings 32; Ugaritic texts 119
underworld 97
Ur III 23
urban 40, 84; urban centres 43, 44; urban society 52
Urim (oracle) 92
Uruk 119
Ushpizin 106

Valley of the Cedar 110
Valley of the Lebanon 119
victory stele 114
vision 93, 94, 96
votive gift 73, 78
votive inscription (for Ištar) 99

Wadi Brissa 118
war, encounter 36, 75, 77, 91, 100
weapons 23
Wen-Amon 84, 118
West 2, 7, 27, 54, 56–62, 66–8, 84, 101, 107, 112–15, 117
West Semitic 1, 2, 22, 23, 27, 32, 34, 36, 41, 42, 44, 46, 47, 49, 54, 55, 58, 70, 77, 79, 80, 84–6, 93, 99, 100, 102, 103, 108, 109; idioms and terms 32, 37, 67, 68; social institutions 48
wine cellar 24
women 11, 12, 90, 91

Xerxes 111

Ya ʿaqob̲-ʾAḥ, Yaʿaqob-Haddu, Yaʿaqob-Har 31 cf. Jacob
Yabni-Addu 58
Yaggid-Lim 10, 107
Yaḫdun-Lim 8, 10, 13, 14, 35, 42, 44, 59, 65, 72, 73, 80, 96, 107, 108, 109, 111–21; Disc Inscription 16; Foundation Inscription 107
Yaḫqub-El 31
Yahwe 50, 72, 79, 119; Yahwistic 104
Yailites 40
Yamama 80
Yamḫad 2, 4, 50, 53, 54, 57–9, 61–5, 112, 116
Yaminites 39, 40, 42, 44, 46, 52, 53, 62, 74, 86
Yamm 109–12
Yanana 83, 84
Yaqarum 101
Yarim-Addu 48
Yarim-Lim 4, 11, 12, 58, 59, 63, 64, 66, 112
Yarmuti 116
Yasmah-Adad 10, 12, 35, 56, 74–6
Yasmah-El 31
Yemen 67
Yered 100
Yiśrāʾēl 31
Yizkōr (Remembrance) 106
Yom Kippur (Day of Atonement) 107

Zakkur 84, 88
Zalmaqum 52
Zedekiah 90
Zelophehad 51
Zimri-Lim 2, 4, 6, 8–16, 24, 25, 35, 49, 50, 53, 57–60, 62–5, 68, 71–3, 80, 81, 83, 86, 88–91, 96, 99, 102, 107, 112
Zion 43, 50
Ziph 44
Zizi 12

INDEX II
AKKADIAN WORDS AND SUMEROGRAMS

A.AB.BA 108, 109, 116
A.AB.BA *rabītum* 118
abi'ānum 33
abum, abbū 42; *ša abbē* 101; *ša abīya* 45
aharātum 33, 63
akālum 71, 77; *īkul* 71
A-KUL 120
ālik idim 60, 61
amārum 94; *āmuru* 93
Amurrum 56, 67
AN 108
anzillum 71
apālum 86, 88
apillûm 86
āpiltum 86, 87, 88, 96
āpilum 50 (*āpilū*), 72, 86, 87, 88, 89
aplûm, aplû 86, 88
aqdamātum 33, 67, 68
ša ištu aqdami 68
[*Ar-ra-*]*ap-ḫi-im* 62
asakkum 70–7, 79, 86
asakkam akālum 71
assinnum 85
awīlum 4
ayaba 108, 109

bārûm 80, 82, 84, 88, 89
baza(ḫā)tum 33
bēlum, ša bēlīya 45
bēl pagrē 97
bērum 59
**binū/banū* 31
binū/banū-yamīna 35
bīt abim 34
bīt hilāni 10
bīt kussî 25
bīt nakkamti 13
bīt rimki 111
bītānu 11
bur-zi 59
burāšum 114, 115

dannātim šakānum 77
dannum 4
dīn napištim 74
DUB.SAR.MAR.TU 76
DUMU.MEŠ 31
DUMU.MEŠ-*sim'al* 35, 67
DUMU.MEŠ-*yamīna* 35, 42, 67

eblum 15
É.DAM.NI 10
É.GAL 10
egerrûm 91
elammakum 108, 112, 113, 119
EN 103
enūtum 94
eqlum, eqlāt^{meš} 48
erēbum 67
erēnum 113, 118; ^{giš}*erēnam* 118
eṭemmum 25, 96, 98, 104
ētiqtum 61

gaba'um 33
GAL.KUD 76
GAL.MAR.TU 76
gāyum, gā'um 33, 38, 39, 42
gāyum Amurrum 39

ḫa(yā)rum 33
ḫabārum 40
ḫabbātum 55
ḫakim 33
ḫakûm 33
ḫalûm 33
ḫalṣum, ša ḫalṣim 45
ḫamāṣum 115
ḫamūṣam iḫmuṣ 115, 120
ḫamqum 33
Ḫana (ḫibrum) ša nāwêm 40, 44
ḪAR-*ra* = *ḫubullu* 56, 98, 113, 117, 119
ḫarāšum 33
Ḫaṣurāyum^{ki} 57
ḫaṣārum 33, 38, 47, 48
ḫaṣīrātum 33, 47
ana ḫaṣārim šaḫātim 47
ḫazzum 33
ḫēn 33
ḫibrum 33, 38–41, 44
ḫibrum ša nawêm 40, 41

ḫiglum 33
ḫimrum 33
ḫīṭum 46
ḫurru-bird 94

ikkibu 71, 72, 79
ilum, i-lu-um 108
isiḫtum 76
isqum, isiqtum 76
išme- 55
ištānu (iltēnu) 67
ittātim 91

k/qaṣûm 33
kallûm 61, 95
kalûm 64
kamānum 22
Kaptarāyum 58
kārum 58
kasāmum 118
kàs-pa ili 72
Kinaḫḫi 66; *Ki-na-aḫ-num^{meš}* 55
kispum 21, 24, 25, 96–106
ana kispim ša abbē 101
kispum ša šarrāni 102
kispa takassip 98
kunukkum 64
^{giš}kur-sa-lu 59
kussû eṭimmē 98

La-ab-na-an 117, 119; *La-ab-na-nu* 113
La-ab-a-an^{ki}, *La-ba-an^{ki}* 117
lamassātum 25, 98
La-Pi-iš 58
lāsimum ša sikkim 61
leqûm 74
libbum, ina ṭūbi libbim 49
LUGAL 103

maḫûm, immaḫu 85, 86
maḫḫûm 85
ma-li-gú-um 102
malikum, maliktum, malik, malku, milki 33; (*malikū*), 102, 103
ana malikī 102
mālikum 102
mār šiprim, mārū šiprim 61
marḫašu 59
mārum 31
Mārū-yamīna 35
mātum 117
merḫûm 33
meteia 103
miksum 2
mubassirum 61
muḫḫûm 85–8, 96
muḫḫūtum 85–8, 90
MUŠEN.ḪURRI 94

naḫālum 33, 48, 49; *inḫil* 38, 49, 50; *inḫilunini* 48; *ittaḫalu* 49
NAM.EN 103
naptan šarrim 20
naqāmum 33
naṭālum, naṭlat 94; *aṭṭulu* 93
nawûm 32, 33, 37, 38, 43, 44, 45, 46
niḫlatum 33, 38, 48, 50, 82
nīš(šarrim) 72 76
NU.BANDA 76

pagrā'um, pagrā'ī 97
pagrûm 97
panûm, ina panītim 68
ina panīya 93
parûm 60
pisannum 8
purrusum 85

qabbātum (qamatum) 85, 87, 96
qabûm 85
qatālum 33
qātum, qāti 118; *ana mīl qātišunu* 76; *ana qāt × mullû* 76

rabiam 108
rāgimu, rāgintu 81
ramākum 111
rimkum 111
ruqqum 75

sabākum 33
saḫātum 33
SAR 71
Sa-ri-a 119
**sim'al* 33, 35, 67
Si-ra-a 114
sissiktum 95
sugāgum 74
suḫrum 33
ṣalmum 118
ṣiṣi 12
ṣuḫarum 93, 102
šadû 67
šakānum 77; *luškunma, luštaknam* 118
šalûm 33
šangûm 85

šapāṭum 33, 34, 77
šāpiṭum 33, 34, 77
šāpiṭūtum 33, 34, 77
šarāqum 74
šarrāni 4, 97, 102
šarrāni[meš] *A*-[*mu*]-*ur-ri-i* 56
šarrum 4, 102
šarrum dannum 4
šārtum 95
šipṭam nadānum/šakānum 77
šipṭum 33, 34, 77
šuḫtum 75
šurmēnum 113, 114
šūtu 67
šuttum, ina šuttim, ina šuttīya 93

targamannum 58
ták-lu 95
tâmtum, [d]*tâmtum* 107, 109; *tiamtum* 108
taskarinnum 113
tebûm 92
terḫatum 12
tubqum 11

ṭēḫītum 60

ummānum 41
ummat Ḫana 42
ummat TUR/DUMU-mi-im 42
ummatum 33, 38, 39, 41, 42

wardum 100
wašābum 33

yābiltum 33
yagātum 33
yalūtum 33
yamīn(*a*) 33 (**yamīna*), 35, 67
yaradu, yarādum 25, 33, 98, 99, 100

zakûm, lizakkû 95

INDEX III
HEBREW AND OTHER WEST SEMITIC LANGUAGES
(according to the Hebrew alphabet)

'eḇyōn 33
'āhōr 33, 67, 68
  *le'*āhōr 68
'aharōn 68
'aḥarīt 68
  'aharīt hayyamīm 68
'eyāl
'ylwt, 'ayyālōt 120
'īš hā'elōhīm 82, 85
'īš ḥermi 78
'īš yemīnī
  'anšē haššem 106
  'anšē milḥāmāh 39
  'anāšīm 77
'kl 73
'ēlleh 49
'elōhīm 87, 104
'ēlōt 120; see *'ylwt*
almog, 'almuggīm 113
'ēm 41, 43
  'ēm hadderek 43
*'om 43
'ummāh 33, 38, 39, 41, 42, 43
'ummōt 43
'umīm 43
'sp
  ne'esaṗ 'el 'aḇōtāw 101
  ne'esaṗ 'el 'ammī 101
'oṣerōt haqqodāšīm 73
'arāzīm 113
'ereṣ yemīnī 35
'ereṣ yardēn 100
'ēšet ḥayīl 12

bādād, lebādād 5
bēt āḇ 34
bēt nekōt 13
  lbỳ[t yhw]h qdš khnm 73
bkh
  bōkiyāh 88
bāmōtām (>bemōtām) 103
ben yemīnī 35
benē Yiśr'āēl 35
benē neḇī'īm 82
benē 'Ammōn 35
benē qedem 35
bṣ' 33
berōš, berōšīm 113, 114
bat qōl 91

gibbēn 85
gibbōrīm 106
gibe'āh 33
gōy 33, 38, 42, 43; *gōyīm* 43
gōrāl 49, 76

drš
  dōrēš 'el hammētīm, 'el 'elōhāw
    yidrōš 105
har naḥalateka 50
hārē merōm yiśrā'ēl 46

zbḥ ymm 105
zeḇaḥ hayyāmīm 105
zeḇaḥ mišpāhā 105
ziḇḥē 'elōhīm 104
ziḇḥē mētīm 104
zkr
  hazkēr šēm, hazkēr šemī 104, 106
zrḥ 67

hēḇel neḇī'īm 86
ḥbr 39, 41
ḥeber 33, 38, 39, 40, 43
ḥōzeh 82, 85, 86
ḥṭ' 46
  'aḥaṭṭenna 46
  teḥeṭa' 46
ḥākōh 33
ḥāḵām 33
ḥālōh 33
ḥalelē ḥereb 99
ḥālōm, baḥalōmī 93
ḥēleq 77
  ḥēleq wenaḥalāh 51
ḥemer 33
ḥāṣēr 33, 38, 47
ḥāṣōr 48
ḥaṣērīm 33, 47, 48
ḥaṣērōt 47
ḥoq u-mišpāt 78
ḥrm 78
ḥērem 70, 71, 73, 74, 78, 79
  hāyā, hāyū leḥērem 71, 74
  hērem leYahwe 72
  kol ḥērem 'ašer yoḥoram 74
  hḥrmth 79
ḥārōš 33

ṭwb
hēṭaḇtā lir'ōt 94

**yaḇal, yūḇāl* 33
yōḇēl 51
yāgōn 33
yād wāšem (lᵉzikkārōn) 104
yōm 'aḥᵃrōn 68
yām 108, 109, 110
hayyām hā'aḥᵃrōn 68
hayyām haggādōl 118
yāmīn 33, 67
yrd 100
yārōd 33, 100; *ērēd, yārᵉdū, hurād* 100; *wayyērᵉdū* 101
yōrᵉdē dūmāh 100
yōrᵉdē 'āp̲ār 100
yāšōḇ 33

kᵉḇōd šᵉmō 120
kawwānīm 22

lᵉ'om 10
lahᵃqat nᵉḇī'īm 86

mabbūl 120
mizrāḥ 67
mayīm rabbīm 120
mek̲es 2, 77
mallē' 'et yādām 76
mlk 120
melek̲ 33, 103
melek̲ 'az 4
malk̲ēhem 103 (ancestral spirits of their kings)
mō'ēd 106
ma'ᵃrāb 67
mērēᵃ' 33
mir'eh 46
maśśā' 87
mᵉšugga' 85
mšl 120
mišpāhā 43, 105
meteg hā' ammāh 43

nᵉ'ōt 'ᵉlōhīm 47
nᵉ'ōt deše 44
nāḇī' 82, 85, 86, 87
nibbā' 86
hitnabbē' 86
nōḇelet nᵉḇū'āh ḥᵃlōm 93

nāweh 33, 38, 43, 44, 45, 46, 47
nᵉwēh Ya'ᵃqōḇ 45
nᵉwēh midbār 44
nᵉwēh ṣō'n 44
nᵉwēh rō'īm 44
bᵉnāweh ṭōḇ 46
min hannāweh 45
nwyt/nāyōt 45
nḥl 51
nāḥōl 33; *naḥᵃlū, yinḥᵃlū, niḥḥᵃlū, niḥḥēl, linḥōl, lᵉnaḥḥēl* 49
naḥᵃlāh 33, 48, 50, 51
naḥᵃlat 'āḇōt 52
naḥᵃlat 'ᵉlōhīm 50
naḥᵃlat Yahwe 50
naḥᵃlat Yiśrā'ēl 50
nᵉ'ārīm 77
nōp̲ᵉlīm baḥereḇ 99
nāqōm 33
nāśī' 42, 51

sābōk 33
sukkāh 106

'ēgel 33
'iwwēr 85
'ēz 33
'oz melek̲ 4
'ayin 33, 44
'ayir 33
'kr 74
'am, 'amm 39, 42, 43, 101
'am ḥermī 79
'am qodeš 79
'ēmeq 33
'nh, 'ānāh, 'ōneh 87
ma'ᵃneh 87
'nyh 88
'ṣb
lᵉha'ᵃṣīḇāh 22
'īr wᵉ'ēm 42
'īr wᵉ'ēm bᵉYiśrā'ēl 43
'īr u-ḇᵉnotehā 43
'rḇ 67
'tq
ha'ᵃtēq 61
pᵉgārīm 103
pigrē malk̲ēhem 103
pᵉnīmā 11
pissēᵃḥ 85
pi'ēl 49

qbb 85
qbh(?); qabboh 85
mah eqqoḇ lō' qabboh 'ēl 85
qedem 33, 67, 68

qdš 73
tiqdaš 70
qodeš, qodāšīm 70–73, 79
qodeš lᵉYahwe 72
qiṭṭēl 85
qāṭōl 33
qāṣeh 33
qr' 105
qᵉrī'ē mō'ēd 106
qārᵉ'ū šēm, qārᵉ'ū bᵉšēm 105
qirbām/qiḇrām 105

rō'eh 82, 85
rō'š 42
rᵉp̄ā'īm 100
rqd
wayyarqīdēm 119
rqḥt mr wkhnh (Deir 'Alla Inscr.) 88

śīm mišpāṭ 77
śᵉmō'l 33, 67
śᵉ'ōrāh 33
śar šel yām 110 (post Biblical)
šᵉ'ār 106
šᵉ'ēr 106
šᵉ'ērīt 106
šaḥat 33
šālōᵃḥ 33
šēm 106
špṭ 77; *šāp̄ōṭ* 33
šōp̄ēṭ 33, 34, 77
šᵉp̄āṭīm 34
šāqēd 93

tᵉhōm 108, 112
tō'ēḇāh 72

ARAMAIC

'aḇra'āh 106
'ummā 42
ḥtm, ḥtmh 20
ḥuṭrā 47
yrt 100
'nh
wy'nny 88
'dd 84
'ddn 88
šurbīnā/šurbānā/šarvainā 113, 114

UGARITIC

'almg 113
ymm
zbl ym 109
ym-'il, ymy, ymn 109
mdd 110
mlk 103
mlkm 103
mt 42
nḥl 48
nḥlt 48
'dd 88
ǵr nḥlty 51
qbṣ 101
rp'um (rapa'uma) 103
ṯpṭ nhr 109

ARABIC

'umm 42
'umma 42
**ḤḌR* (Proto-Semitic) 47
ḥḍr, ḥaḍara 47
hāmūlā 40, 41
**ḤẒR* (Proto-Semitic) 47
ḥaẓīra(t) 47
'ašīra 41
qabīla 41

INDEX IV
BIBLICAL REFERENCES

Genesis

2:9 23
2:10 23
6:4 106
12:6 37
12:8 37, 61
13:11 40
13:18 37
14 62
14:1, 9 38
14:15 67
14:24 77
17:4, 5 38
20:4 38
22:20–24 54
24:10 40, 51
25:6 54
25:13–15 54
25:16 42, 47
26:22 61
26:25 37
31 104
31:14 51
31:39 46
32:38 31
34 36
36:2 54
37:10 43
37:12ff. 45
40:9, 16 93
41:17 93
49 29

Exodus

15 29
15:13 47
15:17 50
15:25 77
29:33 76
32:13 50

Leviticus

21:1–6 104
22:14 73
23:20 73
25:13, 25–28 51
25:31 47
26:30 97
27:21 73
27:28 70, 73
27:29 74

Numbers

10:29ff. 40
10:35 91
12:6 92
16:2 106
18:14 73
21:1–3 78
23–24 29
23:3 87
23:8 85
23:9 5
25 104
25:14 42
25:18 42
26:52–56 49
27:1–11 51
31:27 78
31:28ff. 77
31:28, 37, 41 5
34:6–7 118
34:13, 17, 18, 29 49
36:2 49
36:7 51

Deuteronomy

1:15 76
2:23 47
4:20 50
4:34 38
7:26 70
9:26, 29 50
13:1, 2 92
13:16–17 78
18:10–11 105
18:15 92
18:21–22 95
18:34 10
22:9 70
26:14 104
33 29
33:28 5, 31

Joshua

1:4 118
5:6 39
6:17 78
6:18 74
6:19 78
7 74, 75
7:11–12 74
9:3–6 51
10:13 39
11:1 58
11:1–5 5
11:10 5
13:4 8
13:6 49
13:21 42
13:32 49
14:1–2 49
18:10 49
19:8 47
19:49, 51 49
21:12 47
24:25 77, 91

Judges

1:16 [LXX] 40
4:2, 24 56, 58
4:4 92
4:5 8
4:11, 17 40
4:13, 16 38
5 29
20:6 50
21:5–11 74

1 Samuel

3:3ff. 93
3:7 93
9:17 87
15:3, 21 78
19:18–20:1 45
20:5–6 105
20:5, 18, 24–5 21
20:28–29 105
24 95
28:6, 15 92
28:13 104
30:25 77, 78
30:29 41

2 Samuel

7:8 45
7:11 73
9:7ff. 21
8:1 43
14:7 106
16:21–22 12
18:18 104
20:19 43, 50

1 Kings

2:7 21
4:22–23, 27 [RSV] 21
5:2–3, 7 [MT] 21
7:51 73
8:51, 53 50
10:4–5 21
15:15 73
18:19 21
20:42 79
21 52
22:6ff. 91
22:13 89
22:17 91

2 Kings

6:18 39
9:11 85
9:25 87
12:19 73
19:20ff. 90
19:23 114
20:12–15, 16 13
22:14 92
23:12ff. 90
25:19 76
25:29–30 21

Isaiah

8:18 91
8:19 104
14:8 114
14:22 106
19:4 4
27:11 46
29:7–8 39
30:8 68
32:18 47
33:20 47
34:5 79
34:13 46
35:7 46
37:2ff. 90
37:24 114
41:23 68
42:11 48
46:10 68
51:9–10 110
54:4 43
56:4–5 104
58:14 50
62:12 79
63:18 79
65:1 81

Jeremiah

1:6–7 93
1:11–12 94
1:17 92
2:3 73
3:14 43
5:22 110
7:18 22
9:3 31
10:25 45
11:19 106
15:8 43
20:1, 6 85
20:2 90
21:12 83
22:3 83
23:25ff. 92
23:28 92
23:33, 37 87
27:9 92
28:4 89
28:8–9 95
29:8 92
29:26 85
31:23 47
44:19 22
49:19 46
49:28–33 48
50:44 46
52:25 76

Ezekiel

2:2 92
3:22–24 92
16:46 67
21:26 43
25:5 46
32:20, 21, 22, 24, 28, 30, 32 99
33:33 95
34:14 46
43:6–9 104
43:7–9 97
44:29 73
46:1 49
46:17 51
47:14 50
47:15 118
47:22 49

Hosea

4:5 43
6:9 40
9:7 85

Joel

1:6 39
2:20 68
4:3 76

Amos

7:10–13 90

Obadiah

1:11 76

Micah

2:5 50
3:7 87
4:13 78
6:5 87

Nahum

3:10 76

Zephaniah

2:6 46

Zachariah

10:2 92
14:8 68

Psalms

2:8 50
23:1–2 47
29:5–6 119
45:14–15 11
49:12 105
69:7 45
74:13 109
79:1 51
88:13 106
89:28 50
99:4 4
104:16 119
105:8–11 50
106:28 104
117:1 43

Proverbs

31:25 68

Job

1:14–19 45
5:3, 24 46
7:12 109
18:11 106

23:8–9 67
42:13–15 51

Lamentation

2:2 45
2:14 87

Ecclesiastes

9:5 106

Daniel

6:18 20
8:17–18 92
10:10–11 92

Nehemiah

5:17–18 21
12:29 47

1 Chronicles

6:41 47
16:15–18 50
26:20 73
26:26 73
26:26–28 77

2 Chronicles

15:6 38
24:2 92
26:22 76

NEW TESTAMENT

Matthew

27:66 20

POST BIBLICAL LITERATURE

Genesis Rabba

44:17 93

Babylonian Talmud

Rosh Hashana 25a 106
Hagigah 12a 110

PLATE I

Air-photograph of the Mari palace during excavations, looking north-west.

PLATE II

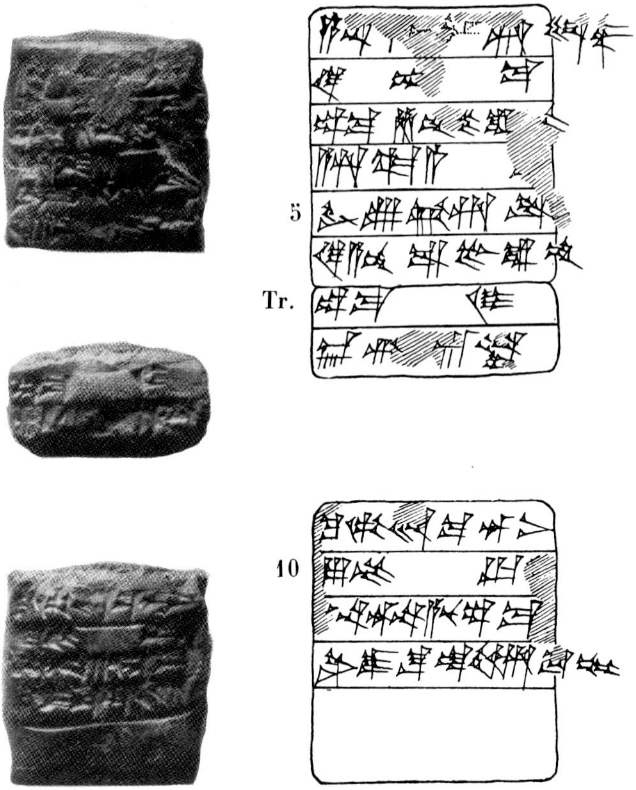

a. The letter concerning the proposed visit of the son (?) of the King of Ugarit to the Mari palace.

b. Tablets as found, *in situ*, in Room 115—part of the 'diplomatic archive'.

PLATE III

a–c. Clay sealings of King Zimri-Lim, Queen Shibtu and Mukkanišum.

d. The initial discovery of tablets in the Mari palace: André Bianquis removing tablets a mere metre below the surface, in Room 5, early in 1936.

PLATE IV

a. Looking through Room 6 to Room 5, from Room 1.

b. Room 7, with two bathtubs and a privy.

Room 116, possibly 'the sealed store-room for fine oil in the Court of the Palm', with Room 115 (the 'diplomatic archive') beyond; Courtyard 106 to the left; and Courtyard 131 to the right.

Wall-painting of a West Semite (leading a sacrificial bull), from Courtyard 106.

a. A cake mould depicting the goddess Ishtar (Astarte).

b. Cake moulds as found among the debris of the upper storey, in Room 77.

PLATE VIII

a. The pottery 'doorbell' of Room 108, *in situ*.

b. Two clay liver-model fragments from Hazor in Northern Israel.